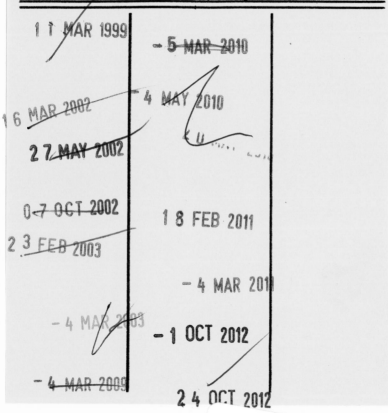

THE
MCFARLANE
LEGACY

STUDIES IN LATE MEDIEVAL
POLITICS AND SOCIETY

THE FIFTEENTH CENTURY SERIES

Advisory Editor: Ralph A. Griffiths, Professor of Medieval History, University of Wales, Swansea

THE FIFTEENTH CENTURY SERIES is a tribute to the vitality of scholarly study of the later Middle Ages (and especially of the fifteenth century) and to the commitment of Alan Sutton Publishing to make its conclusions widely available. This partnership, which Charles Ross did much to encourage, has been extraordinarily productive in the quarter-century since the pioneering colloquium on 'The Fifteenth Century, 1399–1509: Studies in Politics and Society' was held in Cardiff and presided over by S.B. Chrimes. The proceedings of that colloquium, edited by S.B. Chrimes, C.D. Ross and R.A. Griffiths, were published in 1972. Since 1979 Alan Sutton Publishing has published no fewer than twelve volumes of papers, invited especially from younger scholars and discussed at further colloquia, which have become a notable feature of the academic landscape in Britain. Aside from the encouragement given to talented young historians, noteworthy features of these volumes are the breadth of topics addressed, the novelty of approaches adopted, and the participation of scholars from North America and the European Continent. The volumes have proved influential and informative, and there is good reason to include future volumes in a major new series, both to recognize the achievements of the present generation of fifteenth-century historians and to consolidate the interest in later medieval history which they have undoubtedly generated.

It is appropriate that THE FIFTEENTH CENTURY SERIES should be inaugurated by a volume of papers delivered in 1993 at a colloquium, held at Durham, which focused on K.B. McFarlane (1903–66) and the contribution which his teaching and writings have made to later medieval historiography. He gave a unique stimulus to the study of English politics and society, especially in the fifteenth century: his insights have been adapted and developed, sometimes supplemented, and even occasionally challenged. This has been achieved in a spirit of friendly and constructive discussion which has marked the twenty or so colloquia since the first in Cardiff in 1970. *The McFarlane Legacy* is a fitting beginning to THE FIFTEENTH CENTURY SERIES. Subsequent volumes will include:

Crown, Government and People in the Fifteenth Century, ed. R.E. Archer
The North of England in the Age of Richard III, ed. A.J. Pollard.

✧ THE FIFTEENTH CENTURY SERIES   NO. 1 ✧

THE MCFARLANE LEGACY

STUDIES IN LATE MEDIEVAL POLITICS AND SOCIETY

EDITED BY

R.H. BRITNELL AND A.J. POLLARD

ALAN SUTTON PUBLISHING · STROUD
ST. MARTIN'S PRESS · NEW YORK

First published in the United Kingdom in 1995
Alan Sutton Publishing Limited
Phoenix Mill · Far Thrupp · Stroud · Gloucestershire

First published in the United States of America in 1995
St. Martin's Press · Scholarly and Reference Division
175 Fifth Avenue · New York · N.Y. 10010

British Library Cataloguing in Publication Data

McFarlane Legacy: Studies in Late Medieval Politics and Society
  I. Britnell, R.H. II. Pollard, A.J.
  941.007202

ISBN 0-7509-0626-X

Typeset in 10/15 Baskerville.
Typesetting and origination by
Alan Sutton Publishing Limited.
Printed in Great Britain by
Hartnolls, Bodmin, Cornwall.

ACKNOWLEDGEMENT

The editors and publisher gratefully acknowledge the grant towards the cost of publication from The British Academy.

CONTENTS

ABBREVIATIONS

B.I.H.R.	*Bulletin of the Institute of Historical Research*
B.J.R.L.	*Bulletin of the John Rylands Library* (later *Bulletin of the John Rylands University Library of Manchester*).
B.L.	British Library, London, U.K.
Bodl. L.	Bodleian Library, Oxford, U.K.
Borthwick I.H.R.	Borthwick Institute of Historical Research, York, U.K.
Carpenter, *Locality*	M. C. Carpenter, *Locality and Polity. A Study of Warwickshire Landed Society, 1401–1499* (Cambridge, 1992)
C.A.D.	*Calendar of Ancient Deeds* (6 vols, H.M.S.O., 1890–1915)
C.C.R.	*Calendar of Close Rolls* (46 vols, H.M.S.O., 1892–1963)
C.Ch.R.	*Calendar of Charter Rolls* (6 vols, H.M.S.O., 1903–27)
C.H.J.	*Cambridge Historical Journal*
C.I.P.M.	*Calendar of Inquisitions Post Mortem* (19 vols, H.M.S.O., 1904 – in progress)
Commons 1386–1421	*History of Parliament, The Commons 1386–1421,* J.S. Roskell, L. Clark and C. Rawcliffe (eds.) (4 vols, Stroud 1992)
C.P.R.	*Calendar of Patent Rolls*
C.U.L.	Cambridge University Library, Cambridge, U.K.
E.E.T.S.	Early English Text Society
Ec.H.R.	*Economic History Review*
E.H.R.	*English Historical Review*
G.E.C.	*Complete Peerage of England,* H.V. Gibbs and others (eds.), (13 vols, 1910–59)
H.J.	*Historical Journal*
H.L.	Huntington Library, San Marino, California, U.S.A.
H.M.S.O.	Her Majesty's Stationery Office
J.C.H.	*Journal of Contemporary History*
J.R.L.	John Rylands University Library, Manchester, U.K.

McFarlane, *England*	K.B. McFarlane, *England in the Fifteenth Century, Collected Essays*, G.L. Harriss (ed.) (1981)
McFarlane, *Nobility*	K.B. McFarlane, *The Nobility of Later Medieval England* (Oxford, 1973)
Paston L. & P.	*Paston Letters and Papers of the Fifteenth Century*, N. Davis (ed.), (2 vols, Oxford 1971–6)
P.B.A.	*Proceedings of the British Academy*
P.I.M.S.	Pontifical Institute for Medieval Studies
P.P.	*Past and Present*
P.R.O.	Public Record Office, London, U.K.
R.O.	Record Office
R.P.	*Rotuli Parliamentorum* (6 vols, Record Commission, 1783)
R.S.	Rolls Series
S.R.	*Statutes of the Realm* (11 vols, Record Commission 1810–28)
T.L.S.	*Times Literary Supplement*
T.R.H.S.	*Transactions of the Royal Historical Society*
Y.B.	*Year Book*
Y.M.L.	York Minster Library, York, U.K.

INTRODUCTION

K.B. McFarlane was the most influential twentieth-century historian of late medieval English politics. He more than anyone else was responsible for transforming the study of the period, especially the fifteenth century, from the malign neglect which he inherited in the 1920s, to the intense scrutiny which he left on his death in 1966. And yet he wrote only one book, and that the study of Wycliffe and Lollardy which was published in the 'Teach Yourself History' series. The rest of his published work lay in some dozen learned articles; his numerous other unpublished and incomplete papers were printed only after his death. The reasons why he published so little are well rehearsed and alluded to further in this volume. If, as a consequence, his work is less well known beyond the world of his specialism, for decades its influence has nevertheless been ubiquitous and profound throughout the teaching of and research into late medieval English political history. He was, as many have attested, a gifted and inspiring teacher of both undergraduate and postgraduate students. He supervised no fewer than thirty research students, most of whom took up posts in the expanding post-war university system. And they, in their turn, brought on another generation of scholars. In this way he was of central importance in the development of fifteenth-century political history from a virtually uncultivated field at the beginning of the century to a highly productive one at the end. McFarlane himself may have shunned collective research, and would possibly have been horrified at the very suggestion that he would found a school of history, but that is in effect what he did. The current state of the art in the history of late medieval English politics is therefore McFarlane's legacy.

By 1940 McFarlane had clarified the objective of his life's work: a comprehensive analysis of the English governing classes during the later Middle Ages, which itself was to be the key to understanding the history of late medieval England. Such a project proved beyond him as an individual scholar and was left uncompleted. Like the companions of McFarlane's hero Henry V, so the historians of the fifteenth century who have come after him have endeavoured to fulfil his grand design; but like them too, nearly thirty years on, they have lost their direction and found his goal elusive. Now his legacy is being questioned, and rightly so, especially by a younger generation of scholars who are but indirectly his inheritors. Has the very proliferation of theses and narrowly-focused studies, exploiting precisely those rich sources of documentation which he first explored, led his heirs to lose sight of the wood for the trees? Have they followed each other too blindly down the cul-de-sac of 'patronage studies'? Has McFarlane been misconstrued? Was he always correct in his judgements and conclusions? Was he even going in the right direction?

This volume addresses these questions and asks whither now. The papers it contains, which were delivered at a colloquium held at Durham in September 1993, represent mainly the work of a younger generation of scholars who did not know McFarlane. McFarlane's awareness of the importance of interpersonal relationships for the rich political life of the period is echoed throughout the volume. His sense of continuity between the later Middle Ages and succeeding centuries is reinforced by evidence of the way in which elements of later parliamentary and popular politics were foreshadowed in the fifteenth century. At the same time, these papers show that in some respects McFarlane's characteristic interpretations of late medieval politics have become constricting, and that they are currently being modified by changes of emphasis.

In the first essay, Gerald Harriss, McFarlane's successor as a fellow of Magdalen College, presents an overview of where we now stand. He suggests that the framework for the analysis of the governing classes upon which McFarlane embarked is now in place. It is built around four separate but connected sets of social relationships, or 'contexts', in which political action took place. The first is that of the landed society of lords and gentry, the point from which McFarlane himself started, which was essentially localised in character. One may speak, he suggests, of a partnership between the élites that actually ruled the localities in the name of the crown, and the crown that validated that rule. At home in the provinces, the principal concerns of members of this landed society lay in property, family and magistracy. The second is the court and the king's immediate circle. This was the often tense and volatile world of high politics, where peers and parvenues, the natural councillors of the king and privileged members of his entourage, jostled for place and favour. It was a world in which honour, precedence, chivalry and war were issues of intense importance. Landed society and the crown, locality and centre, formally met together from time to time in parliament, where lines of demarcation between the two worlds were drawn. Parliament, the third context of late medieval politics, was almost a regular event as a focus of government and politics between 1340 and 1450. And finally, outside and beyond these worlds, with whom they were nevertheless in constant contact as dependent servants and suitors, lay the common people. The lynchpin, holding these four political contexts together, was the crown. Under an effective king, such as Henry V, all was well; but equally, as under the ineffective Henry VI, all could easily fall apart.

Most of the following essays take up and explore aspects of these four fields of late medieval politics. Simon Payling examines one of the principal concerns of landed society, in which the disposition of property was of fundamental significance for the configuration and continuity of political élites. He provides an analysis of the late medieval development of marriage contracts of male heirs and girls who were not heiresses. Marriages, and the terms in which they were negotiated, were a highly sensitive issue for the governing classes, not only because of the impact they had on landed estates and inheritances, but also because of the royal interest in wardships. Marriage contracts were never the crude matter of bargain and sale which shocked some nineteenth-century historians, but carefully constructed agreements which sought to protect the interests of all parties – grooms, brides, their respective parents, and above all the lineages to which they belonged. Payling lays bare the manner in which from the twelfth to the sixteenth centuries simple dower gave way to jointure, first as a supplement and eventually as a replacement. He shows that the complex entailed use, which settled the whole family patrimony for the next generation, had been evolved by the reign of Henry VIII. Its very success in enabling families to avoid feudal incidents was one reason for the passage of the Statute of Uses in 1536.

In the first of three papers focusing on the court and high politics, Anthony Gross stresses the symbolic role and consecrated status of the monarch. In doing so he questions the adequacy of Harriss's framework. He offers the alternative metaphor, familiar to contemporaries, of society as a body politic. The king did more than hold the ring. He was the head of the body; and without a head the body could not live. Thus the well-being of the community of England as a whole, including the governing classes, depended on the king, who was thus perceived to have a sacred role as protector and guarantor of the realm. For this reason any doubt about the legitimacy of the king threatened the whole of society. The malaise that characterised Henry VI's disintegrating regime in the 1450s, revealed, for instance, in the cult of Archbishop Scrope of York as a victim of the Lancastrian usurpation, and the desperate resort to astrology to restore the health of king and kingdom, had its origins in the flawed Lancastrian title to the throne. In an analysis which echoes an ancient tradition, Gross suggests that the House of Lancaster failed not simply because of Henry VI's incompetence but because the dynasty lacked sacred authority.

Simon Walker explores a different dimension of the sacred trappings of monarchy: the veneration of political saints, and especially saints of royal blood. He argues that the creation of cults surrounding secular politicians and kings, namely Simon de Montfort, Thomas of Lancaster, Edward II, Archbishop Richard Scrope and Henry VI, were not merely successful exercises in propaganda for or against the crown. They depended for their success on touching a responsive chord in their devotees. With the exception of the cult of de Montfort which failed, and thus proves the rule, they projected and reflected a desire for reconciliation and the healing of social rifts. None, whatever their specific genesis, remained exclusively partisan, and all affirmed an ideal of political conduct. Thus the principal attribute of Thomas of Lancaster was that he stood for justice, Scrope for forgiveness, and Henry VI for patience in adversity. Like officially recognised saints they represented idealised role models, but secular rather than religious in character. Kings endeavoured to harness them to their own causes so as to benefit from the sympathetic magic they imparted.

Anthony Tuck approaches kingship on a more down-to-earth level; he tackles the political and diplomatic history of the first critical years of the reign of Henry IV to demonstrate how he dealt with the initial implacable hostility of France and Scotland to his usurpation. By his own clear-sighted astuteness, and profiting from French mistakes, Henry was able to isolate them by securing the neutrality of the Iberian kingdoms and by forging marriage alliances with two powers of northern and central Europe, Denmark and the Empire. Henry's deft and decisive diplomacy to a large extent explains the speedy acceptance of the House of Lancaster among the dynasties of Europe. We are reminded again, if need there is, that international relations and foreign policy were matters of central importance not only to dynasties and kings but also to the political nation at large. More specifically, Henry IV himself emerges with greater stature than McFarlane, for one, was prepared to concede.

Henry IV's relations with parliament are part of the backdrop to Linda Clark's analysis of the relationship between lords and commons between 1386 and 1421, a topic which McFarlane himself famously debated. She examines in detail the patterns of leadership and control that operated in this third context of political life when the leaders and other representatives of provincial élites met together with the agents of the king and his court. Drawing on the kind of collective enterprise that McFarlane distrusted, but which has proved essential for the thorough prosopographical work which he advocated, Clark argues that it is hard to demonstrate that lords exercised a great deal of influence over the election of MPs, and that there is little to show that they controlled the House when it was sitting. Even bearing in mind regional variations and the incompleteness of the surviving evidence, what emerges, as McFarlane anticipated, is a picture of a House of Commons more enterprising and independent than was once supposed. Nevertheless, the House tended to be dominated by a handful of well-connected, high-standing and articulate knights of the shire, who coordinated and steered business in the House. They often led a caucus linked with a particular magnate (notably the house of Lancaster), with a group of peers, or, above all, with the crown. Individual MPs outstanding both in the constituencies and in the house, such as Chaucer, Erpingham, Hungerford, Sturmy and Tiptoft, were parliamentary business managers active on behalf of crown and court. Already, in the parliaments of the late fourteenth and early fifteenth centuries, the time-honoured art of managing the House had manifested itself. MPs were not controlled by the lords, but they were led by those of their number who were in the confidence of king and magnates.

Members of parliament represented the communities of the realm, but the House of Commons was a forum in which the common people had a voice only very indirectly. Isobel Harvey takes up the neglected topic of the influence of the disenfranchised on politics in the fifteenth century, an influence felt not only at a distance through parliament but also more directly through riot, petitioning and pamphleteering. She argues that during the fifteenth century, perhaps in relationship to rising standards of living, especially prosperous husbandmen and artisans were more literate, better informed, and more fully engaged in political debate in alehouse, tavern and market than had previously been the case. As men called to defend the kingdom in crisis and pay taxes to finance the king's wars, they too had a stake in affairs. And this mattered in politics, partly because of the resort to direct action, as in Cade's Revolt and the later tax rebellions, and partly because the crown and governing classes took note either to suppress, control or exploit popular grievances for their own ends. So this fourth dimension of late medieval politics had a real and, indeed, increasing impact on events. Harvey suggests that in the mid-fifteenth century the discrediting of the regime of Henry VI, and of the monarchy itself, served to intensify its importance. McFarlane also recognised that the common people had a distinctive voice in the politics of the kingdom and spoke up more loudly in the second half of the fifteenth century. The many-headed monster was as familiar in the fifteenth-century as in the sixteenth.

Finally Christine Carpenter places McFarlane's intellectual journey in its historiographical perspective. She reflects on the connection between his disenchantment with the received emphasis on constitutional history, indelibly associated with the name of Stubbs, and his own early Marxism, and stresses how later, particularly under the influence of Namier, he took a more catholic and pragmatic view of the past. Taking stock, Carpenter concludes by suggesting that we need a new synthesis to bring together the mass of recent detailed research, some of which is reflected in this volume. McFarlane, she points out, did not reject constitutional history as such; rather he posited a new history which encompassed the political, social and governmental. This has not been achieved largely because his project has been misunderstood and debased by the recent obsession with the politics of self-interest at the expense of ideology. The way ahead, she suggests, lies in a fuller understanding of the *mentalité* of the governing classes and their political culture, especially their perception of the role of law. We need, in short, a new constitutional history.

From these essays, then, there emerges both respect for what McFarlane achieved and a degree of impatience with constraints that have come to be associated with his legacy. In developing his ideas McFarlane's followers have tended not to question an emphasis on personalities and patronage. They have played down the importance of the institutional, intellectual, cultural and economic contexts of political action in favour of a less structured view of politics in which the personalities, attachments and interests of individual kings and their subjects shaped the course of events. Invaluable though this approach has been in sharpening our perceptions of politics, the time is now ripe for renewed interest in the institutions and values within which political activity took place and the social and economic changes which, in various ways, affected political agendas. From the essays in this volume, in particular, it is clear that new directions are being taken in the attempt to understand the *mentalité* of the governing classes, especially in the region of belief in the supernatural. It is clear, too, that the nature of the constitution in which the politics of late medieval England were enacted is once again centre-stage, even though reasons for the central problem of the later Middle Ages, the collapse of order and the onset of dynastic civil war, remain unresolved and disputed.

Whether a new synthesis can emerge is a moot point. Judging by the divergent approaches to the period represented in these essays, one would suspect not. The employment of a wider variety of institutional, intellectual and cultural frameworks of interpretation, must reduce the prospect of a single formula winning general agreement, and it may be that the McFarlane legacy is already too fractured, and his legatees too fractious, for any unity of understanding to be achieved. There are many more voices to be accommodated within any proposed synthesis than there were in McFarlane's time. This is all very much in line with patterns of experience outside the narrow world of late medieval studies. When McFarlane set out on his career, the intellectual world was more confident that a definitive understanding of the past could be erected on generally acceptable foundations. Today we are more inclined to doubt the possibility and even the desirability of such a single interpretative construct. To that extent, we are all post-modernists now.

R.H. Britnell
University of Durham

A.J. Pollard
University of Teesside

1

THE DIMENSIONS OF POLITICS

G.L. Harriss

MAGDALEN COLLEGE, UNIVERSITY OF OXFORD

In his introduction to *The Nobility of Later Medieval England*, Cooper described how, at an early stage, McFarlane's dissatisfaction with Stubbsian orthodoxy had led him to ask how government actually worked, how the interests of individuals and classes affected political attitudes, and how bastard feudal connections operated in late medieval society.[1] If, in 1938, he expected that the exploration of such questions would yield 'the outlines of a new framework', his interest in this subsequently faded.[2] After the war, as his pupils were set to work on the problems of central government and administration, he embarked on his staggering single-handed exploration of the estate records of the nobility. These he read not primarily to unravel their finances or economy, nor even for what they revealed of their political influence (though he had a sharp eye for such), but to find out their concerns, their outlook, and their abilities, and thus to break down the stereotype of the overmighty subject. What he had to say about the political role of the nobility came right at the end of the final Ford lecture, almost as a postscript to his exposition of service and maintenance. Politics was not just about the relations of kings and nobles, but about the interests of the whole political class. War, the inheritance, the family, income and expenditure – the titles of the lectures – were their common concerns and central to their political attitudes.[3]

The investigation of these themes has been undertaken largely by the generation following his death, many taking guidance and inspiration from Ross and Pugh. Thorough and increasingly wide-ranging research into local, legal, and personal records has familiarized us with the structure of local society, the functions of lordship and litigation, the importance of land and family, and the role of friends and patrons. A critical evaluation of the evidence of wills, marriage settlements, feoffments, and arbitration has deepened our understanding of landholding mentality. It has been a productive harvest and has changed the approach to the fifteenth century. From different studies different emphases have appeared: on the vertical bonds of lordship or the horizontal ties of community, on patronage or loyalty as political cement, on the retained affinity or the looser ties of good lordship and service. And so the question is now asked, does this offer a new political framework into which we can place the tensions, conflicts, and adjustments (for that is what politics is about) of the fifteenth century? Can we discern any guiding principle of political development which will help to define the contribution of the period to the development of the early modern state?[4]

We must approach this question in the way McFarlane taught us, from the actual practice of government and politics. If we reject the growth of representation and constitutionalism as key themes of fifteenth-century development, we must be doubly cautious about replacing them with patronage, careerism, lineage, honour, hierarchy, or service. These indeed provided a framework for political life, but when we ask what was politics about and what were its tensions and mechanisms for adjustment at different social levels, it is the diversity and disjunctiveness of political experience that emerges. Let me take what I see as the four main dimensions or arenas of political activity, and briefly explore the culture of each in turn.

The first is the one to which McFarlane directed our attention and on which research has largely concentrated in the last twenty-five years, namely landed society. Here I must gratefully rely on the writings of others. Political society in the localities centred on land, and the lordship and magistracy which land conferred. Land underwrote the family: ancient lineage was the expression of continuous landholding, and the foundation of a new lineage depended on the acquisition of sufficient land. Land created immediate ties with families, neighbours and, where held in tenancy, lords. Invoked particularly in legal and family business, these formed a network of supportive – though at times conflicting – relationships. For while land imparted stability to social relationships, no society is immobile, and late medieval landed society was subject to tensions both intrinsic and extrinsic.

Payling has argued that demographic decline accelerated the transfer of land through heiresses, enabling families which survived in the male line to accumulate land and form a wealthy knightly élite, often at the expenses of the middling and lesser gentry.[5] This not only widened the differentiation within the class but bred contrasting reactions: some families concentrated on survival while the more adventurous, especially newcomers, turned the situation to their advantage, through legal devices to change the rules of inheritance or a marriage policy which sometimes had disruptive consequences. As well as inbuilt stability landed society had an inbuilt fluidity; clinging to and competing for land was at the heart of its politics.

It was thus an intrinsically competitive society, though whether, with Carpenter, we want to depict the gentry 'passing their lives in an intensively competitive atmosphere where momentary inattention could breed disaster' I am not so sure.[6] For the title to the majority of their estates was never challenged and instances of them losing them are relatively few. That was, of course, applicable to the Pastons and they, as Richmond has vividly recounted, must be placed among that species of pushing professionals intent on breaking into gentry society which Carpenter has identified as among its most disruptive and destabilizing elements.[7] Whether land was scarce (as some would have it) or plentiful (according to others), the lawyers, estate officials, top civil servants, courtiers and occasionally men of war were out to get it, and did so by purchase, by marriage to widows and heiresses, by grant from magnates or the crown, and by legal sharp practice. Abrasive and assertive as they were, arousing resentment and jealousy with their new manor houses and claims to lordship, displaying the unacceptable face of ambition and greed, their interests were nonetheless in joining not undermining the political order. This they did not merely by marrying their heirs into it but – often surprisingly quickly – by filling shire office, serving as member of parliament, and acting as feoffees and even arbiters.[8] Society needed their expertise and services, and so did lords under whose favour they often made their entry. Younger sons or second families of the élite might be another acquisitive and disruptive element, but their circumstances were more particular. Finally at the other extreme were the losers, who from misfortune or failings of character were tempted to defy the social mores and resort to illegal and violent acts. Their equals would indeed ostracize them, and lords would be ill-advised to afford encouragement or protection to society's moral outlaws.

What mechanisms contained and resolved the tensions generated in landed society? Disputes were, of course, pursued through the legal machinery of the state, in local and central courts, by civil and criminal actions. But the royal courts and royal justices were a relatively recent importation into a society which had long regulated its disputes by seigneurial and communal courts, and even in the fifteenth century royal law was administered locally through landowners acting as sheriffs and justices of the peace, and their tenants as jurors. The ability of local interests to influence judicial process is well known, even if there were growing opportunities for appeal to, and intervention by, superior courts and authorities. But the resolution of disputes, whether in the central courts or locally, had to take account of local attitudes and the realities of landed power. The natural and primary arena for their resolution was among the local community, through lovedays, mediators, arbitrators, and umpires who might be neighbours, lords, or impartial outsiders. Indeed Carpenter views the incidence of cases reaching the King's Bench from the localities as an index of the failure or weakening of informal local peace-keeping.[9] Ultimately she sees the responsibility for the stability of local society as resting with its lords, those with power to enforce order and settlements. The proclivity of bastard feudalism to escalate gentry disputes has perhaps been exaggerated, for magnates were cautious about committing their influence and honour in local quarrels. Though their lordship and worship depended on affording protection to their followers, that was more usually through the settlement of disputes than in their exacerbation. Within a large affinity the lord fulfilled a natural role as arbitrator, and incorporation into an affinity was more than once employed to restore peace and regulate unacceptable behaviour. Lordship, and the hierocratic principle in general, was a force for stability; leadership of gentry society from above deterred factionalism. Indeed, Carpenter argues that lordship provided the necessary framework within which the competitiveness of the gentry could safely assert itself, and where lordship of this kind was absent a gentry élite had to perform much the same role.[10]

Yet lordship could itself be a disruptive force. Unless it embraced virtually the whole of local political society, lordship could be divisive, restricting favour and rewards to a clique, as in early fifteenth-century Staffordshire and Shropshire, studied by Powell. Alienated outsiders then formed a natural constituency for an intruder to challenge the established leadership, as in Talbot's attack on Arundel's followers in 1413. Other instances readily come to mind.[11] Between long-established nobility of comparable rank disruptive rivalry was less common. Their own estates and areas of influence were usually well defined, and even where these were juxtaposed a tacit recognition of the need for coexistence seems to have obtained: that of Percy and Neville in Yorkshire described by Pollard had lasted for almost forty years before the encircling Neville influence brought a rupture in 1453.[12] Lordship was also an ambivalent force in local society because it reached beyond it and could import the feuds and favours of high politics into its operation. The Blount-Vernon feud of the mid century and the Vernon-Grey rivalry in the 1460s both became linked to, and inflamed by, magnate factions at the highest level.[13] Further, the exercise of favour by the king or others on his behalf could induce a downward spiral of conflict. The award of a royal office to a rival could affront a magnate's local standing, as in the grant of the constableship of Tutbury to Henry, earl of Warwick, rather than to the earl of Stafford. When royal protection was afforded to his enemy, Sir William Tailboys, Lord Cromwell, felt his safety and honour threatened. The redistribution of forfeited estates carried the seeds of mortal enmities, as in the case of the Appellants' lands in 1397 or those of Lord Scrope in 1415. Even the bestowal of a lapsed or disputed inheritance to a royal favourite as in the cases of Ufford and Beauchamp, could arouse jealousy and variance between lords.[14] Lords were not more naturally or frequently disruptive than the gentry, but their potential for damage to society was greater. The internal mechanisms for stability in landed society could thus be negated by factionalism and favour imported from outside.

None the less, the indigenous politics of this society – centred on land, family, and patronage – were essentially localized. Title was protected, inheritance safeguarded, intruders absorbed, disrupters reprobated and disputes settled largely through mechanisms which, if validated from above, drew their effectiveness from the force and approval of landed society itself.

The same principles underlay the exercise of local magistracy. Even manorial lordship conferred jurisdiction of a kind and the shire offices of sheriff, justice of the peace and representative in parliament generally circulated among an élite of 'well connected and affluent landowners, some of them very rich indeed'.[15]

Sheriffs and justices of the peace were, of course, crown appointees and though there is little concrete evidence of how the choice was made, it is clear that local lords exercised an important influence. In counties where a great comital family held the rule of the shire, its retainers might occupy one half to two-thirds of the available posts. Just as we are now realizing that earlier deductions from such affiliations about the packing of parliament were misleading, so we must be cautious about concluding that this represented the absorption and subversion of local government and justice by seigneurial power. For in a longer perspective local magistracy had always been the function of the landlord class and it is the crown that can be seen as increasingly intrusive, seeking to regulate local peace-keeping, social control, and the exercise of authority by local leaders. In any case the interests of the crown and the local landlord élite (lords and gentry) largely coincided, and were certainly interdependent. As Carpenter has emphasized, the crown depended on this élite for effective rule of the locality, its stability and loyalty, while the landlords relied on the crown to validate their authority as its agents.[16] Neither could depart too far from this unspoken pact, the crown by appointing to local office its own creatures who lacked a natural power base, the landlord class by too flagrantly failing in its duties to keep order, administer justice, and respect royal authority. Nor, as Simon Walker has valuably shown, did the crown wholly abandon local administration to them. It could monitor the rule of the county through its assize justices and individual magnates or gentry who had personal access to the king.[17] Essentially these provided fail-safe mechanisms, and the active channels of government, on which both crown and magnates depended, were the leading gentry of the locality. And even they, in practice, depended much on a handful of working justices of the peace, often local lawyers of the quorum, as did the sheriff on his under-sheriff and bailiffs. Government at this level went deep into the political community. Undeniably these men exercised magistracy broadly in the interests of the landlord class (that should cause no surprise) and on occasion specifically to give themselves an advantage in contests in which they were involved. But they had sense enough to see that the social and political fabric which they controlled depended on an ethic of justice by which their rule would be judged.[18] In general local office-holding was not a matter of political contention. Stability characterized the peace commissions, and the office of sheriff was one which men contended to avoid as much as to assume.[19]

In matters of both land and rule, then, this was very largely a locally orientated and self-regulating society, marrying delegated royal authority with regional lordship to deal with its own political concerns by its own standards. Those concerns were with property, family, and magistracy, and for the settlement of the tensions to which these gave rise they principally looked to neighbourhood and local lordship.

The ethos of court politics was very different. This centred on honour and service, and competition for favour, influence, and material rewards. Here the division between peerage and non-peerage was of more consequence than it was in local landlordship, for peers stood in a special constitutional relationship to the crown, with personal obligations to the body politic. Yet their relationship with the king had an inbuilt imbalance which produced strong tensions. They expected their personal fidelity to be reciprocated by the demonstration of royal favour which would validate their own position and status; yet that was at the king's volition. Likewise they took pride in their role as defenders of the realm and natural councillors of the king; yet they received military commands at royal pleasure and kings sought advice wherever they pleased. McFarlane emphasized that kings and lords expected to cooperate and judged that the area of likely conflict was small. Lords had no desire to do the king's work and rule in his place, but he had to afford them opportunities to pursue their careers.[20] Yet animosities within this ruling circle were frequent and periodically lethal. What were the causes of disharmony and the mechanism for their containment?

First war and, with it, foreign policy. I put it first because McFarlane emphasized that 'above all the king needed to lead his nobility in war', and cited the warrior kings, Edward I, Edward III and Henry V, as those who achieved a community of interest between crown and baronage, a point recently underlined by Richmond.[21] If nobility rested on land and lineage, war provided the opportunity to affirm it by deeds of prowess. The gentry felt no such compulsion, as the dramatic decline of knighthood showed. Hence to be denied the chance to fight and win renown dishonoured noble rank and lineage. Not to be given a military command, or to be removed from one, provoked bitter recriminations and even political crises. One may think of Prince Henry's reaction to being sidelined from the 1412 expedition, or Warwick's loss of the captaincy of Calais to Bedford in 1427, or York's loss of the lieutenancy of

Normandy in 1446.[22] The effect on Richard Neville of Edward IV's treaty with Burgundy, despite his own negotiations with France in 1467, was perhaps not dissimilar. A peace policy predictably bred frustration and suspicion among some of the nobility, as when Gloucester and Arundel railed against that of Richard II and Humphrey of Gloucester against that of Henry VI. In both cases this was taken as a sign of disaffection and contributed to their destruction. When such policies brought defeat and the danger of invasion, as in 1386 and 1450, kings and ministers stood accused of treason to the realm. Even controversies over rival alliances, as in 1411–12 and 1467–8, opened deep rifts within the baronage and between some of them and the king. In high politics personal considerations of honour, trust, repute, and favour could never be dissociated from policy.

Another cause of dissension in curial politics was the public expression of honour in terms of title and precedence. Examples of such disputes are manifold. They could rise to something of a crescendo in reigns like those of Richard II, Henry VI and Edward IV when new ranks among the peerage were invented and new titles widely distributed. Henry IV, Henry V and Henry VII were more restrained and sought a consensus for their creations and endowments, emphasizing that titles and money were the rewards for loyal service. These were not merely matters of personal pride and pique; ambitions for title could induce magnates to serve in war, and contentions over title could feed down into territorial conflict in the localities.[23]

In the noble ethic, service and honour should be reciprocal, but ties of blood had also to be recognized and the advancement of members of the royal family in land and dignity was one of the most politically sensitive decisions a king had to make. For the late medieval nobility was not a uniform class; it tended to divide between the old landed families whose estates and wealth were growing inexorably the longer they survived – Beauchamp, Mortimer, Mowbray, Neville, Percy, Stafford – and those with neither ancient lineage nor lands whom the king wished to establish. These were either his relations by blood or marriage Holands, Beauforts, Woodvilles – or those like de la Pole, Talbot, Bourchier, Herbert who were advanced to the upper peerage on grounds of trust and service. (A similar division obtained among the baronage.) It was precisely their lack of traditional and extensive landed estates which freed such families for service at court and in war, and which made them dependent on royal favour for office, income, and rewards. They competed for these with an urgency that was not felt by the great landed families. Their hope ultimately was to establish themselves among the landed nobility, either through marriage or the acquisition of lands, but the opportunities for the crown to provide these were increasingly scarce. Moreover grants of escheated lands, forfeited estates, or heiresses could be highly contentious if they entrenched on the expectations or local influence of the older families. The good lordship which this nobility of service could offer was also of a different political character from that based on lordship over land and men. It rested on their influence in council and in court, and on the offices at their disposal, civil and military, and in this sense was an extension of their own dependence on royal favour. Thomas Beaufort, duke of Exeter, is a good example of one whose patronage and use of such influence consolidated loyalty to the crown, whereas that exercised by the duke of Suffolk was judged factious and disruptive. Here, in the different situation, needs, and outlook of the older landed and newer service nobility, was a fault line along which the unity of the nobility repeatedly split.[24] These *arrivistes* were a more destabilizing element in high politics than their counterparts, the pushy professionals, in local politics. Not merely were the stakes higher but the element of royal favour made the context more volatile. It was the task of the king to stand above the divisions of the nobility, to deal justly with all, and regulate their disputes, and he was repeatedly advised in these terms. But perhaps only war provided the framework of discipline and common purpose in which these profound differences of status and expectation could be subsumed.

Courtiers could represent an even more contentious element at this political level. But the attitude of the nobility to low-born favourites was governed less by honour and emulation than by affront to their own claim to the royal confidence, and fear of machinations against their lives and inheritances. Even the greatest, like John of Gaunt and Richard of York, felt vulnerable. When they challenged the upstart courtiers it was in the name of a prescriptive right to reform the commonwealth, to purge it of those who were plundering it for their private gain. That of course laid them open to the charge of usurping or assuming the royal power to govern, and could lead them ultimately into rebellion.[25]

Although they claimed to be the king's natural councillors with a responsibility for the commonweal, how much the nobility – particularly the landed nobility – concerned themselves with the workings of central government is unclear. We have virtually no record of what the lords in parliament discussed, and little enough of what went on in council. The handful who attended council or appeared at court on more than an occasional basis formed an inner circle of royal confidants with a distinct political role. But the majority of the nobility, in their capacities as rulers of their countries and defenders of the realm, were not in immediate contact with the king except when serving alongside him in the field. Their relationship rested rather on a mutual concern for stable government and reciprocal support for their respective roles.

I therefore see court politics, or high politics, as a distinct political culture. Its agenda was the distribution of honour and favour, and the opportunities for service in war and peace. The bond between the nobility and the crown rested on reciprocal obligations of *fidelitas* and *benevolentia*, but proximity to the royal will imparted tensions and fears which only confidence in the king (as under Henry V) or the suspension of the royal power (as in the minority of Henry VI) could assuage. External pressures, notably the need to fight a war, and the internal requirement for dynastic security and political stability, could impose discipline, but high politics was volatile, with a destructive potential for the whole realm.

There was a third area of politics between those of the court and the localities, what might be termed the politics of government. The focus of this was parliament. It will be objected that parliament was not, like the court and the localities, a continuous area of political activity and was merely an *ad hoc* selection of political society. Moreover some would seek to challenge Maddicott's claim that by the end of the fourteenth century 'it was the parliamentary commons and not the baronage who had come to be regarded as defending the interests of town and country'.[26] Yet parliament was (at that point) a regular event and the only occasion on which the voice of the whole realm was heard through those who collectively represented its communities. They were summoned, as the poet put it, 'forto shewe the sores of the royaulme' so that rancour could be purged before it erupted in rebellion.[27] In order to be able to speak for the common good, expressed through their common petition, the commons should have an independent voice. The assertion that elections should be free, not influenced by the crown or magnates, and the requirement that they be conducted through the whole class involved in the political life of the shire or borough, implies a view of politics as a critical appraisal of government by all those whom it touched.[28] That common petitions were in practice promoted by private interests, that elected members were retained by the king and magnates, that the king's *regimen parliamenti* set limits to what might be discussed, that members might be bribed and parliament as a whole intimidated, did not negate its essential and perceived function, that of expressing the authority of the realm either in support or criticism of royal government.

Parliament's concern with government was wide, but its active scrutiny more restricted. It registered approval of decisions on war and peace and foreign alliances but, as far as we know, only exceptionally were these debated, certainly by the lower house. It could also be the appropriate venue for setting accord between the nobility and defining precedence, but apart from expressing their concern over magnate divisions the commons themselves did not meddle in lords' matters. On exceptional occasions they were moved to criticize the character and size of the court, but Richard II's fierce response in 1397 showed that they trespassed on the royal dignity at their peril. In practice much of high politics was thus beyond the commons' remit. In so far as local society was concerned, the commons did have a legitimate concern with order, law enforcement and justice; with the preservation of social hierarchy and social peace; and with the honesty and effectiveness of local administration. Many of their petitions touched such matters in both particular and general terms. They might reprove lords for distributing badges and liveries and maintaining evildoers. They might complain of rapacious and corrupt royal justices, of sheriffs and their staffs who intimidated freeholders and perverted judicial process, of tax collectors and purveyors who exceeded their powers, of artisans and peasants who were greedy, undisciplined and disruptive.[29] In some sense all this reflected the ever-extending impact of government on local society and its corresponding readiness to seek remedy from the centre. As familiarity with the mechanism of government at Westminster spread, the shire and borough representatives became increasingly well-informed critics.[30] In this sense parliament served to mitigate the tension between government and subjects, between centre and locality.

A third and important concern of the commons in parliament was with the failings of central government. This focused pre-eminently on the crown's finances: first on its demand for and use of taxation, then, by the end of the fourteenth century, on the cost and character of the royal household and administration, and finally on the management of the crown's own revenues. The right of subjects to probe into the *status regis* did not go unchallenged and could only be justified on the ground that the state of the crown touched the welfare of the whole realm. That was evidently so if royal indebtedness impoverished subjects, weakened national defence, and undermined the king's dignity. To argue further that for a king to purge his courtiers, restrain his generosity, and resume his gifts would be an enhancement of his true dignity was a piece of political sophistry well within the commons' grasp by 1450. Yet their role of licensed critics was fraught with tensions and could induce threats of violence; normally both king and commons stayed well on this side of that line.

However much the commons saw themselves as representatives of their communities and custodians of the common good, members of parliament were foremost among that 'predatory governing élite' whose formation in the late Middle Ages has been denounced by Richmond. Is it true that this élite 'cared for the honour of the crown, the French war, birth and title, royal finance and government only because these nourished and enhanced itself'; that 'if they talked of England they talked of themselves'?[31] Doubtless yes, for as they assumed the role of a natural governing class they adopted its blinkered mentality. Yet besides this narrowing and hardening professional élite of successful lawyers, courtiers, rich gentry, and men of business, for whom repeated election to parliament was part of their career structure, the late medieval volumes of the *History of Parliament* have pointed to a widening membership of the commons and signs of increasing competition for a seat. The parliamentary experience was being diffused and the intake broadened; the élite were part of a wider constituency.[32]

Let us descend to the rustic environment of Oxfordshire. Edmund Rede, esquire, like many gentry, had probably attended the Inns of Court and inherited a modest estate, centred on Boarstall. In 1439 he was recruited into Henry VI's local affinity and was eventually knighted by Edward IV in 1465. Five times sheriff but only once a member of parliament (though that in 1450–1), he was

typical of many backbenchers who were governors in their localities.[33] But at
Boarstall he had gathered a well-stocked library of poets (Gower and Lydgate),
chronicles, chivalric romances and manuals, and works of devotion, as well as his
working books on law and estate management.[34] How his culture informed his
political attitude we cannot directly tell, but his friend and lesser neighbour, Peter
Idley esquire, drew on Rede's library for the moral precepts in his *Instructions to his
Son*. Two of these have political relevance. In general Peter Idley is a man of
peace, preaching moral and physical restraint, respect for neighbours, the law,
and religious duty. But he is also a patriot, charging his son

> To stande with thy kynge in the Reawme's defence
> And never to flee in no maner kynde
> But uttirly to abide to the last ende

and this goes with a sense of direct obedience to the king. To this degree the
realm is a meaningful entity to him. Secondly there is his moral economy,
exemplified in that most commonplace of warnings to young men – don't live
beyond your means:

> In mesure to spende, thus Y meane
> Eche man after his astate
> Spende after thy levelode woll strecche
> Worshipfully and not as a wrecche.[35]

It is an exhortation repeated in almost identical words all the way up society; by
William Harleston to young Sir William Stonor, by John Paston to old Sir John
Fastolf, by George Ashby to Henry VI.[36] A commonplace, but political
dynamite when this parliamentary class saw that the king himself did not heed
the advice they gave to their children and practised in their own households
through daily accounts and yearly budgets.[37] Fortescue was to elevate it into a
political programme and invest his council of professionals (like himself) with
the duty of restraining the king's generosity and parliament with a veto on
alienation of the fisc.[38] The parliamentary class doubtless wore the blinkers of a
ruling élite but their concern with good governance and their pride in England

had resonances throughout a wide spectrum of political society. In this sense they spoke not just for themselves.

Indeed the distinctive character of fifteenth-century politics is how the reverberations of political debate extend beyond political society to the yeomen and artisans. Consideration of this fourth political dimension, popular politics, must be left to Harvey's better-informed discussion in chapter 7 below; it seems to reflect the deepening impact of government, increasing familiarity with literate culture, and a growing sense of nationhood and Englishness. What is remarkable about Cade's revolt, Harvey has shown, is first the knowledge which the sub-parliamentary class had of the identity and character of the court group, secondly how it looked to the parliamentary programme of reform for the redress of grievances, and thirdly its use of bills and manifestos to spread its views, and of letters to organize support.[39] If those shipmen who cut off Suffolk's head really had raised the banner of St George and had repudiated the king's letters in the words ascribed to them, viz. 'they did not know the said king but they knew well the crown of England, saying that the aforesaid crown was the community of the realm and that the community of the realm was the crown of the realm', they had absorbed the political culture of a superior class.[40] Nonetheless they had their own agenda and mechanisms. Their agenda was the overthrow of the great extortioners and traitors in Kent who manipulated the local machinery of government to their advantage and who were protected by the false progeny and affinity of the duke of Suffolk. The mechanism was to organize popular risings and demonstrations to remove the oppressors and kill them.[41] Kent may not have been typical; it lacked a resident and active nobility who might have controlled the petty extortioners; it even lacked lords and substantial gentry opposed to the court who could express and lead popular opposition, as did the duke of Norfolk and Sir John Fastolf in East Anglia; but it was clearly not unique in suffering from the tyranny of petty gentry and officials and their protectors. Complaint about such people runs through the parliament rolls and this is a whole dimension of political life which cries out for investigation.

Where has this discussion led? The question 'what was fifteenth century politics about?' can only be answered, it seems to me, by reference to these four political arenas, or perhaps political cultures, each having its typical concerns, tensions, mechanisms, and language. Landed politics was concerned with the inheritance and the family; threats to these from social mobility and political ambition are regulated by law, lordship and neighbourhood, and its political language is of good lordship, friendship, and justice, meaning 'to every man his rights'. The concerns of curial politics were with honour, service, favour, and influence; its tensions arose from an imbalance between favour and service, between new and old nobility, between nobility and courtiers, tensions often expressed in conflicts of policy. War calmed such tensions, and kingship provided the focus of loyalty. Here the language was that of chivalric service, of natural councillors and defenders of church and realm, of fidelity to blood and honour. In the politics of government the concerns were with national security, social and political division, good governance, and the weight of public burdens notably taxation. Tensions could arise between the crown and the communities represented by the parliamentary commons, and the mechanism for resolving these was the parliamentary petition. The language is of the necessities of the king and kingdom, of the obligations of subjects and rulers, of the crown and the commonweal. The overriding concern of the people, as Harvey has said, was for security for their livelihood against those immediately above them who, protected by patrons, could abuse law and office to their own advantage. Economic and social strains fuelled these political tensions. Their mechanisms for redress operated through neighbours, manorial courts, obstructionism and eventually revolt, though exceptionally they might petition. Their cry was for justice, meaning the redress of wrongs.

That still leaves the question of whether there is a national framework into which we can fit these different political cultures, and a pattern of historical development in which the fifteenth century takes its place. Stubbsian constitutionalism derived too exclusively from what I have termed the politics of government; it reflected the world and language of Sir John Fortescue and the rolls of parliament, not that of landlord politics, court politics, or popular politics.[2] We understand better now the particular dynamic, problems, and language of other political arenas. But did these share common assumptions of political behaviour? Did the polity in any sense form a whole? Clearly these were not self-contained worlds. Men inhabited more than one: the nobility those of both curial and landed politics; some of the gentry those of land and government. As we have seen, their concerns and language crossed these boundaries, while disruption in one area could all too easily spread to another and feed its own tensions. There were, too, common concepts of obedience to, and respect for, royal authority, and adhesion to common ideals of honour, justice, hierarchy, property, and commonweal. A coherent philosophy of the state, evolved by the thirteenth-century schoolmen, had become the property of the political classes. Its language had been familiarized by parliamentary dialogue and popular polemic; it could even be employed in protest and rebellion. High politics was the concern of the whole realm, which anxiously watched for any signs of disharmony and misrule that threatened to undermine royal authority and imperil the body politlc.[43] In this sense the whole realm felt itself to be a political unit, a feeling strengthened by continual preoccupation with foreign war, by the spread of literacy and education and common language, by the growth of law and administration, and by the gradual coalescing of centre and locality. The formation of the English state through such forces is undoubtedly what the history of the late Middle Ages is about.

Yet if there existed a common language of politics, it was given different meanings in different political arenas. Honour meant one thing to a royal duke, another to the Pastons; justice had different implications in different social contexts; the fidelity and obedience to the king owed by any peer was of a different order to that of Peter Idley; king and people meant different things when they spoke of 'the crown', and law was both a political principle and a weapon against an adversary.[44] These differences are as important as the common usage, for fifteenth-century England did not operate as a political unit but as a series of political contexts, each with its own problems and rules.

And so, as we might expect, the picture is complex, of a political society still particularized but with interlocking experience and interchangeable language. Yet the identity of the English people and their sense of nationhood was noticeably advanced in this century by a series of formative political experiences. The first was the celebration of English ascendancy and destiny under Henry V, to which Allmand has drawn attention.[45] The second was the multiple crisis of the mid century which uniquely affected all four political arenas. The third was the effective abandonment of the crown's continental ambitions in the second half of the century and the consequent growth of insularity, separating the medieval from the early modern outlook. In the late fifteenth century English politics turned inward to deal with the problems of domestic government and royal power presented by civil war. These experiences of national triumph and national crisis helped to create the political climate in which a unitary polity could evolve.[46]

Notes

1. McFarlane, *Nobility*, pp. viii–xxviii.

2. Ibid., p. 297.

3. Ibid., pp. 119–21.

4. Carpenter, *Locality*, pp. 113; C. Carpenter, 'Who Did Rule the Midlands in the Later Middle Ages?', *Midland History*, XIX (1994), pp. 1–20; M.A. Hicks, 'Bastard Feudalism' in *Richard III and his Rivals: Magnates and their Motives in the Wars of the Roses* (1991), pp. 1–40; R. E. Horrox, 'Local and National Politics in Fifteenth Century England', *Journal of Medieval History*, XVIII (1992), pp. 391–403; E. Powell, 'After "After McFarlane": The Poverty of Patronage and the Case for Constitutional History' in *Trade, Devotion and Governance: Papers in Later Medieval History*, D.J. Clayton, R.G. Davies and P. McNiven (eds.) (Stroud, 1994), pp. 1–16; C. F. Richmond, 'An English Mafia?', *Nottingham Medieval Studies*, XXXVI (1992), pp. 236–43.

5. S.J. Payling, 'Social Mobility, Demographic Change and Landed Society in Late Medieval England', *Ec.H.R.* XLV (1992), pp. 51–73.

6. Carpenter, *Locality*, p. 287.

7. C.F. Richmond, *The Paston Family in the Fifteenth Century* (Cambridge, 1990); Carpenter, *Locality*, p. 402.

8. The penetration of the county élite by new arrivals was more common in some counties than others: G.L. Harriss, 'The Medieval Parliament', *Parliamentary History* (1994), XIII, p. 216.

9. Carpenter, *Locality*, pp. 364, 393–7.

10. Ibid., pp. 365, 396–7, 472–5, 636; S. M. Wright, *The Derbyshire Gentry in the Fifteenth Century* (Derbyshire Record Society, VIII, Chesterfield, 1983), pp. 122–6; I.D. Rowney, 'Arbitration in Gentry Disputes of the Later Middle Ages', *History*, LXVII (1982), pp. 367–76; S. J. Payling, *Political Society in Lancastrian England* (Oxford, 1991), pp. 203ff.

11. E. Powell, *Kingship, Law, and Society: Criminal Justice in the Reign of Henry V* (Oxford, 1989), pp. 208–24; cf. the important remarks on John of Gaunt's position in Lancashire in S. K. Walker, *The Lancastrian Affinity, 1361–1399* (Oxford, 1990), pp. 145, 170–4, 180–1. Other examples of challenges to established leadership are those mounted by William, Lord Ferrers of Groby, and Joan, Lady Bergavenny, against Richard, earl of Warwick, in 1427 (Carpenter, *Locality*, pp. 380ff); by Ralph, Lord Cromwell, against Henry, Lord Grey of Codnor, in Nottinghamshire in 1440 (S.J. Payling, 'Law and Arbitration in Nottinghamshire, 1399–1461', in *People, Politics, and Community in the Later*

Middle Ages, J.T. Rosenthal and C.F. Richmond (eds.) (Gloucester 1987), pp. 143–6); and by James, earl of Ormond, against John, Lord Tiptoft, in Cambridgeshire in the 1430s (R. Virgoe, 'The Cambridgeshire Election of 1439', *B.I.H.R.* XLVI (1973), pp. 97–9).

12.   A.J. Pollard, *North-Eastern England during the Wars of the Roses* (Oxford, 1990), pp. 245–57; cf. Carpenter, *Locality*, p. 396.

13.   Wright, *Derbyshire Gentry*, pp. 71–81; C.D. Ross, *Edward IV* (1974), p. 119.

14.   Carpenter, *Locality*, pp. 412, 433–5, 635; R. Virgoe, 'William Tailboys and Lord Cromwell: Crime and Politics in Lancastrian England', *B.J.R.L.* LV (1973), pp. 459–82; *G.E.C.* V, pp. 426–7; C.D. Ross, 'The Yorkshire Baronage, 1399–1435' (unpub. D.Phil. thesis, Oxford Univ. 1951), ch.vii.

15.   *Commons 1386–1421*, I, pp. 255, 553.

16.   Carpenter, *Locality*, pp. 348, 625, 628–9.

17.   S.K. Walker, 'Yorkshire Justices of the Peace, 1389–1413', *E.H.R.* CVIII (1993), pp. 281–313.

18.   Richmond, *Paston Family*, p. 233 for Sir John Fastolf's expressive letter of 1450.

19.   Carpenter, *Locality*, pp. 272–3; Wright, *Derbyshire Gentry*, p. 86; Payling, *Political Society*, pp. 109–19; E. Acheson, *A Gentry Community: Leicestershire in the Fifteenth Century*, c. 1422–c.1485 (Cambridge, 1992), pp. 107–10.

20.   Carpenter, *Locality*, p. 348; McFarlane, *Nobility*, p. 120–1.

21.   Ibid., p. 121; C.F. Richmond, '1485 and All That, or What was going on at the Battle of Bosworth ?' in *Richard III: Loyalty, Lordship and Law*, P.W. Hammond (ed.) (1986), pp. 172–206. It is of course true, as Carpenter points out (*Locality*, p. 397), that the nobility would only serve abroad once domestic political peace had been established and their inheritances were secure, a sequence evident in the reigns of Edward III, Henry V, and Edward IV.

22.   G.L. Harriss, *Cardinal Beaufort* (Oxford, 1988), p.60; M.K. Jones, 'Somerset, York, and the Wars of the Roses ', *E.H.R.* CIV (1989), pp. 291–5; A. Sinclair, 'The Beauchamp earls of Warwick in the Later Middle Ages' (unpub. Ph.D. thesis, London Univ. 1986), p. 120.

23.   For the discord aroused by the precedence quarrels between the earls of Warwick and Norfolk in 1426 and between the dukes of Warwick and Buckingham in 1446, see Carpenter, *Locality*, pp. 385–7, 413. John d'Arundel secured recognition for his claim to the title in 1433 by virtue of his service in France with the duke of Bedford (*G.E.C.* I, pp. 247–8)

24.   Such tensions are evident in all the major political crises, of 1311, 1340–1, 1386–88, 1397–99, perhaps 1403, 1453–55, 1469, and 1483.

25.   For Gaunt's fear of asassination in 1385, see A. Goodman, *John of Gaunt* (1992), pp. 102–3; for York' s opposition to the court in 1450–2, see P.A. Johnson, *Duke Richard of York, 1411–1460* (Oxford, 1988), pp . 81–108. The ultimate statement of the right to purge the commonwealth is contained in the Yorkist manifestoes of 1459–60, and repudiated in the *Somnium Vigilantis*. For a very similar stance and language adopted by the earl of Essex in 1599, see M.E . James, *Politics, Society, and Culture. Studies in Early Modern England* (Cambridge,1986), pp. 422–3, 454–5.

26.   J.R. Maddicott, 'Parliament and the Constituencies, 1272–1377' in *The English Parliament in the Middle Ages*, R.G. Davies and J.H. Denton (eds.) (Manchester, 1981), pp. 61, 86: 'it had become the chief intermediary between the crown and its subjects'. But cf. M.C. Carpenter, 'Gentry and Community in Medieval England', *Journal of British Studies*, XXXIII (1994), p. 364, and Carpenter, *Locality*, p. 288: 'the nobility provided the essential connecting link between centre and locality'.

27. *Mum and the Sothsegger*, ed. M. Day and R. Steele (E.E.T.S. original series, CXCIX, 1936), p. 59 line 1120 .

28. For a discussion of the legislation regarding electoral practice, see J.S. Roskell's 'Introductory Survey' in *Commons 1386–1421*, I, pp. 55–68.

29. For the Commons' concern with badges and royal justices, see N. Saul, ' The Commons and the Abolition of Badges', *Parliamentary History*, IX (1990), pp. 302–15; J.R. Maddicott, 'Law and Lordship; Royal Justices and Retaining in Thirteenth and Fourteenth Century England', *P.P. Supplements*, IV (1978). For purveyance, see C. Given-Wilson, 'Purveyance for the Royal Household, 1362–1413' *B.I.H.R.* LVI (1983), pp. 145–63.

30. G.L. Harriss, 'Political Society and the Growth of Government in Late Medieval England', *P.P.* CXXXVIII (1993), pp. 34–9.

31. Richmond, *Nottingham Medieval Studies*, XXXVI, pp. 235–6.

32. *Commons 1336–1421*, I, appendix D1 shows an increasing proportion of novices elected. Appendix D2 a decreasing proportion of re-elected members after 1400. The constituency surveys bear this out. Whether the trend continued into the second and third quarters of the century remains to be shown in the succeeding volumes.

33. J.C. Wedgwood, *History of Parliament, 1437–1509. Biographies of Members*, (1936) pp. 711–12.

34. *The Boarstall Cartulary*, H.E. Salter (ed.) (Oxford Historical Society, LXXXVIII, 1930), pp. 286–91.

35. *Peter Idley's Instructions to his Son*, Charlotte D'Evelyn (ed.) (Boston, 1953), pp. 95 (lines 859–61), 84 (lines 204–5, 209–10). Idley was bailiff of the honour of Wallingford, 1441–6, and Controller of the King's Works, 1456–61.

36. *The Stonor Letters and Papers*, C.L. Kingsford (ed.) (2 vols, Camden Society , 3rd series, 1919), II, p. 98; *Paston L. & P.* II, p. 170, cited by Richmond, *Paston Family*, p. 252; G. Ashby, 'Active Policy of a Prince', p. 21 (lines 274–8), in idem, *Poems*, M. Bateson (ed.) (E.E.T.S. extra series, LXXXVI, 1899).

37. *Household Accounts from Medieval England*, C.M. Woolgar (ed.) (Records of Social and Economic History, new series, XVII, Oxford, 1992), I, pp. 18–65.

38. J. Fortescue, *The Governance of England*, C. Plummer (ed.) (Oxford, 1885), pp. 143–4, 154–6.

39. I. M.W. Harvey, *Jack Cade's Rebellion of 1450* (Oxford, 1991), pp. 73–111.

40. R. Virgoe, 'The Death of William de la Pole, Duke of Suffolk', *B.J.R.L.* XLVII (1965), pp. 489–502. It echoes the poem 'God Save the Kyng and Kepe the Crown', *Historical Poems of the Fourteenth and Fifteenth Centuries*, R.H. Robbins (ed.) (New York, 1959), pp. 45–9.

41. Harvey, *Cade's Rebellion*, pp. 80, 83, 105–6, 185.

42. W.E. Ives, 'The Common Lawyers', in *Profession, Vocation and Culture in Later Medieval England*, C.H. Clough (ed.) (Liverpool, 1982), pp. 190–1, points out that Fortescue's 'dominium politicum et regale' probably reflected the common view in the profession.

43. P.C. Maddern, 'Weather, War and Witches; Sign and Cause in Fifteenth-Century Vernacular Chronicles', in *A World Explored. Essays in Honour of Laurie Gardiner*, A. Gilmour-Bryson (ed.) (Melbourne, 1993), pp. 77–98.

44. P.C. Maddern, 'Honour among the Pastons: Gender and Integrity in English Provincial Society', *Journal of Medieval History*, XIV (1988), pp. 357–72; C.M. Crowder, 'Peace and Justice

around 1400: a Sketch', *Aspects of Late Medieval Government and Society. Essays Presented to J. R. Lander*, J.G. Rowe (ed.) (Toronto, 1986), pp. 53–82.

45. C.T. Allmand, *Henry V* (1992), pp. 404–25.

46. James, *Society, Politics, and Culture*, p. 460: 'The desire and pursuit of the whole can be seen as a dominant theme of English sixteenth century political aspiration.'

2

THE POLITICS OF FAMILY: LATE MEDIEVAL MARRIAGE CONTRACTS[1]

Simon Payling

HISTORY OF PARLIAMENT

T he story of the arrangements made by English landed families at the marriages of their children, from the appearance of recognizable marriage contracts in the early thirteenth century to the invention of the 'strict settlement' in the late seventeenth, is one of ever-increasing sophistication and elaboration.[2] As landholders sought to free themselves from the restraints placed upon their freedom of disposition by common-law rules and to anticipate an ever-increasing range of future contingencies when they arranged the marriages of their children, the land law and the legal devices it sanctioned became progressively more complex. Since these devices determined the form marriage contracts assumed, this increasing complexity was mirrored in the arrangements made at marriage. Nevertheless, this chain of development does not disguise the fact that the simple contracts of the thirteenth century deal with the same basic questions with regard to the future of the contracted couple as do the advanced contracts of the seventeenth century and beyond. What changed was the complexity of the answers they were designed to provide. In this paper I will be concerned with the two most fundamental questions addressed in the commonest form of contract, that for the marriage of a son and heir to a non-inheriting daughter drawn up between their respective fathers, and the answers found to these questions in contracts from the early thirteenth century to the early sixteenth.[3] The first question is how the bride was to be maintained in the event of her widowhood; and the second, how the groom's inheritance was to be guaranteed to him and the future of the couple's issue assured.

These questions are best examined in the context of the two principal interests involved, those of the fathers of bride and groom. The concerns of a father in marrying his male heir are too obvious to warrant extensive discussion. Evidently he was seeking to perpetuate his lineage and to realize the asset represented by the marriage before it could fall into the hands of his superior lord. Equally clearly he was concerned with status and political advantage, wanting for his heir a bride who would add lustre to the family name and bring with her valuable political connections. If he was looking for advantage in a more tangible form he might hope to extend the family estates by marrying his son to an heiress or heiress apparent. Yet while it is not difficult to discern what a sensible father wanted from the marriage of his heir, there were limits to what he was prepared to sacrifice to obtain it. The more desirable the bride in terms of status and connections, the greater the jointure settlement needed to secure her hand, and hence the greater the loss of landed income to the groom's father consequent upon the marriage. Although this loss could be limited by a jointure settlement in remainder expectant on the death of the groom's father, not only was the degree to which this could be done limited by the couple's immediate need for a competence, but an over-generous settlement could seriously compromise the future interests of the couple's son and heir if the bride long survived the groom.[4] Heiresses demanded yet greater sacrifices, for not only could they command handsome jointures but they did not bring with them the compensatory money portion that came with a landless bride, the portion passing instead from the groom's to the bride's father.[5] The male heir's marriage thus became a source of immediate financial loss rather than profit to his father, and while, considered in the long term, such outlay was justified in that it was cheaper to marry land than to buy it, in the short term it could have unpleasant consequences, particularly if the groom's father were dependent, as so many were, on his heir's portion to finance good marriages for his daughters.[6]

What the father of a bride required when he gave his daughter in marriage is rather more complex. If she was his heiress apparent, he required money; if she was not, he had other demands to make in return for the money portion he would bestow upon her. Plainly for him the same considerations concerning status and political connection applied as they did for the father of the groom. It needs to be emphasized that the marriage of a daughter represented an opportunity just as did that of a male heir. Recent studies of local society in late medieval England have shown that the marriages of non-inheriting daughters played a crucial role in extending a family's political and social horizons.[7] This is why, as McFarlane once remarked, 'among the first claims on his pocket which no self-respecting father thought it right – or wise – to shirk was the provision of adequate marriage portions for his daughters'.[8] The father was compensated for the expense by the acquisition of distinguished sons-in-law who added both to his political capital and his worldly repute. This is one reason why strikingly few daughters of baronial or greater gentry families found their way into nunneries, despite the fact that disposing of a daughter in this way was a far cheaper solution to the problem of her future maintenance than finding her a husband.[9] The basic point here is that if a father were rich enough to arrange suitable marriages for his daughters he would do so, particularly after the mid-thirteenth century when the money portion came to replace the portion in land, and he would probably consider it a prudent investment in his own and his family's worship. Yet if the urge to contract marriages for his daughters was strong, so was the determination that his married daughters should, in the material sense, be well provided for. It was to this end that he made demands of the fathers of prospective grooms, the most important of which was the settlement of land in jointure to provide, amongst other things, for his daughter's immediate comfort and for her potential widowhood. In crude terms the greater the jointure the groom's father was ready to settle, the greater the sum the bride's father was prepared to pay for the marriage. Thus if a father with a male heir to marry were to realize the capital value of that marriage, he needed to balance his own interests against those of the bride's father. It was to strike this balance that a formal contract was necessary.

The interests of the contracting parties did not, however, exist in a vacuum. They were played out in the context of the rules governing the descent of real property and the incidents attendant upon a system of feudal tenure which bound landed society together by ties of obligation and service. By the early thirteenth century the most important of these incidents were those of wardship and marriage. They made it strongly in the interests of a tenant to marry his heir young to avoid the disagreeable prospect that the choice of bride and, more importantly, the cash value of the marriage would fall into the hands of his lord in the event of the tenant's early death.[10] By the same token, early marriage was very much to the disadvantage of lords, and the greatest loser, always lord and never tenant, was the crown. Early marriage cost the crown both revenue and a valuable source of patronage. Canon law came to its aid in part. Marriages contracted under the age of consummation, fixed by presumption at fourteen for boys and twelve for girls, could be repudiated by either bride or groom when they reached those respective ages.[11] Thus, if a married male ward under fourteen came into its hands, the crown could exert pressure on him to repudiate his bride in favour of one of royal choice. But such pressure was, from the late thirteenth century until the early Tudor period, the only redress the crown possessed. Not until the reign of Henry VII did it take the obvious step of insisting that it would not be bound by marriages contracted before the age of consent.[12] In this situation it is not surprising that one of the prevailing characteristics of late medieval marriage was that couples were contracted young. Nor was this the only way that prevailing marriage customs worked to the disadvantage of lords in general and the crown in particular. Jointures deprived the crown of the wardship of valuable lands since, when a tenant-in-chief died leaving an under-age heir, the crown lost the wardship of those lands in which the widow had a joint interest together with the dower lands bestowed on her by common law;[13] a loss which outweighed the compensatory gain represented by the cash value of any future marriage of the widow which accrued by right to the crown. It was thus in the crown's interests to restrict the volume of land in the hands of widows, but again the late medieval crown, driven by political rather than financial expediency, indulged its tenants. It was not until the promulgation of the Statute of Uses in 1536 that the crown intervened to reduce its loss. The main points to appreciate here are that late medieval landed families could draw up contracts for the marriages of their their children largely ignoring the interests of their lords, even when that lord was the king; and that it was not until the Tudor period, when the crown became more aggressively interventionist in the way landed families dealt with their inheritances, that marriage contracts came to include legal charms to ward off the evil of the crown's feudal rights.

What, however, late medieval families could not ignore were the rules that regulated the descent of land. As Painter long ago remarked, these 'seriously hampered a family's control over its property and relationships',[14] and while this hindrance was felt more strongly in the earlier than the later medieval period, it long retained some force. As far as marriage was concerned the most important of these rules was that relating to dower. Common-law dower was a landed provision for widowhood that arose by operation of the law and it needs to be distinguished from those older forms of dower, important in the marriage contracts of the thirteenth and early fourteenth centuries, that arose out of an agreement between the contracting parties.[15] By the middle of the thirteenth century, a widow's common-law dower entitlement had come to comprise a third of all those lands of which her husband had been seised at any time during their marriage, rather than the more restricted entitlement that had prevailed in the late twelfth century.[16] A rule so generous to widows was an important factor in determining the structure of landed society, ensuring that a significant part of the kingdom's wealth was always in their hands,[17] and, from the point of view of landed society in general, could only be tolerated because of the tendency of widows to remarry. Thus what a family temporarily lost through a widow's dower, it potentially gained through marriage to a dowered widow. The rule also had an effect on the form of marriage contracts, limiting the size of that other provision for widowhood, namely jointure.

The interplay between the arrangements landowners made at the marriages of their children and other relevant aspects of the land law beyond dower, particularly the rules relating to conditional gifts and entails, is best understood by looking at typical contracts from a range of dates. The first two contracts abstracted in the appendix to this paper illustrate two very important developments: the decline in the *maritagium*, or marriage portion in land, in favour of the money portion as the bride's father's side of the contract, and, on the groom's father's side, the decline of the older forms of dower in favour of jointure.

The first of these contracts, dated 1236, is an early example of a post-Conquest marriage contract recognizable as such in that it contains in one document mutual obligations on the part of both fathers.[18] Its terms are fairly basic. The obligations assumed by the groom's father extended no further than to giving his son land worth £40 *per annum* with which to dower the bride. Anciently, indeed almost certainly as late as 1217, such an endowment at the time of marriage was sufficient to extinguish a widow's claim to common-law dower, but this was seemingly no longer the case by 1236.[19] In this contract the purpose of the agreement was to provide for the bride should the groom die before coming into his patrimony, a role soon to be usurped by jointure. For his part, the groom's father also gave the couple £40 *per annum* of land, said to be 'in free marriage', and undertook to pay the groom's father 200 marks. Here is a stage in that key transition from land to money as the contribution of the bride's father to the material establishment of the new couple or, put another way, the shift from land to money as the non-inheriting daughter's share of her father's inheritance.[20] This transition was well advanced by the mid-thirteenth century and it would be difficult to overstate its importance in the history of the marriage contract. It greatly added to the range and flexibility of arrangements that could be made at marriage. The money portion was a very different thing from the *maritagium* in that it went not to the new couple but to the father of the groom. The marriage of a male heir thus became what it had not been before, an occasion of financial profit for his father. In return he was expected to extend his commitment to the landed foundation of the couple. Whereas with the *maritagium* both fathers contributed to this foundation, under the system of the money portion this burden fell on the groom's father alone. On marrying his son, in exchange for a cash sum from the bride's father, he committed himself to either an immediate or a future loss of income in the form of a settlement of land on the couple greater than that represented by the older forms of dower. He had, in short, to make good the couple's loss of the *maritagium*. It is important to note that he also forwent something that was of long-term advantage to his family: since the *maritagium* was an heritable estate, intended to provide for both the widow and her issue, it represented, potentially at least, a permanent addition to the lands of the groom's family.[21] It was these losses that justified his receipt of a money portion that was, amongst the greatest families, a very substantial sum. The average portion given with baronial daughters between 1300 and 1500 was in excess of 1,000 marks, and individual portions were not infrequently very much greater.[22]

Thus, from the mid-thirteenth century, the marriage of an heir was, in cash terms, a valuable commodity to his father, but it was one for which he paid in the form of a greater landed settlement in favour of the couple than he would otherwise have made. Moreover, in the case of many fathers, the money they received on the marriages of their heirs they later paid out when they married their daughters: a father with only a son was in a singularly fortunate financial position. On balance, from the point of view of the father of a groom, the benefits of the new system are to be seen in the form of the greater flexibility it gave him: one might say that he now had the option of mortgaging land, in the form of the settlement he made on the couple, on favourable terms without the danger of a permanent diminution of his family's landed base since the lands so settled would be reunited with the patrimony on his death. It is, however, from the point of view of the part of the bride's father that the advantages of the new system are most obvious. While the *maritagium* represented an increase in the landed resources of the groom's family, it represented a reduction in those of the bride's. Clearly her father would prefer to keep his estates intact and make instead the sacrifice of raising a money portion. This is particularly true when one considers that there is no evidence for the late medieval period that the raising of portions led in any significant degree to the mortgaging or selling of land.[23] Portions were generally paid in instalments over several years and could thus generally be met out of income.[24] Only after the great portion inflation of the late sixteenth and seventeenth centuries was this no longer the case.[25]

The argument is not, of course, quite as straightforward as this. After all, a father who had a daughter to marry, one, that is, who was not his heiress, also had a son, and hence what he lost in granting land to her, he, or more precisely the family he headed, gained by receiving land on the marriage of his son. The most important point, then, is not the advantage of the system in endowing daughters with money as against land from the viewpoint of the father of either bride or groom, but rather its advantage from the viewpoint of landed society as a whole. That advantage lay in the fact that the money portion brought a greater stability of inheritance. As McFarlane pointed out, 'Daughters, unless they were heiresses, were not, in the later middle ages, an occasion for the dispersal of land'.[26] Instead, the land that was dispersed on marriage was dispersed within the male line of the groom's family in the form of a gift from father to son subject to the life, and hence the temporary, interest of the son's bride.

The second contract in the appendix is drawn from a period when the money portion was already the usual, though not the invariable,[27] form of the bride's father's contribution, but before jointure had displaced the older forms of dower as that assumed by the father of the groom. In this 1277 contract the groom's father undertook to dower the bride with land worth £100 *per annum* which was to stand as her total endowment if the groom should predecease him, but which would become only part of her common-law dower should the groom outlive him and she her husband. In addition to this endowment, he also undertook to convey seisin of these lands to the groom when the latter reached the age of twenty. The purpose of this future grant was to enable the couple to set up an independent household when of an age to do so, and it meant that the groom's father was committing himself to a not inconsiderable loss of income should his son either live to be twenty or die before that time leaving the bride a widow. In return for this sacrifice, the bride's father was to pay him 600 marks but to make no landed provision for the couple. Beyond this absence of *maritagium*, the most significant point to notice here is that the 600 marks was not to be paid unconditionally. Two-thirds of it was to be repaid if the bride died childless and under the age of thirteen. One reason for this is clear: if the bride should have the misfortune to die young, she would never enjoy the endowment that her father's financial sacrifice had purchased for her and he was thus entitled to some repayment. More interesting, however, is the fact that repayment was conditional not only on her early death but on her death without issue. This gives an insight into what the money portion was considered as buying beyond provision for the bride's potential widowhood.

The more detailed repayment clause in the third contract in the appendix makes the same point more forcefully. The point to notice here is that if the Montagu bride were to die in the lifetime of the groom's father without issue by the groom, the whole of the thousand-mark portion was to be repaid. The 'without issue' is the critical phrase for it demonstrates that the portion was perceived as a contribution to the future security not only of the bride but also of her issue.[28] A further stipulation of the contract was that if the bride were to die with issue by the groom in the lifetime of her father-in-law then only 600 marks would be repayable, the other 400 marks remaining in suspense to be repaid if that issue were to die in the lifetime of the groom's father. These repayment terms reflect a hard bargain driven by Lord Montagu, who, as a close personal friend of the king, was in a strong negotiating position, and they are not entirely typical. But it is a standard clause in marriage contracts from the late thirteenth century, as soon in fact as portions began to be paid almost exclusively in money, that part of the portion, usually a half, was to be repaid if the bride died within either a certain number of years of the marriage or before a certain age, varying between thirteen, as in the 1277 contract, and, more commonly, eighteen or twenty,[29] and always one finds the proviso 'without issue'. In short, it was the bride's childlessness rather than the mere fact of her premature death that justified repayment,[30] not least because her childless death restored to the groom's father the marriage of his son at its full market value, whereas the survival of her issue would significantly devalue the marriage.

Against this background it is easier to see the real significance of the new feature introduced by the Montagu contract, namely, jointure. Here the groom's father does not, as he does in the two earlier contracts, dower the bride with certain lands; instead he undertakes to settle lands worth £100 *per annum* on the couple and their issue. This form of settlement had two advantages from the point of view of the bride and her father. First, it was a more secure form of provision than the older forms of dower for her premature widowhood, that is, if she were widowed in the lifetime of her father-in-law and hence not entitled to common-law dower out of her husband's inheritance. Jointure was a legal estate. She had joint seisin of the land with her husband and, on his death, the law protected her seisin even, from the late fourteenth century, if her husband suffered forfeiture for treason.[31] Second, and more important, is the consideration that, while the older forms of dower were subsumed within it, should the bride ever become entitled to common-law dower,[32] jointure was not. Thus, assuming the groom lived to inherit, his widow was entitled both to her jointure and a third of the remaining and, almost invariably, the larger part of his inheritance. It is this which explains what McFarlane described as the 'new and sometimes disproportionate weight' of widows in late medieval society,[33] and was the culmination of a process that had seen a steady improvement in their position since the late twelfth century.

Yet if jointure is viewed only in terms of an evolution out of the older forms of dower and a further improvement in the position of widows, an important part of its purpose is neglected. It was not simply a settlement of land on the bride for her life; it was a settlement upon her and her issue by the groom. In this sense it evolved not out of the older forms of dower but out of the *maritagium*. Since, with the move from land to money as the bride's father's contribution to the material establishment of the couple, he no longer contributed to the maintenance of the bride or her issue, it was reasonable that the groom's father should increase, both in extent and type, the landed contribution he made to the couple, and so it was that jointure emerged out of the decline of the *maritagium*.

This raises the question of why, while the money portion came to supersede the *maritagium* in the mid-thirteenth century, jointure did not replace the older forms of dower until towards the end of that century. Part of the answer probably lies in the obscure timing of the process by which the latter lost all vestige of their power to bar a widow's claim to common-law dower and so became less attractive to the fathers of grooms. More important, however, is the consideration that it was not until the promulgation in 1285 of the second Statute of Westminster, with its famous first chapter, *de donis conditionalibus*, that jointure became a form of settlement well-adapted to answer the concerns of the fathers of brides. Before *de donis*, if a father granted lands jointly to his son, his son's wife and their issue, the grantees were restrained from alienation only until they had issue because common law interpreted the grant as one in fee simple, conditional only upon that issue's birth.[34] If one looks at this rule with reference to marriage contracts, it was unsatisfactory from the point of view of the bride's father, who had paid a money portion to ensure, amongst other things, that his daughter's issue would inherit part at least of her husband's lands. Badly drafted as it undoubtedly was, *de donis* restrained alienation by the grantees and so protected the inheritance of their issue and, as it came to be interpreted by the mid-fourteenth century, the issue of the issue and so on until issue failed.[35] The importance of this protection is illustrated by the following common scenario. Suppose the bride died leaving only female issue, the groom subsequently having male issue by a later wife. Before *de donis* the groom could disinherit the female issue of his first wife of any jointure settled upon them in favour of his son; after *de donis* he no longer could do so. The effect of *de donis* was thus to complete the decline of the *maritagium* for the bride's issue could no longer be disinherited of their mother's jointure and so no longer required the security given to them by a settlement of land by the bride's father to which they were inheritable but to which their father's issue by a later wife were not.

By the end of the thirteenth century marriage contracts had already taken on the basic form that was to characterize them until the early sixteenth century and beyond. The groom's father settled a joint estate on the couple and their future issue, while the bride's father paid him a sum of money proportional to the size of this jointure, part of which sum was repayable if the bride died without issue within a defined period. There is, however, a centrally important aspect of the marriage contract that we have not yet touched on. This is illustrated by the fourth contract in the appendix, dating from 1372. The groom's father undertook not to disinherit the groom by any feoffment or other deed of any lands which he held in present possession or in reversion expectant upon his step-mother's death – she held part of his inheritance in jointure and dower – except one named manor which was to be settled on a younger son in tail male, saving reversion to the main line of the family. Here we see the other important consideration, beyond the size of the jointure, that weighed upon the mind of a wise father in marrying a daughter. This was a calculation of the landed wealth the groom could expect to enjoy on his father's death, a wealth that would determine the extent of the bride's potential common-law dower and the social position of any heir of the marriage. The bride's father thus had a strong interest in ensuring that the groom's father would not subsequently diminish the groom's expectations by alienating any part of the family patrimony. Even a temporary alienation, such as a life estate to provide for a younger son or a generous jointure in favour of any future step-mother of the groom could have an adverse effect on the bride's dower. Moreover, a thoughtful father on marrying his daughter was looking beyond her security to the future interests of the heir of the marriage, for both would suffer from any permanent alienation by the groom's father subsequent to the marriage. It was for these reasons that marriage contracts came to place restrictions on the freedom of alienation of the groom's father.

Such restrictive settlements became common in the second decade of the fourteenth century[36] – the 1372 contract is a later example of interest because of its exception in favour of a younger son – and this early date is in itself a clue to the reasons behind their adoption. While it is certain that such settlements were designed to control alienation by the fathers of grooms and were incorporated into marriage contracts at the insistence of fathers of brides, this begs an important question: why should the fathers of grooms be considered liable to disinherit, either partially or worse, their newly-married heirs? McFarlane's answer is well known: in the emotional links that bound fathers to their younger sons he saw a genuine threat to an inflexible primogenitary law which left younger sons with nothing, and in the enfeoffment-to-use he found the means by which fathers could satisfy these emotional links without the need for *inter vivos* alienations that meant an immediate loss of income to themselves. Their readiness so to devise lands by will at the expense of their heirs, the argument runs, provoked a reaction on the part of fathers of brides who were understandably anxious not to see the expectations of their sons-in-law diminished. 'What', McFarlane asked, 'was the point of a man's offering a large portion in order to secure for his daughter the hand of an heir, if the value of the match could be subsequently depreciated by an excessive provision for the heir's younger brother?'[37] He dated this reaction to the second half of the fifteenth century because he believed that only then did restrictive marriage settlements become common, and this led him to the conclusion that, by 1500, 'primogeniture, having outlasted two centuries of confusion, was once more securely enthroned'.[38]

Such an analysis, attractive though it is in its simplicity, cannot be accepted. McFarlane did not realize that the restrictive settlement predated the rise of the use, and he underestimated by more than a century and a quarter the date at which restrictive settlements came into common usage. Moreover, recent research has made it very clear that the use did not pose a serious threat to primogeniture.[39] As Carpenter has remarked in her exhaustive study of landed society in late medieval Warwickshire, 'there is no evidence that direct male heirs [were ever] in any danger from dismemberment of the [paternal] estate; there was in fact an almost reverential attitude to their rights, which often cost their younger brothers dear'.[40] How then is the restrictive marriage settlement to be explained? Carpenter has suggested that it was not designed to protect the heir and his bride against his father's generosity to his younger brothers, at least not in the way McFarlane imagined, but rather to any future wife his father might take and any issue he might have by her.[41] In insisting that the contract for the marriage of the heir incorporated a restriction on alienation, it is likely, therefore, that the bride's father had in mind a scenario in which the groom's mother died and the groom's father married again, settling a significant part of his inheritance upon his new wife in jointure and so potentially delaying – perhaps long delaying – the moment the groom came into his full inheritance. If he were given to pessimism he might envisage a scenario yet more unpalatable from his point of view in which the later wife came so to dominate the affections of her husband that he became minded to disinherit his heir in favour of his issue by her.[42] Even if one considers this latter scenario too uncommon an occurrence to inform the conditions of marriage contracts, it remains true, as Carpenter has pointed out, that jointures were the greatest single cause of serious loss of property to the heir,[43] and that second jointures were a common phenomenon.[44] Further, if the second jointure incorporated some measure of provision for the issue of the second marriage by being settled in joint tail, the survival of this issue would involve a measure of disinheritance for any son of the first.

Carpenter's explanation for the emergence of the restrictive settlement certainly fits the known chronology better than does McFarlane's, and this adds strength to her argument. While she accepts McFarlane's claim that the restrictive settlement became common only as late as the second half of the fifteenth century and is led to wonder if there is any significance in its emergence immediately following 'a period when dowagers had been having a field day',[45] the correct chronology, dating the emergence of the restrictive settlement to the early fourteenth century, makes her explanation more rather than less compelling. It is striking that the restrictive settlement became common at about the same time as it became almost invariable practice for the groom's father to settle a jointure on the marriage of his heir, and it is difficult to accept this as mere coincidence. Nor should we imagine that for the great majority of such fathers, who had no intention of seriously diminishing the expectations of their heirs, whether in favour of younger sons or future wives, at the time they undertook not to alienate, this undertaking simply represented the loss of an unnecessary freedom. In fact it was a hostage to an uncertain future and could in certain circumstances imperil the continuation of the patrimony in the male line. Suppose, for example, the groom died in the lifetime of his father, leaving only female issue but with a surviving younger brother. Here a restrictive settlement entered into on his marriage would restrain his father from perpetuating the patrimony in the male line through that brother.[46]

It is only in this field of restricting a father's freedom of alienation when he married his heir that one observes any growth in sophistication in the marriage contract from the early fourteenth century to the early sixteenth. The tendency over this period was for these restrictions to become more narrowly defined as they came specifically to exempt an ever greater range of acceptable future charges on the lands of the groom's father. The apparently strict restraints on alienation in contracts of the early fourteenth century lacked the flexibility necessary to the family situation, but this was progressively remedied over the next two centuries. By the early sixteenth century the bulk of the terms of some contracts was given over to defining the exceptions to the groom's father's promise not to alienate. One routinely finds exceptions in favour of future wives of the groom's father limiting how much jointure he might settle upon them, and of his younger sons, who were almost invariably to be given life estates with reversion to the groom and his heirs. Less routinely one finds a whole range of other exceptions in favour, for example, of bastard children and other relatives, illegitimate and otherwise, of trusted servants, who were to enjoy life annuities, of various religious and charitable purposes and so on.[47] Moreover, many contracts allow the groom's father to set aside lands of a certain value for a certain period, which might be as long as twenty years, for the implementation of his last will and testament.[48]

In these elaborate definitions of allowable alienations in the contracts of the late fifteenth and early sixteenth centuries, one can perceive the beginnings of a change in the nature of the marriage contract. When the fathers of bride and groom came together to negotiate terms, they were now concerned with something more than the immediate financial implications of the impending union, namely, the fixing of the respective sizes of jointure and portion. They were also concerned to anticipate a wide range of contingencies. The groom's father was asked to lay down how much land he would settle on a potential future wife, what he would give to his younger sons and other male members of his family still to be provided for, what volume of land he would set aside for the implementation of his will, and so on. Hence, if a father lived to contract his heir in marriage it was at the time of the negotiations with the heir's prospective father-in-law that the orderly transmission of the patrimony to the next generation was regulated.[49] Here we are witnessing both an advance in the way landholders dealt with the future disposition of their estates and a coming together of the interests of the fathers of bride and groom. While it was clearly to the advantage of the bride's father that future alienation by the groom's father be restrained and defined, and it was at his insistence that the non-alienation clause was first introduced into marriage contracts, yet it is not difficult to see how later the non-alienation clauses, rendered less restrictive by their long lists of exceptions, had compensating attractions for the groom's father. He would at some point have to address such questions as how much to give his younger sons, so why not do it when he married his eldest son and in negotiation with the father of the chosen bride? Further, the fathers of most grooms were as anxious to protect the inheritance of their heirs as fathers of brides were that their daughters should not suffer from over-generous provision for other members of the groom's family. Non-alienation clauses were thus a necessary insurance against a conflict of interests that only infrequently arose in practice, and, as they came to include a greater number of exceptions, the potential for conflict was further reduced. Only when the groom's father's circumstances dramatically changed through some unlooked-for eventuality, such as the groom's death leaving only female issue, could serious conflict arise.

This brings us to the last and most complex of the settlements in the appendix, that of 1531 for the marriage of the heir of the Hastings earl of Huntingdon. Just as the non-alienation clause was attaining its maximum refinement in the late fifteenth and early sixteenth centuries so it was already giving way to a more adaptable and secure alternative in the entailed use. This conveyancing device, the most sophisticated conceived by the late medieval lawyer, is very clearly exemplified in this 1531 contract. It brought together the two principal tools of the late medieval conveyancer, the entail and the feoffment-to-use. Its development in the second half of the fifteenth century was prompted by changes in statute and case law, principally the emergence of the common recovery as an efficient method of barring entails, the statute of 1

Richard III, ch. 1, which allowed the beneficiary of a simple use to convey the
legal estate, and the evolution of the equitable doctrine that prevented a feoffor
altering instructions given to feoffees in the case of feoffments made upon
consideration.[50] But the technical details need not concern us. More important
here are the purposes the entailed use was designed to serve and its applicability
to marriage contracts.

The mechanics of the device are fairly straightforward. While in the simple
use the feoffees were seised to the use of the *cestui que use* and his heirs, in the
entailed use they were seised to the use of the *cestui que use* and a prescribed class
of his heirs. Hence, for example, the jointure in our 1531 contract is not
entailed, as it might have been earlier, directly on the couple and their issue or
the issue of the groom, but rather it was conveyed to feoffees to hold to the use
of the couple and the groom's issue. Such involved conveyances, as far as they
relate to marriage contracts, had three purposes. First, the entailed use was the
successor of the non-alienation clause in that it was more effective than its
predecessor in ensuring that the groom's father would implement the promises
he made in the contract. The lands conveyed to the feoffees at the time of the
marriage generally involved, as in this 1531 example, the whole inheritance of
the groom's father, and these feoffees were not seised solely to his use but rather,
for the bulk of the inheritance, to him for life and then to a variety of entailed
uses, the beneficiaries of which were protected against any alienation that lasted
longer than his lifetime.[51] In other words, by conveying his lands to feoffees who
were not seised to his own use alone, the groom's father had deprived himself of
the ability to alienate any of the enfeoffed lands. In effect, the feoffees, some of
whom would have been nominated by the bride's father, became trustees for the
implementation of the marriage contract. Only in extreme circumstances, such
as his capture in war and subsequent ransom – hence the final clause in the
1531 contract[52] – did the groom's father retain the right to vary the uses laid
down at the time of the contract. For the rest he was deprived of all power to
make any disposition of his lands contrary to these uses, and also, it is worth
noting, to allow common-law dower to any future wife he might take.[53]
Moreover, and equally importantly, if the feoffees were seised to the use of the
couple and their issue, that issue was protected against alienation by the groom
as long as the feoffees remained so seised,[54] for, as an Exchequer Chamber

judgment of 1489 makes clear, a feoffment by *cestui que use* in tail could bind the feoffees only during the *cestui's* life.

The second purpose of entailment to uses at marriage takes us back to the question of the interaction between the crown's feudal rights and the form assumed by marriage contracts. As is well known, the late fifteenth century witnessed what one commentator has described as 'a revolutionary change' in the attitude of the crown to the loss of its feudal revenues.[55] I have already mentioned one result of this changed attitude: the rule that if the son and heir of a tenant-in-chief were married but below the age of consent at the death of his father, the right to marry him nevertheless came to the crown. Such royal aggression in the matter of its feudal dues put landowners on their guard and led the conveyancers they employed to devise arrangements more finely tuned to revenue avoidance. And it is thus probable that one purpose of a feoffment to the entailed uses of a marriage contract was to achieve a long-lasting division between the legal estate and the beneficial enjoyment of it: the feoffees being intended to act as an undying corporation, adding to their numbers as they died out, and remaining seised of the legal estate, on which the feudal rights of the crown and other lords depended, while the groom's father and his descendants retained the beneficial or equitable estate, to which no such rights appended.[56] All that would change as generation succeeded generation would be the uses to which the feoffees were seised. For example, when the groom came to marry his son and heir, new arrangements would have to be made concerning the jointure of the new bride, the implementation of the groom's will, and so on, and this could be done by the simple expedient of issuing new instructions to the feoffees. It may have been this prospect of a permanent division between legal and equitable estates, with its serious revenue implications for the crown, that led Henry VIII to force through the Statute of Uses in 1536. By executing the use, this statute rendered nugatory the revenue effects of this division.[57]

Finally, we come to the third purpose of the employment of entailed uses in marriage contracts. Just as the feudal rights of the crown suffered from the division of equitable and legal estates, so too did the dower rights of widows: a bride could have no dower in her husband's inheritance if the feoffees enfeoffed by his father at the time of their marriage remained seised until the groom's death. This raises two questions. Why was there this reaction against dower in the late fifteenth century,[58] and why were the fathers of brides prepared to condone something so potentially detrimental to their daughters' future interests? The answer to the first lies in a general perception that widows with their jointures and dowers held too much land, a perception which was part of a wider reaction against women as landholders, whether as heiresses or widows, that was to gather pace during the early sixteenth century. This reaction is reflected in the changing pattern of jointure settlements. Throughout the fourteenth and early fifteenth centuries jointures were generally settled on the couple and their issue, but in the early sixteenth century it became the fashion to give the bride only a life interest with remainder to the groom in fee simple or fee tail.[59] By such settlements, the issue of a marriage that produced only daughters was effectively disinherited of the jointure in favour of any male issue the groom might have by another wife, and this was a symptom of the declining level of female inheritance in the early sixteenth century.[60] The answer to the second lies partly in this general perception, and partly in the consideration that what the father of a bride lost in the sacrifice of her dower rights the male line of his family gained by the parallel sacrifice of those of his heir's bride.[61] It should also be noted that, as in our 1531 example, a bride's loss of dower could be, and sometimes was, compensated by an increase in her jointure: here she was allowed 1,000 marks *per annum* out of an inheritance worth 2,550 marks *per annum*, a similar proportion to that which she might have enjoyed with dower and jointure. Most brides, however, were not as saleable as Katherine Pole – note that a future wife of the groom's father was to have only 500 marks *per annum* – and it is clear that the general effect of the exclusion of dower claims was to diminish the volume of land held by widows. Nor did their position recover after the Statute of Uses had deprived the entailed use of its efficacy against both dower and feudal incidents. Clause four of the statute decreed that a widow jointured at her marriage could not subsequently claim dower.[62] Widows thus once more found themselves in the position they had been in the early thirteenth century: their husband's endowment at the time of marriage was sufficient to extinguish their claims to common-law dower.

The end of dower in the form it had existed for three centuries – although not until 1925 was it finally extinguished[63] – brings us to the end of the story of the late medieval marriage contract. In the early thirteenth century it had been concerned only with the immediate financial implications of the union, chiefly how much the groom was worth in terms of his expectations, and the provision his father would make for the bride's potential widowhood. Three centuries later it had evolved into something much more important. The drawing up of the heir's contract had become the occasion at which a father laid down the form in which the family patrimony was to descend to the next generation, and hence it was already what it was to continue to be down to the nineteenth century, the most important moment in the life-cycle of a landed family.

APPENDIX

SOME EXAMPLES OF MARRIAGE CONTRACTS, 1236–1531

1. Agreement between Humphrey de Bohun, earl of Hereford, and Ralph de Toeni, for the marriage of Bohun's daughter, Alice, to Toeni's son and heir, Roger (1236).[64]

Bohun will give £40 *per annum* of land *'in liberum maritagium'* to Roger, retaining the land in his own hand until the marriage takes place. Toeni will give Roger £40 *per annum* of land *'ad dotandam'* Alice, retaining that land in his own hand until the marriage. On marrying, the couple are to have full seisin of both *maritagium* and dower. Bohun will pay Toeni 200 marks of silver.

2. Agreement between Robert FitzRoger and Robert de Tybetot for the marriage of FitzRoger's son and heir, John, to Hawisia, daughter of Tybetot, before quinzaine of Martinmas next (11 September 1277).[65]

John will dower the bride at the church door on the day of the wedding with lands worth £100 *per annum* so that she may not exact more in name of dower during the life of John's father if John predecease him. But if John survives his father she shall be entitled to her common-law dower. When John reaches the age of twenty his father shall be bound to enfeoff him of the said land and cause him to have seisin thereof. For the execution of the marriage, dower and enfeoffment, Tybetot will pay John's father 600 marks, on condition that if the bride die under the age of thirteen without issue, John's father shall be bound to repay him 400 marks of said 600 marks. For the observance of this agreement the parties have given faith in the king's presence.

3. Agreement between William, Lord Montagu, and Roger, Lord Grey of Ruthin, for the marriage of Grey's son and heir, John, to Montagu's daughter, Anneys, before Whitsuntide next (12 June 1335).[66]

Before the marriage Lord Grey will give the couple £100 *per annum* of land to hold to them and the heirs of their bodies, saving the reversion to Lord Grey and his heirs. For the performance of this marriage and gift, Lord Montagu will give Lord Grey 1,000 marks, i.e. 200 marks on the day of the marriage and 200 marks *per annum* thereafter, on the following conditions: (i) if the groom should predecease his father so that the bride is not by law dowable from the lands Lord Grey holds, then all but 200 marks of the said 1,000 marks are to be repaid; (ii) if the bride should die in Lord Grey's lifetime without issue by the groom then all 1,000 marks are to be repaid; (iii) if she should die during Lord Grey's life with living issue by the groom, 600 marks are to be repaid, the remaining 400 marks to be in suspense, to be repaid if that issue die in Lord Grey's lifetime. The contracting parties have entered into mutual bonds in £2,000 for the observance of these covenants.

4. Agreement between John, Lord Northwode, and Sir Arnold Savage, for the marriage of Northwode's son, Roger, to Eleanor, daughter of Savage, before Christmas next (31 August 1372).[67]

Lord Northwode will settle specified lands on the couple for their lives on condition that, if either he or his step-mother die in the lifetime of either Roger or Eleanor, the couple's estate is to cease. He is also to settle his manor of Northwode Sheppey on himself for life, with remainder to the couple and their male issue; and the reversion of another manor, expectant on the death of his step-mother, on the couple and their issue. He grants that he will not disinherit Roger, by any feoffment or other deed, of any lands which he holds at present in demesne or in reversion expectant on the death of his step-mother, except a specified manor, which he may give to a younger son in tail male, with reversion to the main Northwode line. He grants that if he contravenes any of these covenants he will pay Savage £200. Savage, for his part, undertakes to pay £200 as his daughter's portion.

5. Agreement between Margaret, countess of Salisbury, and Henry Pole, Lord Montagu, on the one part, and George Hastings, earl of Huntingdon, on the other, for the marriage of the earl's son and heir, Francis, Lord Hastings, to

Montagu's eldest daughter, Katherine, before the feast of Purification next (3 July 1531).[68]

The earl is to convey to persons nominated by himself and the countess lands worth £900 *per annum* to the following uses. The feoffees are to stand seised of lands worth: (i) 200 marks *per annum* to the use of the couple and the groom's issue; (ii) 150 marks *per annum* to the use of the earl during the life of his step-father (d.1534) and then to the use of the couple and the groom's issue; (iii) 650 marks *per annum*, after the deaths of the earl and his step-father, to the use of the couple and the groom's issue in full recompense of the bride's jointure and dower; (iv) 350 marks *per annum* after deaths of the earl and his step-father and the seven-year performance of the will of the earl's mother, to the use of the groom and his issue. The earl is to convey lands worth £800 *per annum* to another set of feoffees to the following uses. The feoffees are to stand seised of lands worth: (i) 300 marks *per annum* to use and intent that the earl may give lands worth 100 marks *per annum* to each of his three younger sons for their lives, with remainder, after the deaths of the earl and his younger sons, to the use of the groom and his issue; (ii) £400 *per annum* to the use of the jointure of the groom's mother, with remainder, after the deaths of the groom's parents, to the use of the groom and his issue; (iii) 300 marks *per annum* to the use of the performance of the earl's will for 15 years after his death and then to the use of the groom and his issue. If the groom's mother die in the lifetime of the earl, he may set aside lands worth 500 marks *per annum* for the jointure of any future wife he may have. For the assurance of the above covenants, the countess will pay the earl 3,000 marks at 500 marks *per annum*. Despite the uses above, if the earl is taken prisoner in France or elsewhere by reason of the king's wars, he may set aside his lands, except the £900 *per annum* conveyed to the first set of feoffees, for the raising of his ransom.

Notes

1. I am very grateful to the British Academy for funding the research on which this article is based, and to Dr G.L. Harriss and Prof. R.A. Griffiths for their comments on an earlier draft. What follows is a preliminary survey of work in progress. I hope to deal with many of the points raised in greater detail elsewhere.

2. For the later part of this story: L. Bonfield, 'Marriage, Property and the "Affective Family" ',

Law and History Review, I (1983), pp. 297–312; idem, *Marriage Settlements, 1601–1740: The Adoption of the Strict Settlement* (Cambridge, 1983).

3. Contracts involving younger sons, heiresses and widows raise a different set of problems, as too, although to a much lesser extent, do those contracts in which the groom is arranging his own marriage. Both will concern me only very peripherally in this paper.

4. Jointures were also settled in reversion on a range of other contingencies such as, not uncommonly, the death of the groom's grandmother or step-grandmother. For an example, see the 1372 contract in appendix.

5. For typical contracts involving heiresses apparent: eg. *C.C.R. 1360–4*, p. 148; *C.A.D.* V, A13222, p. 470; VI, C6405, p. 340; Lancashire R.O. DD B 12/4; H.L. Hastings MS. HAP Box II (6). The loss of portion involved in the heir's marriage to an heiress gave a younger son his only advantage over the heir in the competition for heiresses.

6. For the interdependence of the marriages of heirs and those of their sisters: L. Stone, *The Crisis of the Aristocracy, 1558–1641* (Oxford, 1965), p. 632; *Sir Christopher Hatton's Book of Seals*, L.C. Loyd and D.M. Stenton (eds.) (Northamptonshire Record Society, XV, 1950), no. 486, pp. 336–7; *Lisle Letters*, M. St. Clair Byrne (ed.) (6 vols, Chicago, 1981), III, no. 510, pp. 10–11; *Yorkshire Deeds*, W. Brown and others (eds.) (10 vols, Yorkshire Archaeological Record Series, 1909–55), IV, no. 211, pp. 58–9; *Stonor Letters and Papers, 1290–1483*, C.L. Kingsford (ed.) (2 vols, Camden Society, 3rd series XXIX, XXX,1919), I, no. 54 pp. 47–9; W.O. Massingberd, *History of the Parish of Ormsby-cum-Ketsby* (Lincoln, 1893), p. 390; B.L. Additional Ch. 53638; Derbyshire R.O. D 185 B/Ashburne M 20. For a strong statement of the potential disadvantages of heiresses: Carpenter, *Locality* pp. 106–9.

7. S.J. Payling, *Political Society in Lancastrian England; The Greater Gentry of Nottinghamshire* (Oxford, 1991), pp. 80–1.

8. McFarlane, *Nobility*, p. 84.

9. B.J. Harris, 'A New Look at the Reformation: Aristocratic Women and Nunneries, 1450–1540', *Journal of British Studies*, XXXII (1993), pp. 92–8. For the cost of placing a daughter in a nunnery, see E. Power, *Medieval English Nunneries, c.1275–1535* (Cambridge, 1922), pp. 17–24.

10. S.L. Waugh, *The Lordship of England: Royal Wardships and Marriages in English Society and Politics, 1217–1327* (Princeton, 1988), p. 56. Bean suggests that the development of marriage contracts in itself added a further encouragement to fathers, if any were needed, to arrange marriages for their heirs during their lifetimes: J.M.W. Bean, 'Landlords' in *The Agrarian History of England and Wales, III: 1348–1500*, E. Miller (ed.) (Cambridge, 1991), p. 558.

11. R.H. Helmholz, *Marriage Litigation in Medieval England* (Cambridge, 1974), p. 98.

12. That the old rule prevailed as late as 1495 is confirmed by Constable's reading on *Prerogativa Regis* and it seems to have continued to be held in theory after that date: *Prerogativa Regis; Tertia Lectura Roberti Constable de Lyncolnis Inne anno 11 H 7*, S.E. Thorne (ed.) (New Haven, 1949), pp. xxxiv–v, 122–133, especially pp. 128–9, n. 316; Coke on Littleton, 80a. But that this was not taken to be the rule from the first decade of the sixteenth century is made clear both by those marriage contracts which make provision for repayment of the portion if the crown refused to honour the marriage of a groom married *infra annos nubiles* and by examples of such refusals: *C.I.P.M. Henry VII* (3 vols, 1898–1955), III, no. 198; *Letters and Papers, Foreign and Domestic, Henry VIII*, I, (2nd edn,

H.M.S.O., 1920), part 2, no. 2964 (80), p. 1285; T.D. Whitaker, *An History of Richmondshire* (2 vols, 1823), I, p. 384; *C.A.D.*, V, A12274, pp. 275–6; *Antiquarian Repertory*, F.Grose (ed.), IV (1809), p. 671, Cf. P.R.O. Early Chancery Proceedings, C.1/1226/44. See also the earlier discussion of the question in *Y.B.*, Mich. 7 Hen. VI, ff. 10–12, pl. 36.

13. Waugh, *Lordship of England*, pp. 101–2. This is not the same thing as saying that jointure arose as a tax avoidance device. As such it was deeply flawed. While it could deprive the crown and other lords of the wardship of land, it could do so, in normal circumstances, only at the cost of placing a disproportionate amount of land in the hands of a widow who might survive long into the heir's majority. Only if her interest could be terminated at the heir's majority would jointure have real potential as an instrument of tax avoidance. Theoretically this could be achieved through a conditional feoffment, but I know of only one example of jointure being settled on condition the widow relinquish her interest on the heir coming of age: B.L. Cotton Charter, XXVI. 38 (contract of 1347).

14. S. Painter, 'The Family and the Feudal System in England', *Speculum*, XXXV (1960), p .13.

15. W.S. Holdsworth, *A History of English Law*, III (3rd edn, 1923), pp. 189–95.

16. For the complex story of this change, see J. Biancalana, 'Widows at Common Law: The Development of Common Law Dower', *Irish Jurist*, new series, XXIII (1988), pp. 255–329.

17. Waugh, *Lordship of England*, pp. 21–3; R.E. Archer, 'Rich Old Ladies: The Problem of Late Medieval English Dowagers', in *Property and Politics: Essays in Later Medieval English History*, A.J. Pollard (ed.) (Gloucester, 1984), pp. 15–35.

18. Since they do not contain mutual obligations I have not considered earlier marriage settlements (such as that printed by J.H. Round, 'A Great Marriage Settlement', *Ancestor*, XI (1904), pp. 153–4) as contracts proper.

19. Biancalana, *Irish Jurist*, new ser. XXIII, pp. 260–1, 313–28. For mid-thirteenth-century contracts which specifically state that endowment at the time of marriage was not to bar a claim to common-law dower: *C.Ch.R. 1226–57*, pp. 438–9; *C.Ch.R. 1257–1300*, pp. 90–1. By the end of the thirteenth century, when the older forms of dower were, in any case, giving way to jointure, such stipulations had become unnecessary for they reflected established law.

20. For the idea of a marriage portion as the daughter's share of the patrimony: Waugh, *Lordship of England*, p. 24. As Bonfield has pointed out, 'inheritance practice must be conceptualized in terms of the division of wealth rather than the descent of land': L. Bonfield, 'Affective Families, Open Élites and Strict Family Settlements in Early Modern England', *Ec.H.R.* XXXIX (1986), p. 350.

21. For the rules governing the descent of *maritagia*: S.F.C. Milsom, *Historical Foundations of the Common Law* (2nd edn., 1981), pp. 171–2.

22. McFarlane, *Nobility*, pp. 87, 201; T.B. Pugh, 'The Magnates, Knights and Gentry', in *Fifteenth-Century England, 1399–1509*, S.B. Chrimes, C.D. Ross and R.A. Griffiths (eds.) (Manchester, 1972), p. 118 n. 11 (although the portion of Anne, daughter of Richard, duke of York, was 4,500 marks not 6,500 marks: P.R.O. Duchy of Lancaster, Miscellanea, D.L. 41/2/8); *C.C.R. 1354–60*, p. 93; *C.C.R. 1385–9*, pp. 472–3; *Register of Edward the Black Prince* (4 vols, H.M.S.O., 1930–3), III, pp. 480–1. Note that Thomas Holand, earl of Kent, paid as much as 6,000 marks to purchase the hand of the royal ward Roger Mortimer, earl of March, for his daughter Eleanor: *C.C.R. 1381–5*, p.572;

McFarlane, *Nobility*, p. 86. For portions in general: J.P. Cooper, 'Patterns of Inheritance and Settlement by Great Landowners from the Fifteenth to the Eighteenth Centuries', in *Family and Inheritance: Rural Society in Western Europe, 1200–1800* (Cambridge, 1976), pp. 306–12. I hope to deal with the subject at length elsewhere.

23.   Evidence of borrowing to pay portions is hard to come by, but is not non-existent: P.R.O. C.1/229/1; *C.I.P.M. Henry VII*, III, no. 1002, pp. 512–13. For a case of poverty apparently engendered by overgenerous marriage settlements: *Calendar of Papal Registers: Petitions, I, 1342–1419*, W.H. Bliss (ed.) (H.M.S.O., 1896), pp. 133–4.

24.   McFarlane, *Nobility*, p. 87; S.M. Wright, *The Derbyshire Gentry in the Fifteenth Century* (Derbyshire Record Society, VIII, 1983), p. 45.

25.   For a recent discussion of this inflation: R.B. Outhwaite, 'Marriage as Business: Opinions on the Rise in Aristocratic Bridal Portions in Early Modern England', in *Business Life and Public Policy*, N. McKendrick and R.B. Outhwaite (eds.) (Cambridge, 1986), pp. 21–37.

26.   McFarlane, *Nobility*, p. 64.

27.   Indeed, even in the fifteenth century one finds occasional examples of portions, in whole or part, in land: eg. *C.C.R. 1441–7*, pp. 423; B.L. Egerton Ch. 1232. Nevertheless, McFarlane was right to claim that the *maritagium* had 'practically died out before the end of the thirteenth century': *Nobility*, p. 64.

28.   J.R.L. Mainwaring Ch. 325, a contract of 12 November 1512, is an excellent illustration of this point. A widower making his own marriage agreed that the portion, payable in ten instalments over five years, would cease to be paid if the bride either died without issue or his son and heir-apparent had issue inheritable alive at her death.

29.   For the diversity of arrangements: W(est) Y(orkshire) A(rchive) S(ervice), WBS/4; Cheshire R.O. DL T/A1/8; B.L. Add. Ch. 16939, 51091; *C.C.R. 1369–74*, pp. 556–7.

30.   Only a small percentage of contracts provide for a measure of repayment in case of the groom's premature and childless death (eg. J.R.L. Cornwall Legh 873) because in these circumstances the bride would still enjoy her jointure. A contract of 30 September 1493 is unique in ordaining a diminution of the bride's jointure should the groom die without issue within a certain period, in this case within twelve months of the marriage. In return for this reduction from £20 *per annum* to 10 marks *per annum* the bride's father was to pay only £50 of the 220 marks portion: P.R.O. Exchequer, Ancient Deeds, E.40/7247. See also J.R.L. Mainwaring Ch. 238 which provides for the reduction of a 400 marks portion to 200 marks should the groom die without issue before the age of sixteen.

31.   Archer, in *Property and Politics*, p. 20; C.D. Ross, 'Forfeiture for Treason in the Reign of Richard II', *E.H.R.* LXXI (1956), pp. 561, 567.

32.   Coke on Littleton, 36b. Interesting in this context is the 1354 Mortimer/FitzAlan contract, which is unique in providing for a reduction of the jointure if the bride should become dowable from the groom's patrimony: *C.C.R. 1354–60*, pp. 924. It is a mystery why such an eminently sensible arrangement was not common.

33.   McFarlane, *Nobility*, p. 66. Given-Wilson's recent suggestion that jointure may have represented 'an attempt to restrict the amount of land held by a widow after her husband's death' must be rejected: C. Given-Wilson, *The English Nobility in the Late Middle Ages* (1987), p. 200 n. 52.

34. A.W. Simpson, *A History of the Land Law* (2nd edn, Oxford, 1986), pp. 65–6.

35. S.J. Payling, 'Arbitration, Perpetual Entails and Collateral Warranties in Late Medieval England', *Journal of Legal History*, XIII (1992), p. 33.

36. The earliest restrictive settlement I know of dates from c.1243. The groom's father undertook that '*nullam terram dabit, invadiabit in Judeasmo vel aliquo alio alienabit*' to the disinheritance of the groom, and that he would make security to this end in the king's court: *Curia Regis Roll*, XVII, no. 1514, p. 296. But this is an isolated example of a contract unusually sophisticated for its date, although see also *Early Yorkshire Charters*, W. Farrer and C.T. Clay (eds.) (12 vols, Edinburgh 1913–16 and Yorkshire Archaeological Society Record Series, extra series, I–III, V–X, 1935–65), X, no. 109, pp. 164–5. When such settlements became common in the early fourteenth century they generally took this form of a promise not to alienate, with a penal bond to be paid if the promise were broken: eg. *C.C.R. 1313–18*, p. 468; G.W. Watson, 'Marriage Settlements', *Genealogist*, new series, XXXVII (1921), pp. 220–1 (printed in part in *G.E.C.* V. 454 n.a.); Lancashire R.O. DD Sc 28/1. There were also two less common forms. The first was the entailment of the whole or nearly the whole of the groom's father's inheritance at the time of the marriage: G.A. Holmes, *The Estates of the Higher Nobility in Fourteenth-Century England* (Cambridge, 1957), pp. 1212; *C.P.R. 1313–17*, p. 491; T. Madox, *Formulare Anglicanum* (1702), pp. 92–4; *C.C.R. 1346–9*, pp. 2467; Magdalen College, Oxford, Corton 92(1). Such settlements were, however, probably considered too inflexible, particularly after the mid-fourteenth century when the entail was interpreted by the law as a perpetually inalienable estate, and they are only occasionally met in practice. The second, which had a much longer history, consisted of an undertaking, secured by bond, on the part of the groom's father that lands of a specified value would descend to the groom: *C.P.R. 1301–7*, p. 327; Lancashire R.O. DD B 12/1; Leicestershire R.O. 26 D 53/2552; W.Y.A.S. WBS/12.

37. McFarlane, *Nobility*, p. 81.

38. Ibid, p. 278.

39. On closer examination the evidence quoted by McFarlane for the view that it does rather fades away: J.M.W. Bean, review of *Nobility* in *Speculum*, LII (1977), pp. 154–5

40. Carpenter, *Locality*, p. 259. See also Bean, in *Agrarian History of England and Wales*, III, pp. 556–7.

41. Carpenter, *Locality*, p.259.

42. For early fourteenth-century examples of attempts at such disinheritance: *The Grey of Ruthin Valor of 1467–8*, R.I. Jack (ed.) (Sydney, 1965), pp. 1–3; Payling, *Political Society*, p. 72. For later examples, see ibid., pp. 208–12; Carpenter, *Locality*, pp. 110, 464, 535–6.

43. Carpenter, *Locality*, pp. 107–13, 259; McFarlane, *Nobility*, pp. 64–6.

44. Statistics relating to remarriage make this clear. Between 1300 and 1499 baronial husbands left 601 widows, 269 (44.8 per cent) of whom remarried. This, however, tells only part of the story: while, from 1300 to 1349, the remarriage rate was only 36.1 per cent, it was 50 per cent thereafter, an increase indicative of a dawning realization, in the mid-fourteenth century, of the greater economic attractiveness of widows in the age of jointure and dower. Widowers were even more likely to remarry than widows: 61.9 per cent remarried between 1300 and 1499, although the figure was only 52.4 per cent for the period 1300 to 1349. These statistics are drawn from an

analysis of baronial marriages that I hope to publish elsewhere. For the period before 1300, see Waugh, *Lordship of England*, p. 46.

45.   Carpenter, *Locality*, p. 259.

46.   For an excellent example: P.R.O. C.1/13/162–4; 15/124–6; 22/114; E. Acheson, *A Gentry Community: Leicestershire in the Fifteenth Century, c.1422–c.1485* (Cambridge, 1992), pp. 148, 241–2.

47.   B.L. Add. Ch. 51183; Durham R.O. D/St/D5/1/33; William Salt Library, HM 20/5; J.R.L. Arley Ch. 12/29.

48.   E.g. R. Halstead (pseudonym of Henry Mordaunt, earl of Peterborough), *Succinct Genealogies of the Noble and Ancient Houses of . . . Mordaunt of Turvey* (1685), pp. 507–8, for a twenty-year term. Ten years was the commonest term: e.g. Nottinghamshire Archives Office, DD FJ 4/7/1; B.L. Add. Ch. 51210.

49.   For the same point for a later period: Bonfield, *Marriage Settlements*, pp. 6–7. For examples of feoffees at death of feoffor being seised to the use of the implementation of the heir's marriage contract: *C.I.P.M. Henry VII*, II, nos. 406, 423–4, 442, pp. 253, 261–4, 274.

50.   For the doctrine of consideration: A.W.B. Simpson, *A History of the Common Law of Contract* (Oxford, 1975), pp. 327–74.

51.   The same protection, as far as the heir was concerned, could not be achieved at common law. If the father had simply settled the legal estate on himself for life with remainder to his heir in fee tail, the fee tail would have vested in him rather than his heir and hence have been barred if he suffered a recovery. Such settlements were so interpreted because, by making the heir take from his father by purchase rather than descent, they had great potential for tax evasion: Simpson, *Land Law*, pp. 95–7.

52.   A similar clause is found in B.L. Add. Ch. 46060, another contract in which the whole of the groom's father's inheritance is settled to various uses. See also A.J. Pollard, 'The Burghs of Brough Hall, c.1270–1574', *North Yorkshire County Record Office Journal*, VI (April 1978), p. 28.

53.   Significant in this context is the letter dated 18 May 1519 of Thomas, Lord Dacre, to Cardinal Wolsey. In it he asks Wolsey to be his 'good lord' in securing a licence to alienate his inheritance at the marriage of his son to feoffees to hold to his use for life and then to the use of the couple in tail male 'so the effect of the matter is that if it fortune me to marie my wife shall not be indowable': P.R.O. State Papers, Henry VIII, S.P.1/18, f. 165v.

54.   See here *Y.B.* Mich. 4 Hen. VII, f. 18, pl. 9, where it was determined in Exchequer Chamber that a feoffment to *cestui que use* in tail would bind the feoffees only for his life. Five judges came to the same conclusion in *Y.B.* 19 Hen. VIII, ff. 13–114, pl. 11, but three dissented. The question was a controversial one: *The Reports of Sir John Spelman*, J.H. Baker (ed.) (2 vols, Selden Society, XCIII–XCIV, 1976–7), II, pp. 207–8. Barton has pointed out that it was not as important as it seemed for *cestui que use* in tail could oblige his feoffees to convey the legal estate to him and then suffer a recovery: J.L. Barton, 'The Medieval Use', *Law Quarterly Review*, LXXXI (1965), p. 572. But the important points from the perspective of entailed use made at the time of marriage were that (1) this was not an option for the groom's father if the feoffees were seised, as they generally were, to his use for his life only; (2) if the groom obliged the feoffees to reconvey to him the lands conveyed would be rendered liable to the bride's dower. Only if the bride predeceased the groom would reconveyance and recovery become a worthwhile option.

55. J.M.W. Bean, *The Decline of English Feudalism, 1215–1540* (Manchester, 1968), p. 235.

56. Some landowners at least appear to have envisaged just such a permanent division: *C.I.P.M. Henry VII*, III, no. 960; P.R.O. Prerogative Court of Canterbury, PROB 11/8, f. 149. See also the remarkable contract of 15 December 1527 for the marriage of Cecily Gage to George Baynham, where specific provision is made for the seisin of the feoffees to last throughout the lifetimes of the groom and his father and, for part at least of the lands, for twenty years after the groom's death: East Sussex R.O. SAS/G21/5.

57. For an excellent account of this statute and its wide-ranging effects: Milsom, *Historical Foundations*, pp. 218–30, 234–9.

58. The first signs of this reaction are to be discerned in those contracts of the mid- to late fifteenth century which limit the combined value of jointure and dower to be enjoyed by the groom's mother or step-mother: H.L. Hastings MS. HAP Box IV (18); W.Y.A.S. WBS/4; Lancashire R.O. DD Sc 28/lB. What these contracts left unsaid was how such a restriction was to be made safe at law, and it must be assumed that much depended on the goodwill of the widow. A contract of 30 September 1493 conceded as much when it limited to the groom's mother in jointure and dower lands worth 80 marks *per annum* 'if it so shall plese her'; if not, she was to have the 40 marks *per annum* already appointed for her jointure together with her common-law dower: n. 30 above.

59. I hope to publish elsewhere figures to demonstrate this change.

60. S.J. Payling, 'Social Mobility, Demographic Change and Landed Society in Late Medieval England', *Ec.H.R.* XLV (1992), p. 62.

61. Nevertheless, some parents were not prepared to accept a diminution of their daughter's rights. When Dorothy Bothe of Barton (Lancs.) contracted her daughter to James, son and heir-apparent of Thomas Scarisbrick of Scarisbrick (Lancs.) in 1528, she insisted that, although the whole Scarisbrick estate was to be enfeoffed to uses, the feoffees were to stand seised of a third of the lands to the use of the bride's dower just as if the feoffment had not been made: Lancashire R.O., DD Sc 28/5. See also Lancashire R.O., DD Hu 55/4.

62. Coke on Littleton, 36b.

63. J.H. Baker, *An Introduction to English Legal History* (3rd edn., 1990), p. 309.

64. *The Beauchamp Cartulary Charters*, E. Mason (ed.) (Pipe Roll Society, new series, XLIII, 1980), no. 379, pp. 214–15.

65. P.R.O. Chancery, Close Rolls, C.54/95, mem. 15d (calendared in *CCR 1272–9*, pp. 487–8).

66. P.R.O. C.54/156, mem. 24d (calendared in *CCR 1333–7*, pp. 491–2).

67. B.L. Harleian Ch. 54 C 56.

68. H.L. Hastings MS. HAP Box VII (1), printed in *The Antiquarian Repertory*, F. Grose (ed.), IV (1809), pp. 677–80, and with many errors, in J. Nichols, *History and Antiquities of the County of Leicester* (4 vols, in 8 parts, 1795–1815), III, ii. p. 576. The contract was redrawn on 20 June 1532 in almost identical terms: B.L. Harl. Ms. 3881, ff. 33–33v.

3

K.B. McFarlane and the Determinists: The Fallibilities of the English Kings, *c*.1399–*c*.1520

A.J. Gross

London School of Economics

'Assuming one has a fish pond', wrote Nietzsche, 'then possessing opinions is like possessing fish'. Those lucky enough to catch fish would have their own opinions. 'I am speaking of live opinions, of live fish. Others are satisfied if they own a cabinet of fossils'.[1] As a scholar who never stopped changing his view of history, McFarlane shared this love of live fish. Nor were his attitudes less proprietary than Nietzsche's, though the great medievalist's fish pond would undoubtedly have been a rectangular one which needed to be guarded assiduously against the incursions of neighbours. But poachers are no problem for the dead. It is the ownership of the entire pond that is at stake now. McFarlane's ideas are increasingly seen as a legacy, the right to which is open to dispute. Thus, Carpenter's suggestion that McFarlane's successors have so distorted the roles of patronage and personalities that we must now build anew on the first principles of what he said has prompted one reviewer to refer pointedly to McFarlane's intellectual heirs.[2] Apart from the doubt that he wanted such heirs, there is always danger in the posthumous interpretation of the work of great teachers. The fact that McFarlane's assembled work is plainly an unfinished development should not encourage others to take the view that they can step in and fulfil his programme. Any such attempt to set his views in stone will deprive our students of the limited sight of the man they still have. Instead we encourage in some the idea of an overseeing presence with which they can quarrel but never get a reply and in others the picture of an idol at twilight awaiting those who would write history with hammers.

If we are to dispense with the idea of anything so fixed as a legacy, then we need to retain our awareness of the continuous change and development at the heart of McFarlane's work. In this respect it is not enough to read Cooper's illuminating historiographical and biographical introduction to the lectures on the nobility.[3] It is no less important, when considering the widely read collection of his published articles, to recognise, despite meticulous reproduction, the drawback of removing the articles from their original contexts.[4] 'Bastard Feudalism', for example, was originally read to a conference of English and French historians at the Institute of Historical Research a few months after the end of the war. At the same colloquium Perroy read his own influential paper, 'Princes and Principalities in Fifteenth Century France'. The views of Perroy and McFarlane had not a little in common. While the French scholar wished to show that the fifteenth-century dukes of Burgundy, Brittany and the like were Renaissance princes in embryo rather than renegade feudal barons, McFarlane set out to dispel the idea that the relationship between lord and retainer characteristic of the same period was a decadent one which promoted political upheaval and signified the closing of an age.[5] These views reflect one of the medievalist's abiding difficulties: the subject is perceived as dominated by passages first out of antiquity and then into modernity. Scholars at the extremes of the medieval centuries have always particularly resented working in the hallway while others sat in the parlour. For historians of McFarlane's generation these problems were underlined by the prevalance of a school of Marxist determinism which seldom reached beyond the simplistic. The Christian Socialism of Tawney provided a social and intellectual corrective to the ideologies of post-Victorian textbooks and formed part of a milieu which strongly influenced McFarlane in his early years.[6] But by the 1940s he had recognised that this approach simply compounded the existing difficulties of the late medievalist by confirming that the coming of the Tudors brought in not only a new age, but also the beginnings of bourgeois monarchy, and he rejected it with the vigour of one who felt he was seeing clearly for the first time. It was perhaps socialist sentimentality which persuaded him to continue presenting his argument as a repudiation of Stubbs.[7]

From this perspective McFarlane set out what has become the órthodox interpretation of the phases of instability which occasionally inflicted late medieval English monarchy. The theory which set the king at the head of a doomed system precipitated through a series of accelerating conflicts towards its economically determined Armageddon was subverted by the removal of key pieces of argument which were manifestly at odds with the evidence. There was no plague-induced economic crisis of the aristocracy which drove it into a potentially violent quest for additional resources. Nor was there a crisis of mortality promoted by endless blood-lettting which would eventually provide the Tudors with a free hand in their dealings with associates and advisers.[8] Rather, the interests of crown and aristocracy stood in rarely disturbed alignment. Magnates turned their power against the crown only when circumstances left little choice and then usually as isolated individuals. And as for power, what power? McFarlane's work on retaining by magnates began the process which displaced the motif of the marauding band in favour of that of the series of concentric circles expanding in time of war or at rare moments of crisis, contracting in peacetime into a core of family estate officers and friends which posed no intrinsic threat to social harmony.[9] All of this had implications for the task of kingship itself. A tricky and demanding job it may have been, but, as Henry V demonstrated, not impossible. If kings failed, it was through personal inadequacy and political miscalculation. The trouble was that any dynasty would throw up some rulers who were not up to the job, so that it was the institution of monarchy, rather than the individual failed kings of the fourteenth and fifteenth centuries, who now appeared as victims of the *damnosa hereditas*. 'Edward II, Richard II, and Henry VI', McFarlane concluded, 'were the penalties that monarchy paid for its dependence upon the chances of heredity'.[10] The absence of Yorkists from this list of troubled monarchs is striking. By 1964 in 'The Wars of the Roses' McFarlane was ready to incorporate them. Edward IV may not have been entirely to blame for the quarrel with Warwick but the affair encapsulated that 'accidental' quality which characterised the problems of the polity after 1450. Only 'our latter-day Baconians', the brothers and sisters of the boar, would doubt that Richard III's fears and ambitions were responsible for the Yorkist demise.[11]

This reduces McFarlane's celebrated thesis to its fundamentals. It is his view of monarchy as it is usually remembered. Yet, when we read his work with any care, we find unmistakable acknowledgment that the story was more complex. In fact, one of the most impressive, and for those inclined to take issue, perhaps the cruellest of McFarlane's writing skills, was the remorselessness with which he disarmed counter-argument by anticipating it in his own synthesis. 'Had the war any other origins?' That memorable question about the Wars of the Roses might epitomise the comprehensiveness of his approach.[12] It is this incorporation of alternative patterns of explanation which gives his work much of its subtlety and balance, so that it never becomes monolithic or didactic in tone.

McFarlane recognised that while an initial breakdown in the political order might be attributed to the inadequacy of the king, the evidence suggested that once the Pandora's box of disorder was open, it was difficult for a monarch to close it, whatever his ability. Take Edward IV's first reign: a government troubled by pockets of resistance, a land riven by suspicion and confused allegiances, a second king in captivity and an alternative court over the water.[13] Worse still, the dethroned Lancastrians could be considered representive of the plight of the wider ranks of dispossessed hoping to recover lands which had provided rich but insecure fortunes for those preferred under the Yorkists. Here issues of patronage elided, as they often did, with prevailing concepts of law and the sanctity of the inheritance. Civil war disrupted the landholding order, posing problems which could hardly be resolved without engendering further conflict. This combination of difficulties threatened to make the kingdom ungovernable. Edward's fall in 1469–70 could not be blamed on his quarrel with Warwick alone. As McFarlane acknowledged, 'civil war bred civil war', not only because the ineffectiveness of any containing measure meant that an unreliable king was a source of conflict until he was removed, but also because 'a new king had to restore the crown's shaken authority. A change of dynasty made that all the harder'.[14] Nor was this principle restricted to the rapid changes of succession at the end of the fifteenth century. In 'Bastard Feudalism', McFarlane blamed the governmental instability of the fifteenth century on the 'bad fortune which cut short the life of Henry V just when the inevitable ill effects of the Lancastrian usurpation were wearing off'.[15] This is a noteworthy quotation. McFarlane recognised that even after almost a quarter of a century and the divine approval conferred at Agincourt the aftershock of the events of 1399 had not yet completely disappeared. Despite McFarlane's emphasis on the capacities of individual kings, it was difficult not to see some continuity in a period during which as he himself put it, 'kings were seven times driven from the throne by force, while five rulers and two heirs presumptive met with violent ends'. Indeed, a few moments earlier in these Ford Lectures he had mooted a playful explanation for the judicial murders of Henry VIII's reign by suggesting that the king might have 'inherited some of his less amiable-characteristics of his great-uncle Richard III'.[16]

This issue, forming what was almost a sub-text in McFarlane's work, continued to figure prominently in debate in the years following his death especially among his former students. It was one of the principal issues underpinning Wolffe's examination of the minority period in his celebrated essay on the personal rule of Henry VI.[17] The same question lay at the heart of the debate between Prestwich and Maddicott as to whether Edward II, in respect of relations with the baronage, began his reign *tabula rasa*.[18] In the longer term McFarlane's emphasis on the individual capacities of the late medieval English kings faced a serious challenge from a sophisticated revision of the Marxist determinist position. The exchanges between Brenner and Bois, while still very theoretical, advanced the economic determinism of earlier generations by closely articulating the ties between politics and the developing economy.[19] The keystones of the argument remain war and inflation but the decisive moment of their impact was now defined as the late thirteenth century and early fourteenth, when these acquired a new intensity because the landlord economy was no longer buoyed up by the capacity to create new rent-paying tenements from virgin land. As rival jurisdictions vied with one another in their attempts to secure a greater share of resources that were no longer expanding, princes were drawn into a series of expensive and risky conflicts which in turn demanded that they expose themselves to domestic hazards by drawing more heavily than before on the assets of their subjects.

In the context of English historical scholarship a critical response to this thesis may be traced in two important volumes of essays. *Before the Black Death* had implications for McFarlane's political synthesis which were important if indirect, since some of its contributors take issue with the view that irreversible economic contraction had set in before the onset of plague.[20] More apparently relevant to questions arising from McFarlane's work, *Politics and Crisis in Fourteenth-Century England* questioned the view that the landlord class was riven by an unhealthy degree of endemic conflict and examined individual reigns, by and large restating the view that if princes failed it was their personal inadequacies which let them down.[21] In both these works contributors advanced arguments which, by implication at least, supported McFarlane's position as it had come to be understood. But the theory of crisis has been more radically undermined in seminal essays by Gillingham and Harriss.[22] Their views differ in significant respects especially since Gillingham confines himself to the period before the accession of Henry VI, but I hope that I am not distorting the view of either in saying that they have the following in common. It is accepted that war was characteristic of this period and that this placed a strain upon both royal finances and administration. But the notion that the resulting pressure damaged royal authority is decisively rejected. On the contrary, even at the very end of the fifteenth century, finance was still available for foreign campaigns. Tensions produced within the kingdom proved to be creative by encouraging the government to forge new machinery and involve itself more fully with the lives and aspirations of its subjects.

Harriss and Gillingham might accept that the intensity of the engagement between the king and the wider community did not inherently strengthen kingship. After all, no king, including Henry VI, was deposed because he was powerless but rather because the authority of the office had such wide reaching ramifications that it could not be left in unsafe hands.[23] But while they agree that an inadequate ruler would have to be replaced, they conclude, and here both disregard McFarlane's understanding of the long-term damage which usurpation could inflict, that such a replacement could be engineered without weakening the monarchy itself. Indeed Harriss, summarising and supporting Gillingham's view, tells us that the Lancastrian usurpation of 1399 'strengthened the monarchy, in that it aimed to restore the tradition of Edward III'.[24] For Harriss, who henceforward begins to part company with Gillingham, this conclusion is inextricably associated with the view that the monarchy existed co-dependently with a widening political nation. The effectiveness of royal government should not be assessed through the history of the monarchy in an insular sense but rather in terms of the development of the 'society which government had to serve'.[25] This concept of monarchy dedicated to serve a political nation with an identity separate from itself comes very close to suggesting that in the aftermath of 1399 the king had become *roi des Anglais*. But Henry Bolingbroke was no Louis Philippe. On the contrary, as Gillingham reminds us, he aimed to be and succeeded in being 'as free in his powers and regalities as his ancestors before him'.[26]

Harriss's understanding of monarchy also differs significantly from one of McFarlane's key axioms. Harriss and McFarlane certainly agree that 'England depended for its healthy functioning on the exercise of kingship', but McFarlane said that 'England was a monarchy': he did not say that it was a state in which the monarchy acted interdependently with a political society.[27] This distinction is more than semantic. For an age which visualised its political structure as a human body or a ship, monarchy is the only appropriate term for the whole. In the body the head determined all, even if it acted most effectively when it had the willing participation of all its members; in the ship the navigator alone set the course. Even Fortescue, who championed the view that the people were the source of political life and who also echoed the centuries old differentiation between crown and king, did not make the critical distinction between crown and polity. 'In political terms' he wrote 'a community without a head has no corporate capacity whatever'.[28] Even the Digby manuscript, on which Harriss relies heavily for evidence of the contemporary political mentality clearly denies any separation between crown and people:

> The leste lygeman with body and rent
> He is a parcel of the crowne.[29]

The defence of the view that the limitations of individual kings do not denote a weakness in the monarchy has therefore reinforced one aspect of McFarlane's agenda but only by disengaging very gradually from others. It has also entered very awkward territory. The negative impact of usurpation is minimised by relating it to the well-being of a broader political society whose evolution provided opportunities which in the longer term secured the monarchy's role and helped it to avoid the perils of absolutism. Far from avoiding the determinism which McFarlane eschewed, this thesis carries a determinist scheme of its own. At one point Harriss refers to 'the tide of English politics'.[30] This phrase might serve as a warning that where constitutional history, however redefined, enters, Whiggery will not be far behind. But that does not necessarily follow. After all, as Burns indicates, all monarchies regarded as legitimate during the fifteenth and early sixteenth centuries ruled according to laws and customs which by definition made them, in some sense, constitutional.[31] But there is a difference between speaking of a monarchy governing according to the accepted principles of its internal organisation and one contained by the constitutional objectives of a society which stood outside it. The second approach invites both the assumption of a progress towards national democracy and a premature temptation to conjure up the state as an agency for change.

In the final analysis, the case against theories of crisis fails for a mundane reason. It remains difficult to put seven depositions down to coincidence. If an adequate analysis of long-term structural causation has not yet been produced from a purely economic perspective, we should remember that, as Doyle pointed out when he considered the 'desacralisation' of monarchy in a timely review, 'society and economics were only real in the ways people understood them'.[32] In attempting to describe a pattern of causation which reflects contemporary beliefs, it may be more effective to take the institution of monarchy as a starting point, rather than economic change *per se*. It is perfectly possible to take a structural view here while avoiding organic theories, associated with Toynbee, which invest institutions with an instinct for self-preservation. In its long history, monarchy has displayed an exceptional adaptive capacity but adaptation often involves a degree of specialisation which could set limits upon the future, particularly when authority depended on popular belief.

An overview of the crown's fiscal history shows how such a point might be applied. The concept of redress of grievances before supply may have been new in the fourteenth century, but the trade-off between promises of good government and increasing demands upon the resources of subjects had a long history. The relationship was understood in the time of Alfred.[33] Eadmer's report of the promises given to Lanfranc by Rufus and the coronation charters of Henry I and Stephen were developments on an established motif, one which recurs in the reissues of Magna Carta and then in the chancellors' opening addresses to parliaments.[34] It was not that these promises bound the king's actions. It was proved time and again that in practice they did not. But by advancing the accretion of ideas of good kingship they shaped expectations of monarchy, ideals which often fell short of practice. Broad notions of justice, imprinted by canonical and classical traditions, sat uneasily with the dogged and occasionally ruthless pursuit of regalian rights which kings often found indispensable for political or financial reasons.

Whether we accept Joliffe's argument that the king was able to manipulate feudal law because he stood outside it, or prefer Warren's view that the king's power stemmed from his position at the head of the feudal hierarchy, there can be no doubt that a predatory attitude towards the great estates made a major contribution to the success of late Norman and Angevin kingship.[35] The rapid consolidation of a national system of extraordinary taxation, which secured the consent of the landlord classes by sparing their pockets, advantaged the English kings during the north European conflicts of the fourteenth and early fifteenth centuries and led to the temporary obliteration of the more predatory aspects of government.[36] But this precocity created an ossification of custom which meant that the English monarchy faced the consequences of its inadequate tap upon the resources of its wealthiest subjects at a moment when the tax structures of the rival European monarchies still retained a significant degree of fluidity.[37] By the end of the fifteenth century monarchy was once again showing a predatory side. It is true that the machinery had changed and that lesser landowners were now targetted as vigorously as the magnates, but in the reign of Henry VII, as in that of Henry I, *novi homines* made their political fortunes by raking the country, seeking out the king's rights where they could and extorting payments for his goodwill where they could not.[38] Earlier than this, Edward IV had manipulated magnate inheritances with an insouciance unsurpassed even by Edward I.[39] Carpenter has correctly observed the similarity between the kings of the late fifteenth century and their distant forebears, suggesting that from the 1470s they were able to 'terrorise their nobility in a manner not seen since the days of Edward I and his predecessors'.[40] On the other hand, it does not necessarily follow that the kingdom was becoming easier to rule. It is more reasonably argued that the urgent need for political leverage and increased revenue impelled resort to old expedients, what Fortescue called 'exquisite means'.[41]

For it can be argued that, alongside other sources of revenue, the English kings were heavily dependent on a series of dramatic windfalls, often the by-products of political upheaval. The dynastic changes of 1399, 1461 and 1485, as well as Richard III's usurpation in 1483, were the principal components of a pattern of accumulation which vastly increased the extent of royal holdings and enhanced the role of land as a source of revenue.[42] But the last and the greatest windfall came with the sixteenth-century religious dissolutions. That even the seizure of the lands of every chantry in the kingdom proved insufficient to transform the Crown's endowment into the single perpetual chantry envisaged by Fortescue towards the end of the fifteenth century had a great deal to do with the pressures for dispersal which ran alongside acquisition.[43] During the Wars of the Roses, the need to buy and reward support, and the tendency to restore fallen families, meant that attainder and resumption were more successful as political weapons than means of swelling the royal domain.[44] In the mid-sixteenth century the demand for desirable land from those able to exploit contacts with the administration played a part in persuading the Crown to release its grip on the monastic lands.[45]

It is worth noting that, until recently, the vested interests which did so much to promote the redistribution of the Crown's newly acquired land would have sat uncontroversially under the heading of patronage. Similarly, in 1610, when the Reformation bounty was running out, the failure to negotiate a parliamentary alternative to permanent landed endowment was largely the result of opposition from those within the Bedchamber who benefited most from fines and escheats.[46] The collapse of this package meant that the Crown's vigorous pursuit of its fiscal rights remained an area of controversy, while even Cranfield's attempts to improve the sufficiency of these revenues by restricting expenditure were scuppered by his factional rift with Buckingham.[47]

Apart from complaints about the distortion which inevitably results from compression on this scale, this synthesis lies open to the accusation that, despite its declared intention of anchoring the materialist aspects of causation in the context of contemporary belief, it sits unashamedly on the side of money and graft, taking no account of evolving ideologies and cynically reducing the complex web of motivations and actions to a simple series of causes and effects. The problem should not be artificially reduced to the emphasis placed on the role of patronage by pointing to its important part in the evolving pattern of royal finance. Carpenter, who has done as much as anyone to warn against the sweeping assumption of venal motivation, implicitly acknowledges that very association when, as a corollary to her debunking of patronage as the key to late medieval politics, she tells us that there has been an 'over emphasis on the importance of the state of the royal finances'. After all, Edward II and Richard II were rich when they fell and as Carpenter points out in a footnote 'it was as much as anything the way they made themselves rich that caused their downfall'.[48] There is of course a significant distinction between the broad issue of revenue management and the simple question of whether an individual king had full coffers, so that neither royal finance nor patronage is so easily removed from the equation. The real puzzle which confronted most English rulers between the eleventh and seventeenth century was the difficult task of raising money to fund their commitments and ambitions without placing themselves at odds with contemporary ideals of kingship.

While this conclusion, along with much of the preceding argument, apparently confirms Carpenter's broader advice against ignoring the underlying effects of a political culture and its dominant values, it leaves the nature of that culture open to question. In her view, landowning society was cemented by a consensual respect for law sustained by a leavening of Anglo-Saxon reciprocity.[49] If this premise is accepted then Harriss's view of a monarchy buoyed up by a society's growing political consciousness and collegial mentality emerges as more convincing than any theory of continual crisis. Yet Carpenter's statement of society's values is too limited to be used to sustain such a broad analysis. She herself acknowledges that those who fail to grasp that, in seeking through law and custom protection for the integrity of their estates her gentry were developing values which set the collective good above individual ambitions, might regard her position as 'too materialist'.[50] So far as it goes, this concern is prudent, but the issue of materialism cannot be restricted to the simple question of the balance between ideas and vested interests as aspects of human motivation. A materialist interpretation of action and intent can also emerge from an uncritically positivist reading of the evidence. In this respect, it is damaging that Carpenter's argument tends to confuse the functioning of institutions, particularly those of the law, with the ideologies which underpinned them, assuming that by examining the former we will understand the latter. The consequence is that she presents an artificial analysis of political morality.[51]

When we read Carpenter's views, we should be constantly aware that respect for law was rooted in an understanding of the social order which was holistic and cosmological. If the law was the sinews of the body, then the king was, after all, its head.[52] Despite her references to reason, justice, conscience and consistency, Carpenter's view remains essentially utilitarian.[53] In seeking to grasp the perspective in which the aristocratic and merchant classes held the law and their king, we need to enter their libraries as much as the chests which held their accounts. This is made difficult by the degree to which readers relied on the circulation rather than the ownership of manuscripts. But we know enough of both to tell that Carpenter has fallen short of the objective: when she refers to literary sources at all, she does so in the expectation that, rather like some medieval George Eliot, the author will directly address the mores of her gentry and, when she finds that they do not, she rapidly turns aside disappointed.[54] We can also safely say that a broad view of contemporary ideology and literature reinforces the thesis of continual crisis rather than undermining it.

In fact, contemporary literature expresses fatalism and moral pessimism which strongly challenge the validity of using *mentalité* as a counter to the notion of continual political crisis. It is perhaps understandable that the cosmological sciences, alchemy and astrology, do not form part of the world picture of Carpenter's gentry. It is less comprehensible that her assessment of fifteenth-century political mentalities omits John Lydgate. Quite apart from the volume of surviving manuscripts, William Caxton, Wynkyn de Worde and Richard Pynson were shrewd enough observers of their market for us to trust the inclusion of Lydgate in the choice of works for their presses.[55] They aimed at a literate class dieted on mutability and the evil consequences of division.[56] Lydgate's poetry reflects a cultural trend which circumvented the discomforts of blind chance by manufacturing and swallowing heavy doses of moral fatalism.[57] It is true that, taking the example of the lustful and murderous Messalina, Lydgate followed the tradition of free will by denying that man could blame the stars for his sins. But at the same time his description of Astyages' futile efforts to prevent the young Cyrus ascending his throne shows that human sin and the heavens usually acted in concert to provide an ineluctable fate. Despite Astyges' efforts to withstand God's ordinance,

> This was his fate he might it nat refuse,
> The hevenli cours but it dede faile.[58]

Lydgate's poetry was typical in using history as a source of *exempla* by which princes faced a struggle to avoid the pitfalls which had undone their predecessors. Even Commynes, who wryly observed the English predilection for prophecy and who was down to earth enough to keep his choice of *exempla* close to home, enthusiastically asserted that history moved according to predictable patterns.[59] On a more general level, Armstrong and most recently Carey have reminded us of the central role which astrology played in the outlook of the aristocratic classes.[60]

Such fatalism does not exclude the possibility of free will, but it does temper freedom with a heavy burden of destiny and sin. Nor is such fatalism comparable to determinism in the historical sense, but a society that invested so heavily in providence was liable to produce decisions which fulfilled its own prophecies. The young McFarlane's comments about the lack of personal freedom in late medieval England spring to mind here and it should not be forgotten that at the end of 'The Wars of the Roses' he cast more than a glance at the sinister edge which magical fatalism could assume when mixed with politics, noting quite rightly that necromancy flourished 'since it promised to influence events'.[61] It is not difficult to find examples of the belief that the supernatural could do just that. The government-sponsored accusations against Walter Langton, the Coventry plot of 1323–4 against the life of Edward II, and the fate of Joan of Navarre spring to mind.[62] But the later fifteenth century was the high water mark of such activity: the duchess of Gloucester, George, duke of Clarence, and Lord Hastings all found themselves at the centre of controversies related to witchcraft.[63]

Chroniclers, admittedly with some self-conscious literary artifice, specialised in discovering a prophetic irony in the most unsuspected turns of events.

Eleanor Cobham's astrologer Thomas Southwell, accused of predicting Henry VI's death, fulfilled his own prediction that he would escape a violent end by dying in his bed on the night before his execution. Having learned that he would die in the Tower, William de la Pole fled the building only to face death on a ship of the same name. Fearing the prophecy that G would reign after E, Edward IV protected his sons by executing his brother George only to ignore the threat of his other brother Gloucester.[64] Hard as men might try to discover its secrets, fate could not be tricked. If this was the ambience that shaped expectations, did those expectations not help to shape political actuality? Prophecies, as Hobbes would later comment, 'were many times the principal cause of the event foretold'.[65]

For kings this prevalent sense of destiny had special ramifications which suggest some broad speculations about monarchy. Head of the body politic on the one hand, and the physical expression of the *corpus mysticum* on the other, the king was the guarantor of his kingdom's moral well-being. As a result, the ills of the king betokened difficulty for the kingdom while the ills of the kingdom, if severe and prolonged enough, reflected upon the king. Through the ages, monarchs have acted as lightning conductors for the conditions of their kingdoms. Writing in the year after McFarlane delivered his chapter for the *Cambridge Medieval History*, but about an age four and a half millenia earlier, Childe made one of those shrewd anthropological observations which stand independently of his more rigid economic determinism. It will have powerful resonances for any student of the Middle Ages who has read Barber's survey, *The Two Cities*. 'Man, let us insist again, was still dependent on the incalculable chances of rain, flood, sunshine, still exposed to disaster from droughts, earthquakes, hailstorms, and other natural but unpredictable catastrophes. He still sought to control the beneficent forces and to ward off noxious powers by rituals, incantations and charms. Anyone who could successfully claim to control the elements by his magic would, of course, earn immense prestige and authority'.[66] For the priest kings of the primitive age even instances when magic apparently failed them could be turned to advantage by an insistence that future success could be ensured by the further elaboration ceremony, a development which bastioned the authority of the priestly class as the sole masters of the intricacies of ritual. Before we even begin to consider late medieval kings in a similar light we should recall a ringing admonition of Maitland that would have been more familiar to the generation of McFarlane and Childe than it is today. Maitland recognised the degree to which the king embodied the state but he would have no truck with magical capacities. 'The medieval king was every inch a king, but just for this reason he was every inch a man and you did not talk nonsense about him. You did not ascribe to him immortality or ubiquity or such powers as no mortal can wield'.[67]

But we do not need to define medieval kings as the direct inheritors of the magician's wand in order to believe that it had an important mediatory role between the seen and unseen. If this sacred aspect of monarchy was threatened by the personal deficiencies of the king, damaged by usurpation or clouded by doubts about dynastic legitimacy, then it had to be reasserted with ever greater vigour. It would be rash to suggest a linear correlation between the dynastic and financial difficulties faced by the English monarchy and the its increasingly elaborate symbolic profile, but the image of order and virtue in the court culture of Charles I's reign, brilliantly described by Sharpe, though not necessarily a culmination, was certainly a logical if somewhat demystified development of what had gone before.[68] Cultural materialists might stigmatise this argument as Tillyard-like in its tendency to treat as evidence of collective mentality what were in fact didactic elements of ideological struggle. It is true that it is almost impossible to conceive of ideology without struggle and that by the early seventeenth century the concept of providence was challenged by a firmly rooted margin of scepticism.[69] In the fifteenth-century disputes over kingly virtue and dynastic right, however, scepticism had little or no part. Indeed, if Dollimore's view is to be accepted, the echoes of dynastic uncertainty which reverberated through the sixteenth century played some part in crystallising the sceptical attitudes which were emerging by its close.[70] The shift in attitudes is easily exaggerated. The history of the Civil War and Interregnum shows that far from stifling the magical arts the sceptical challenge invigorated efforts of both royalists and radicals to bolster their cause by extracting the grain of uncorrupted truth from amid the mass of false prophets and charlatan alchemists.[71] As late as the reign of James II, no less a scientist than Robert Plot could suggest that the king remedy his situation by founding a hermetic college to furnish him with enough alchemical gold to make parliament obsolete.[72]

Of the many books of prophecy, alchemy and astrology which survive from the fifteenth and early sixteenth centuries to testify to the concerns of that age, let me choose just one. It is interesting because of the social connections which arise from it and because it elucidates a strange parallel between the travails of the last Stuart king and the last Lancastrian. It belonged to the mercer John Frost and is referred to in his will, where it is noted as the place of record of debts owed by Frost's friend, Thomas Cook the younger, and referred to simply as 'my book'.[73] The book survives but it is no account book or commonplace collection. Aside from a list of debts due from Cook and others, it consists entirely of astrological receipts.[74] Now it is especially interesting that both the Thomas Cooks, father and son, had connections with alchemy. They were among the series of commissioners appointed between 1456 and 1458 to search learned texts for the elixir which would remedy both the king's health and his financial difficulties. They probably owed their positions to contacts with the world of book production derived from their association with the Bridge House.[75]

It is not suggested that Frost or the two Thomas Cooks or any other of the eminent men associated with these commissions were distinguished by their mysticism. It would also be an oversimplication to conclude that these were desperate men driven to dangerous measures by the pitiable state of the Lancastrian regime. The hopes pinned in these commissions are pitiable, not because the enterprise was dark, but because, given the social and literary context, it was utterly banal. Nothing reveals this better than the title carried by that accretion of pseudo-Aristotle, the silver paint for many mirrors, the *Secretum Secretorum*. Copied and reproduced, particularly in respect of its astronomical and medical passages, drawn upon by poets and advisers too numerous to list, added to, most notably in an English context by Roger Bacon, the secret was most definitely out.[76] But when it came to alchemy, nothing extinguished the hope of an undiscovered secret in ancient text, or a new efficacy derived from a new level of mathematical or mechanical elaboration.[77]

It is true, that in issuing licences to the court alchemists, Henry VI's regime had to justify the cancellation of prohibitions of alchemical practice issued by Henry IV. It is in the management of this obstacle that much of the significance of Henry VI's approach to alchemy resides. Overtones of theological unorthodoxy were diminished by an association with the common weal. In the case of astrology, it had long been accepted that the practice was more acceptable if it was directed to the common good rather than the divination of an individual destiny.[78] Thus measures taken to enrich Henry VI and provide a cure for his individual physical ills – and it should be recalled that approvers, probably with some encouragement, implied more than once that his sickness had been induced by necromancy – were justified by reference to the benefit (*commodum*) and use (*utilitas*) of the community (*res publica*) of the kingdom.[79] This suggests an intriguing double identification between the body of the king and the body of the realm on the one hand and between fiscal and physical well being on the other, demonstrating that it was more than rhetoric when the Digby poet had likened 'a kingdom in good astate' to a 'stalworthe man mygty in hele' and Gower stated that sickness of the head betokened a sickness of the entire body.[80] Since these were years in which England's chronic shortage of bullion suddenly became acute as silver drained away to the Burgundian mints, reality reinforced the principle. For Gower physical malaise and moral decrepitude were hardly less closely associated than they had been for Roger Bacon who believed that both old age and death were the products of sin. Bacon taught that the decay of the flesh was passed down through the generations as 'corrupt fadres gendren corrupt sones and sones bi the same defaute of rule corrupten hem silf and therefore gendren sones of double corrupcion corrupt and so is corrupcioun multiplied an lif abreviate and shortened as we sen and feelen in thiese tymes'. This rendition from Bacon's *Six Bookes of Sentences in the Four Degrees of Sapience* is taken from a extract almost certainly translated in about 1458, along with *De Retardatione Senectutis*, by the man most aptly described as Sir Thomas Cook's secretary.[81]

It should not be doubted that the malaise which characterised Henry VI's disintegrating regime was intertwined with latent but deep-seated doubts about the legitimacy of the Lancastrian dynasty's ascent to royal status which finally became open in 1460. It is true that Adam of Usk's sensational tales of lice which grew out Henry IV's coronation oil could be dismissed as characteristic only of the period before Henry V set the seal of divine approval upon Lancastrian rule, though judging by the gloomy final passage of his chronicle, even the French conquests did not persuade Usk that the auspices were benevolent.[82] A more certain sign of residual doubt about its legitimacy appears in the tenacious cult which grew up around the Archbishop of York, Richard Scrope, who had been executed on the orders of Henry IV after the rebellion of 1405.[83] Hughes has stressed the role of York's civic identity in the development of the Scrope cult, while Pronger showed long ago how the cult was nurtured by a kinship group of northern gentry, families which were not inherently hostile to the Lancastrian dynasty.[84] If, as Harriss suggests, the screen in York Minster with its imposing portrait of Henry V, was built partly in response to the cult which had proved resistant to outright suppression, then it certainly did not succeed in counteracting it for long.[85] The mid-fifteenth-century texts of the London-based *Brut* make reference to the 'many grete miracles' worked 'for this worthy clerk', showing that the story retained a currency beyond the diocese of York.[86] It was also at this moment, when the souring of Henry V's achievement renewed the vulnerability of his dynasty, that Thomas Gascoigne, drawing on his contact with Yorkshire families personally associated with Scrope, and his acquaintance Clement of Maidstone gave the legend of divine retribution imposed for the execution its most sinister edge. Henry IV is not only struck down with leprosy but finally shrunk into a doll-like totem of sin. Gascoigne's fullest version of the story carries a note of the first battle of St Albans appended in his own hand.[87] By this time the events of Henry IV's reign were remote enough for Scrope's own part in the usurpation to be forgotten, so that the veneration of the Archbishop as a defender of ecclesiastical liberties, which had permitted contemporary commentators to deplore the execution while remaining sympathetic to the Lancastrian succession, had elided with a general unease about the dynasty's origins.[88] Talk of 'miracles' was dangerous to the incumbent regime because they could be interpreted as a source of validation for renewed political upheaval.[89]

Of course, a form of government so resilient and flexible as monarchy possessed the means of attempting to deal with this sort of difficulty. But the Lancastrian dynasty's last-ditch attempt to ring-fence the sacred powers of kingship by damning rivals who claimed providential backing as 'supersticious traitours and rebelles' lacks conviction and reflects the difficulty of restoring lost credibility.[90] Nor could a change of dynasty be relied upon to reinstate the sacred reputation of the monarchy. Such a change might have unlooked for and potentially long-term side effects, legitimating one troublesome cult only by transforming another into a source of antagonism. After the deposition of Henry VI, the tomb of Thomas of Lancaster, setting store upon genealogy rather than political sympathy, began to shed blood.[91] Henry V, in typical mode, had tackled the underlying issue of his dynasty head on, showing his repentance at the fate of Richard II with a ceremonious reburial celebrated in verse by Hoccleve.[92] Like the Scrope legend, this is recounted in the *Brut* but, in some of the continuations at least, it is given an emphasis removed from its original purpose. By associating the reinterment with a list of papal penances for the exoneration of the sins of his father that 'was a lepre er he died', Henry V's piety is emphasised chiefly as a counterpoint to the tainted stem of his dynasty.[93]

The reference to universal papal authority, like the efforts of the Yorkist lords to manipulate the authority of the legate Coppini, or Fortescue's appeal to papal authority in *De Natura*, is a reminder that that even in the late fifteenth century there was no such thing as monarchy in one country.[94] This has manifest implications for Henry V's triumphant exploits in France which allayed the problems of his monarchy only by profiting from crisis in another branch of that universal estate. More telling is the way in which the king's polemicists justified the war by appealing to the ultimate goal of a Christendom united in peace. Of course, the theme of the Christian *rex pacificus* wielding the sword of justice in order to restore the true order was a persistent one, with a history going back well before Henry V's time and a future which, even in kingdoms where Protestantism prevailed, stretched ahead well beyond the Reformation. This survival reflects the ambivalence of the long relationship between the western principalities and *Romanitas*.[95] But rather than outright rejection the prevailing tendency here was consistently towards the utilisation and ultimately the annexation of the universal *imperium*, objectives which were often at their most acute when the succession was at issue. The edge which moments of dynastic uncertainty brought to relations with what could be construed as the superior judicial authorities of papacy and empire makes it easier to comprehend how Henry V could be addressed as 'the likenesse of Constantyn' on the one hand and seek the Emperor Sigismund's endorsement of his claim to the French kingdom on the other.[96] It also assists in rationalising the course set by Henry VII who sought papal canonisation for his ancestor Henry VI and simultaneously asserted his own imperial status by displaying on

his coinage the closed crown first used at the coronation of Henry IV.[97] While
the assertion of imperial right at moments of dynastic crisis might be taken as
part of a process which augmented royal authority, the gradual undermining of
external sources of validation and sanctification helped to raise the stakes of
kingship by further concentrating moral authority and the accompanying
responsibility on the person of the king. Here was another explanation for the
high relief in which contemporaries cast the failings of their kings. If political
necessity required the monarch's removal then the act had to be explained
either as a sacrifice redeemed by the victim's sanctity or, as in the case of
Richard III, the cathartic purging of a monstrous and aberrant product of sin.
Canonisation and demonisation were two sides of one coin. Both contributed to
an awkward environment in which to practise the art of politics.

The intention here has not been to provide a new synthesis for the
development of late medieval English history, but rather to provide a corrective
to the view that a resort to contemporary systems of belief can lend new force to
McFarlane's view that every king was responsible for his own fortune. A broad
appreciation of this evidence suggests that, at least after the dynastic upheaval
caused by the usurpation of 1399, there was an entrenched moral and
ideological malaise that was beyond the capacity of any one monarch to rectify.
But even this limited objective can be sustained only if a few concluding words
are said to explain the success enjoyed by the Tudors against this unpromising
background. In part this achievement has already been explained. As well as
exploiting the fear and pessimism inspired by past division, the Tudor regime
benefited at different times from the last of the great windfalls and from the
perceived leadership of a northern Protestant Europe without ever fully
confronting the difficulties which would later flow from those two
developments.[98] But most of all it was the relative absence of war which
advantaged the Tudors. It may still have been possible to finance the odd
impressive campaign but the disappearance of the restive independent
principalities of northern France shifted the cockpit of warfare to the south of
the continent and robbed cross-channel intervention of the practical edge which
it had during the fourteenth and early fifteenth centuries. Sentimentalists still
associate the foundation of Tudor success with the field of Bosworth.
Revisionists prefer that of Stoke. The case for Nancy remains to be made.

The strains imposed by the wars with Scotland and France during the mid-sixteenth century and by conflict with Spain during the 1590s presaged the familiar range of problems that would recur once the focus of military activity returned north. 'I am Richard II know ye not that,' Elizabeth I opined to William Lambard in 1601, as authors like Hayward and Daniell looked back to the nemesis of 1399, sensing that the gulf between grim social reality and a monarchy replete with esoteric symbolism threatened to set off a new train of disasters.[99] Providential destiny and the claim to represent an imperial universal authority, factors which had both accentuated the weaknesses of individual kings and long enabled the monarchy itself to transcend them, were becoming the topics of ironic play.[100] In 1604 James I, unifier and descendant of the Trojan Brutus, made his triumphal entry into a London adorned with imperial arches and with the Thames transformed into the Tiber for the occasion; within two years another version of Rome had been presented to London, in which it was suggested that the city might as well be left to melt into the Tiber and the arch of empire allowed to fall. The emperor, set on launching war *à l'outrance*, trots out the traditional justification of the proximity of universal peace, prophecies which seem to be fulfilled prove false on close inspection and, for all their ethereal pretensions, princes are compelled to 'stay....in this vile world'.[101]

Despite the complexity of its manifestations, in its rudiments this is a simple story. We do not need to share Carpenter's belief that the Tudors succeeded because the kingdom had become easier to govern as a result of the nobility's shrinking role as mediators between the crown and the gentry. The crown's capacity to intervene in the localities by making direct contact with the gentry was not a novelty, and if some change in balance did occur as a result of the demise of military recruitment by indenture and the scarcity of princes of the blood it must be doubtful whether the need to deal directly with larger numbers of subjects would itself have made the kingdom easier to govern.[102] Doubtless, these 'other and more profound reasons' as Carpenter calls them, will continue to be weighed for some time to come.[103] But when, like the Egyptian Queen transformed into an Elizabethan magus, we find profound longings in us, then we should allow McFarlane, ever the master of the elements, to bring us back to earth with that sonorous warning that makes as good an epitaph as any: 'In talking of causes it is necessary to avoid the temptations of profundity'.[104]

Notes

1. Epigram 317 from *The Wanderer and His Shadow*, second sequel to *Human All-To-Human* (my translation). See *Basic Writings of Nitezsche*, W. Kaumann (ed.) (New York, 1966), p. 165.

2. Carpenter, *Locality*, pp. 5–8; S.J. Gunn, review in *H.J.* XXXV (1992), p. 1001.

3. McFarlane, *Nobility*, pp. vii–xxxvii.

4. McFarlane, *England*, passim.

5. K.B. McFarlane, 'Bastard Feudalism', *B.I.H.R.* XX (1945), pp. 161–80; E. Perroy, 'Feudalism or Principalities in Fifteenth-Century France', ibid., pp. 181–5.

6. McFarlane, *Nobility*, pp. xi–xii.

7. McFarlane, *Nobility*, pp. xvii–xviii.

8. McFarlane, *Nobility*, pp. 179–181; idem, England, pp. 257–9.

9. McFarlane, *England*, p. 27.

10. McFarlane, *Nobility*, p. 120.

11. McFarlane, *England*, p. 241. McFarlane had previously described the wars as 'accidental': ibid., p. 42.

12. McFarlane, *England*, p. 238.

13. The most widely read examination of these conditions is still C.D. Ross, *Edward IV* (1974), pp. 99–103, 122–4. It can be argued that by subsuming evidence of plots within his discussion of antipathy towards the Woodvilles, Ross understates the instability of Edward's regime and the extent of residual Lancastrianism. Some further light will be shed by the present author's forthcoming *The Dissolution of the Lancastrian Kingship: Sir John Fortescue and the Crisis of Monarchy in Fifteenth-Century England*.

14. McFarlane, *England*, p. 255 . McFarlane's point about the long-term consequences of deposition could be extended into the fourteenth century. Although the fall of Edward II did not produce the dynastic upheaval of 1399, Edward III was constantly aware of the need to restore stability. When Gloucester and Arundel wanted to remind Richard II of the need to rule responsibly, they used the example of Edward II as a warning: W.M. Ormrod, *The Reign of Edward III: Crown and Political Society in England 1327–1377* (Yale, 1990), pp. 45–6; A.J. Tuck, *Richard II and the English Nobility* (1973), pp. 103–4.

15. McFarlane, *England*, pp. 41–2.

16. McFarlane, *Nobility*, pp. 2–5.

17. B.P. Wolffe, 'The Personal Rule of Henry VI' in *Fifteenth-Century England, 1399–1509*, S.B. Chrimes, C.D. Ross, R.A. Griffiths (eds.) (Manchester, 1972), pp. 29–49.

18. J.R. Maddicott, *Thomas of Lancaster* (Oxford,1970), pp. 67–70; M.C. Prestwich, *War Politics and Finance under Edward I* (1972), pp. 272–7.

19. G. Bois, *The Crisis of Feudalism: Economy and Society in Eastern Normandy, c.1300–1550* (Cambridge, 1984); R.S. Brenner, 'The Agrarian Roots of European Capitalism' in *The Brenner Debate: Agrarian Class Structure and Economic Development in Pre-Industrial Europe*, T.H. Aston and C.H.E. Philpin (eds) (Cambridge, 1985), pp. 212–327. The following passage is an extrapolation from one aspect of Brenner-Bois debate and should not be taken as a summary of the debate as a whole.

20. *Before the Black Death: Studies in the 'Crisis' of the Early Fourteenth Century*, B.M.S. Campbell (ed.) (Manchester, 1991). It has been stressed to me, quite correctly, that this volume, and the conference debate from which it resulted, should be seen primarily in the context of Postan's work rather than McFarlane's. This acknowledged, the approach taken in *Before the Black Death* stands in marked contrast to the links between economic problems and political turmoil explored by recent generations of Marxist determinists. As such, it helps to support an overall interpretation of late medieval kingship of which McFarlane's view of kingship forms a major part.

21. *Politics and Crisis in Fourteenth-Century England*, J. Taylor and W. Childs (eds.) (Gloucester, 1990).

22. J. Gillingham, 'Crisis or Continuity? The Structure of Royal Authority in England, 1369–1422', in *Das Spätmittelalterliche Konigtum im Europäischen Vergleich*, R. Schneider (ed.) (Konstanzer Arbeitskreis für mittelalterliche Geschichte, Vorträge und Forschungen XXXII, Sigmaringer, 1987), pp. 59–80; G.L. Harriss, 'Political Society and the Growth of Government in Late Medieval England', *P.P.* CXXXVIII (1993), pp. 28–57.

23. For fuller discussion of this point see A.J. Gross, 'The King's Lordship in the County of Stafford, 1312–1322', *Midland History*, XVI (1991), pp. 24–44.

24. Harriss, *P.P.* CXXXVIII, p. 31.

25. Ibid., p. 33.

26. Gillingham, 'Crisis or Continuity', p. 80.

27. McFarlane, *England*, p. 42.

28. J. Fortescue, *De Laudibus Legum Angliae*, S.B. Chrimes (ed.) (Cambridge, 1942), pp. 30–1, cited in translation in J.H. Burns, *Lordship, Kingship and Empire: The Idea of Monarchy, 1400–1525* (Oxford, 1992), p. 67, n. 75. Even the distinction between king and crown needs to be made with caution and reserve. See S.B. Chrimes, *English Constitutional Ideas in the Fifteenth Century* (Cambridge, 1936), pp. 35–8.

29. From 'God Save the King and Keep the Crown' (1413), in *Twenty-Six Political and Other Poems*, J. Kail (ed.) (E.E.T.S. original series, CXXIV, 1904), p. 51; *Henry V: The Practice of Kingship*, G.L. Harriss (ed.) (Oxford, 1985), pp. 1–29.

30. Harriss, *P.P.* CXXXVIII, p. 31.

31. Burns, *Lordship, Kingship and Empire*, p. 158.

32. W. Doyle reviewing R. Chartier, *The Cultural Origins of the French Revolution* in *The Times Higher Education Supplement*, 6 March 1992.

33. See for example, R.H.C. Davis, 'Alfred the Great, Propaganda and Truth', *History*, LVI (1971), pp. 169–182.

34. F. Barlow, *William Rufus* (1983), p. 56 n. 15; *English Historical Documents, 1042–1189*, D.C. Douglas and G.W. Greenaway (eds.) (1981), no. 19, pp. 432–6; A. L. Brown, 'Parliament, c. 1377–1422' in *The English Parliament in the Middle Ages*, R.G. Davies and J.H. Denton (eds.) (Manchester, 1981), p. 121.

35. J.E.A. Joliffe, *Angevin Kingship* (1955), pp. 33–5; W.L. Warren, *The Governance of Norman and Angevin England, 1086–1272* (1987), pp. 18–21.

36. For a summary view of these developments see M.H. Keen, *England in the Later Middle Ages* (1973), pp. 142–65; A.J. Pollard, *The Wars of the Roses* (1988), pp. 48–50. McFarlane, *Nobility*, p. xiv.

37. J.R. Lander, *The Limitations of English Monarchy in the Later Middle Ages* (Toronto, 1989), pp. 8–10. Attempts to introduce alternatives to the tax upon movables proved shortlived: J.A.F. Thomson, *The Transformation of Medieval England* (1983), pp. 260–3, K.B. McFarlane, *Lancastrian Kings and Lollard Knights* (Oxford, 1972), pp. 98–9; Ross, *Edward IV*, pp. 214–16. For comparison with other European kingdoms see P.S. Lewis, 'France in the Fifteenth Century: Society and Sovereignty' in *Europe in the Late Middle Ages*, J. Hale, R. Highfield and B. Smalley (eds.) (1965), pp. 276–300, pp. 280–4; A. MacKay, *Spain in the Middle Ages: From Frontier to Empire* (1977), pp. 145–6.

38. J.R. Lander, *Government and Community* (1980), pp. 351–61; see also D.A. Luckett, 'Crown Patronage and Local Administration in Berkshire, Dorset, Hampshire, Oxfordshire, Somerset and Wiltshire, 1485–1509' (unpub. D.Phil. thesis, Oxford Univ. 1992); R.W. Southern, 'King Henry I' in idem, *Medieval Humanism and Other Studies* (1970), pp. 206–33.

39. McFarlane, *Nobility*, pp. 248–67; Ross, *Edward IV*, pp. 189–90, 248–9.

40. Carpenter, *Locality*, p. 636.

41. J. Fortescue, *The Governance of England*, C. Plummer (ed.) (Oxford, 1885), p. 119.

42. A.L. Brown, 'The Reign of Henry IV' in *Fifteenth-Century England*, Chrimes, Ross and Griffiths (eds), pp. 19–20; C.D. Ross, 'The Reign of Edward IV', ibid., pp. 55–8.

43. Lander, *Limitations*, pp. 12–14; Fortescue, *Governance*, pp. 154–5.

44. B.P. Wolffe, *The Royal Demesne in English History: The Crown Estate in the Governance of the Realm from the Conquest to 1509* (1971), pp. 156–8, 198–9.

45. However, in respect of the dispersal of the monastic lands, it is important to distinguish demands for political favours from the broader and ultimately more influential pressures of the land market: J. Youings, *The Dissolution of the Monasteries* (1971), pp. 117–131.

46. N. Cuddy, 'The Revival of the Entourage: The Bedchamber of James I, 1603–1625' in *The English Court from the Wars of the Roses to the Civil War*, D.Starkey (ed.) (1987), pp. 206–8.

47. M. Prestwich, *Cranfield: Politics and Profits under the Early Stuarts* (Oxford, 1966), pp. 359–64.

48. Carpenter, *Locality*, p 5, n. 22. See also W. Childs, 'Finances and Trade under Edward II' in *Politics and Crisis*, Taylor and Childs (eds.), pp. 19–37.

49. Carpenter, *Locality*, pp. 622–3.

50. Ibid., pp. 627.

51. Ibid., pp. 8–10.

52. Burns, *Lordship, Kingship and Empire*, p. 69.

53. Carpenter, *Locality*, p. 623.

54. Ibid., pp. 48–9.

55. E.G. Duff, *The Printers. Stationers and Bookbinders of Westminster and London from 1476 to 1535* (1906), pp. 10, 32, 62.

56. A.S.G. Edwards, 'The Influence of Lydgate's Fall of Princes, c.1440–1559: A Survey', *Medieval Studies*, XXXIX (1977), pp. 424–39.

57. For the changing relationship between chance and providence, see K. Thomas, *Religion and the Decline of Magic* (1971), pp. 109, 129–30.

58. J. Lydgate, *The Fall of Princes*, I, H. Bergen (ed.) (4 vols, E.E.T.S. extra series, CXXI–CXXIV, 1924–7), I, p. 285.

59. For Commynes' views on the English, see P. de Commynes, *Mémoires*, M. Jones (trans.)

(Harmondsworth, 1972), p. 258. For his view of history, see ibid., p. 180: 'And yet people say "God doesn't punish men like he used to in the time of the Children of Israel" . . . I firmly believe that he no longer speaks to men as he used to do because he has left sufficient examples in this world to instruct us'. On the general question of the relationship between prophecy and history see the comments of A.F. Sutton and L. Visser-Fuchs, 'Richard III's Books, VIII: Geoffrey of Monmouth's Historia Regum Britanniae with The Prophecy of the Eagle and Commentary', *The Ricardian*, VIII, no. 107 (1989), pp. 290–304.

60. C.A.J. Armstrong, 'An Italian Astrologer at the Court of Henry VII', in *Italian Renaissance Studies*, E.F. Jacob (ed.) (1960), pp. 433–54; H.M. Carey, *Courting Disaster: Astrology at the English Court and University in the Later Middle Ages* (1992).

61. McFarlane, *Nobility*, pp. ix–x; idem., *England*, p. 260, n.103.

62. J.G. Bellamy, *Crime and Public Order in England in the Later Middle Ages* (1973), pp. 60–3; A.R. Myers, 'The Captivity of a Royal Witch: The Household Accounts of Queen Joan of Navarre, 1419–21' in *Crown, Household and Parliament in Fifteenth-Century England*, C.H. Clough (ed.) (1985), pp. 93–133.

63. K.J. Vickers, *Humphrey, Duke of Gloucester, a Biography* (1908), pp. 269–80; Myers, 'Captivity', pp. 102–6; R.A. Griffiths, 'The Trial of Eleanor Cobham: An Episode in the Fall of Humphrey, Duke of Gloucester', *B.J.R.L.* LI (1968–9), pp. 381–99; M.A. Hicks, *False, Fleeting, Perjur'd Clarence: George, Duke of Clarence, 1449–1478* (Gloucester, 1980), pp. 133–5.

64. H.A. Kelly, 'English Kings and the Fear of Sorcery', *Medieval Studies*, XXXIX (1977), pp. 206–38; *An English Chronicle of the Reigns of Richard II, Henry IV, Henry V, and Henry VI*, J.S. Davies (ed.) (Camden Society, old series LXIV, 1856), p. 69; A.F. Sutton and L. Visser-Fuchs, 'The Prophecy of G', *The Ricardian*, VIII, no. 110 (1990), pp. 449–50.

65. Cited in Thomas, *Religion and the Decline of Magic*, p. 501.

66. V.G. Childe, *Man Makes Himself* (1936), p. 153; M. Barber, *The Two Cities: Medieval Europe, 1050–1320* (1992), pp. 5–23, 421–40.

67. F. W. Maitland, 'The Crown as Corporation', in *The Collected Papers of Frederic William Maitland*, H.A.L. Fisher (ed.) (3 vols, Cambridge, 1911), III, p. 246.

68. K. Sharpe, *The Personal Rule of Charles I* (Yale, 1992), pp. 209–35.

69. J. Dollimore, *Radical Tragedy* (1984), pp. 6–7, 83–107.

70. Ibid., p. 90.

71. Thomas, *Religion and the Decline of Magic*, pp. 485–91; J.A. Mendelsohn, 'Alchemy and Politics in England, 1649–1665', *P.P.* CXXXV (1992), pp. 30–78.

72. Mendelsohn, *P.P.* CXXXV, p. 74.

73. Prerogative Court of Canterbury, 13 Godyn (Frost's will).

74. Trinity College, Cambridge, R 14 44. At p. 185 there is a list of debtors, of whom Cook is the most prominent.

75. C.P. Christianson, *Memorials of the Book Trade in Medieval London: The Archives of Old London Bridge* (Manuscript Studies, 3, Cambridge, 1987), pp. 3–21, 48–53 and plate 13.

76. *Secretum Secretorum: Nine English Versions*, M.A. Manzalaoui (ed.) (E.E.T.S. original series, CCLXXVI, 1977); M. Grignaschi, 'La diffusion du Secretum Secretorum (Sirr al-'asrar) dans l'Europe occidentale', *Archives d'histoire doctrinale du Moyen Age*, XLVII (1980), pp. 7–70; C.M. Meale,

'The Middle English Romance of Ipomedon: A Late Medieval Mirror for Princes and Merchants', *Reading Medieval Studies*, X (1984), pp. 136–79.

77. Bacon's writings encouraged the belief that the secret to the discovery of the philosopher's stone could be traced through the meticulous analysis of ancient texts: F.M. Getz, 'To Prolong Life and Promote Health: Baconian Alchemy in the English Learned Tradition' in *Health, Disease and Healing in Medieval Culture*, B. Hall and D. Nausner (ed.) (Toronto, 1992), p. 146. See also E. Brehm, 'Roger Bacon's Place in the History of Alchemy', *Ambix*, XXIII (1976), pp. 53–8.

78. This distinction between legitimate and illegitimate forms of practice was emphasised in Bacon's additions to the *Secretum Secretorum*: Carey, *Courting Disaster*, p. 35.

79. D. Geoghegan, 'A Licence of Henry VI to Practise Alchemy', *Ambix*, VI, (1957), pp. 10–17. For the testimony of the approvers in respect of the king's illness, see R.L. Storey, *The End of the House of Lancaster* (2nd edn, Gloucester, 1986), p. 136, n.12 citing P.R.O. KB. 9/273, nos. 2 and 7. Storey details two examples from this source. In the third (P.R.O. KB. 9/273 no. 7) the abbot of Rievaulx and one of his monks are appealed of paying for spells to be cast to bring about the king's death.

80. Cited by Harriss in *Henry V,* Harriss (ed.), p. 5.

81. It is found in the medical compilation Trinity College, Cambridge, R 14 52, f. 53. The manuscript is dated to 1458 and carries the monogram of John Vale. For Vale's association with Cook, see B.L. Add. Ms. 48031a and P.R.O. Early Chancery Proceedings, C.1/66/400.

82. *Chronicon Adae de Usk, A.D. 1377–1421*, ed. E.M. Thompson (2nd edn, 1904), pp. 119, 132–3, 298, 319–20.

83. J.W. McKenna, 'Popular Canonisation as Political Propaganda: the Cult of Archbishop Scrope', *Speculum*, XLV (1970), pp. 608–23.

84. W.A. Pronger, 'Thomas Gascoigne', *E.H.R.*, LIII (1938), pp. 606–11. For a recent consideration of this point, see J. Hughes, *Pastors and Visionaries: Religion and Secular Life in Late Medieval Yorkshire* (Woodbridge, 1988), pp. 311–15.

85. *Henry V*, Harriss (ed.), pp. 28–9, n. 69.

86. *The Brut or the Chronicles of England*, F.W. Brie (ed.) (2 vols, E.E.T.S. CXXXI, CXXXVI, 1906–8), II, p. 367.

87. T. Gascoigne, *Loci e Libro Veritatum*, J.E.T. Rogers (ed.) (Oxford, 1881), pp. 225–9. Both these accounts and the revival of attempts to secure Scrope's canonisation also antedate the active promotion of his cult by the Yorkist kings, so that we may question the extent to which the 'political Scrope was largely the creation of the Yorkist publicists'; cf. McKenna, 'Popular Canonization', pp. 619–22; see also P. McNiven, 'The Problem of the King's Health, 1405–1413', *E.H.R.C* (1985), pp. 747–72.

88. For the interpretation of Scrope's death in the early chronicles, most notably Walsingham, see: H.A. Kelly, *Divine Providence in the England of Shakespeare's Histories* (Cambridge, Mass., 1970), p. 25.

89. For the use of the supernatural in the validation of political change, see Thomas, *Religion and the Decline of Magic*, pp. 176–8.

90. The phrase was used in February 1460 on behalf of King Henry VI in an attempt to quell rumour-mongers in Coventry: *The Coventry Leet Book*, M.D. Harris (ed.) (E.E.T.S. CXXXIV, CXXXV, CXXXVIII, CXLVI, 1907–13), III, p. 309.

91. McKenna, *Speculum*, XLV, p. 622.

92. *Hoccleve's Works: The Minor Poems*, F. J. Furnivall (ed.) (E.E.T.S. extra series, LXI, 1892), p. 48; Henry also apparently encouraged the belief 'that St. John of Beverley's body distilled precious drops of liquid for sixty-one days and nights' in approbation of Henry Bolingbroke's landing at Ravenspur. The Bridlington prophecies which had previously been used to support beliefs that Richard II was still alive were reinterpreted as predictions of a benevolent destiny for the house of Lancaster: Hughes, *Pastors and Visionaries*, pp. 360–5.

93. *Brut*, pp. 373, 495. Similarly Thomas Gascoigne and Clement of Maidstone probably helped to fuel the belief that Henry V's monastic foundations at Syon and Sheen were acts of atonement for his father's execution of Archbishop Scrope: Hughes, *Pastors and Visionaries*, p. 312.

94. B.P. Wolffe, *Henry VI* (1981), p. 325; J. Fortescue, 'De Natura Legis Naturae', in idem, *Works*, Lord Clermont (ed.) (1863), pp. 187–346.

95. F. A. Yates, *Astraea: The Imperial Theme in the Sixteenth Century* (1975), pp. 1–87.

96. *Henry V*, Harriss (ed.), p. 25; E.F. Jacob, *Henry V and the Invasion of France* (1947), pp. 109–24.

97. Wolffe, *Henry VI*, pp. 352–7; S.B. Chrimes, *Henry VII* (1972), p. 225; P. Grierson, 'The Origins of the English Sovereign and the Symbolism of the Closed Crown', *British Numismatic Journal*, XXXIII (1964), pp. 118–34; W.H. St. John Hope, 'The King's Coronation Ornaments', *The Ancestor*, I (1902), pp. 127–59; cf. S. Anglo, *Images of Tudor Kingship* (1992), p. 119.

98. Yates, *Astraea*, pp. 48–59.

99. Although Elizabeth's comment is normally related to performances of a play of Richard II arranged for the earl of Essex, it was probably intended as a more general reflection on the history of her ancestors, since it was made as she perused Lambard's pandect of the rolls from the reign of John to that of Richard III. It was Lambard who, in his reply, took the remark as a reference to Essex and the play: J. Nichols, *The Progresses and Public Processions of Queen Elizabeth* (3 vols, 1823), III, pp. 552–3; M.E. James, *Society, Politics and Culture: Studies in Early Modern England* Cambridge, 1986), pp. 417–19; S. Daniell, *History of the Civil Wars between the Houses of York and Lancaster* (1595); John Hayward, *The Life and Raigne of King Henry IIII*, J. Manning (ed.) (Camden Society, 4th series. XLII, 1992).

100. For the increasing flow of political prophecy from the 1580s and some sceptical reactions to it, Thomas, *Religion and the Decline of Magic*, pp. 486–500.

101. W. Shakespeare, *Antony and Cleopatra*, I, i, ('Let Rome in Tiber melt . . .'), IV, vi, ('The time of universal peace is near'), V, ii, ('What should I stay . . .'). In this last scene Iras predeceases Cleopatra even though the prophecy in I, ii ('Your fortunes are alike') implies that she will survive her. For James I's entry into London, see R. Strong, *Art and Power: Renaissance Festivals, 1450–1650* (Woodbridge, 1984), p. 72.

102. Carpenter, *Locality*, pp. 633–7. For the mediation of the crown's influence within the shires at an earlier date see Gross, *Midland History*, XVI.

103. Carpenter, *Locality*, p. 633.

104. McFarlane, *England*, p. 241.

4

POLITICAL SAINTS IN LATER
MEDIEVAL ENGLAND

Simon Walker

UNIVERSITY OF SHEFFIELD

At one period two distinct tombs containing Esmiss Esmoor's remains were reported: one by the tannery, the other up near the goods station. Mr. McBryde visited them both and saw signs of the beginning of a cult – earthenware saucers and so on. Being an experienced official, he did nothing to irritate it, and after a week or so, the rash died down. 'There's propaganda behind all this,' he said . . .[1]

This paper is an investigation of the nature of political society in later medieval England, though the angle from which it approaches the question will be notably oblique. Its starting point is an attempt to investigate the nature and significance of the religious sanction enjoyed by the political order through an examination of the changes in the definitions of sanctity that occurred within this period. Such definitions provide an important collective representation, less of reality than of an imagined and widely approved ideal of private and public life; properly understood, they can help to make an important point about the nature of the later medieval polity. That ideals of sanctity were in a state of flux during this period, at both the officially approved level of papal canonisations and at the level of unsanctioned local cults, is common ground to most of the historians who have examined the issue.[2] In thirteenth-century England, there existed a general agreement over the qualities desirable and necessary in a saint. Taking example and inspiration from the martyrdom and subsequent canonisation of Thomas Becket, a number of conscientious diocesan bishops, several of them distinguished by their defence of the liberties of the English church against lay encroachment, were recognised as saints by the Holy See: Hugh, bishop of Lincoln (1220), Edmund of Abingdon, archbishop of Canterbury (1246), Richard Wych, bishop of Chichester (1262), and Thomas Cantilupe, bishop of Hereford (1320). In addition, several other bishops who conformed more or less closely to the 'Becket model' were the subjects of local veneration and ultimately unsuccessful petitions to the Curia on their behalf: Robert Grosseteste, bishop of Lincoln (died 1254), William de March (died 1302); Robert Winchelsey, archbishop of Canterbury (died 1313), and John Dalderby, bishop of Lincoln (died 1320).[3] From the middle of the fourteenth century, however, there is, if not a breakdown in the previous consensus over the qualities necessary for sanctity, then an interiorisation of the criteria for Christian perfection that made sanctity less straightforward to define, with the result that it is possible to identify a number of divergent, and occasionally competing, ideals of sanctity in later medieval England.

The episcopal model of sanctity was not abandoned entirely. Two bishops of Exeter, James Berkley and Edmund Lacy, enjoyed a local cult, while at Norwich cathedral the tombs of bishops Suffield and Salmon were both objects of devotion.[4] In none of these cases was the cult widespread, however, and the rapid decline of offerings to Suffield and Salmon, to be replaced by a remarkable pluralism of altars and shrines within the cathedral by the end of the century,[5] suggests that the English episcopate did not in general escape the crisis of definition and purpose that affected the western Church as a whole. Richard Fitzralph, archbishop of Armagh, was the only contemporary bishop to attract a persistent cult,[6] while the long-delayed canonisation in 1457 of Osmund, the first bishop of Salisbury (died 1102), was as much a recognition of the institutional influence and distinction of the Salisbury chapter as it was a promotion of an ideal of episcopal sanctity. Saints drawn from the religious orders, a particular feature of the era of Avignonese papacy across Western Europe as a whole, were only patchily represented in England. Besides the successful canonisation of John, prior of the house of Augustinian canons at Bridlington (1403),[7] the local cults of the religious do not suggest a consistent pattern to their appeal. Thomas Hale, a monk of the Benedictine priory at Dover, killed by French raiders in 1295; John Went, provincial minister of the

Franciscans in England (died 1348); and Thomas Gresham, abbot of Thornton: each was reported to have performed miracles and to be the object of veneration, but there is little in common between their cults.[8] Equally, a third model of sanctity, the 'mystical invasion' of the calendar that is so notable a feature of European religious life after *c.* 1370, was represented in England only by the solitary figure of Richard Rolle of Hampole.[9] More numerous were the parish priests whose qualities of life and ministry earned them a localised veneration; indeed, there is a sense in which they seem to have replaced the conscientious diocesan bishop as the favoured type of clerical sanctity among the laity. They include Philip Ingleberd, rector of Kaylingham (Yorks.), and Richard Caister, vicar of St Stephen's, Norwich, besides the better-known figure of John Shorne, rector of North Marston (Bucks.).[10] In addition, later medieval England was unusually rich in one further group of candidates for sanctity, the 'political' saints; men whose claim to sanctity rested initially, and more or less exclusively, on their violent deaths in the course of a political conflict. The principal representatives of this group, who will receive more detailed attention in this paper, are well known: Simon de Montfort (died 1265), Thomas of Lancaster (died 1322), Edward II (died 1327), Richard Scrope, archbishop of York (died 1405), Henry VI (died 1471). It should not be forgotten, however, that there are other figures who fall into the same category. Simon de Montfort's companions, killed with him at Evesham, were sometimes associated with him in popular veneration, while a cult of Edward of Windsor, the only son of Henry VI, was maintained at Tewkesbury; even Richard II's favourite, Robert de Vere, earl of Oxford, was thought a worthy object of devotion.[11]

This veneration of laymen as 'political' saints had precedent in England; its greater frequency in the later Middle Ages represents a change of emphasis rather than a wholesale shift in the paradigms of sanctity. The considerable devotion that grew up around the figure of Waltheof, earl of Northumbria, at Thorney in the early twelfth century finds an echo in the miracles reported at the tombs of Henry, the Young King, and William Fitzosbert, leader of the London opposition to the rule of Hubert Walter.[12] Nevertheless, there are two important respects in which the uniqueness of these political cults from the twelfth century onwards should be emphasised. Firstly, the degree to which their appearance marks a decisive break with the pre-Conquest past, in which sanctity was especially closely allied to the ruling dynasties of Anglo-Saxon England.[13] Secondly, they represent an especially English phenomenon, for in no other country was the connection between involvement in secular politics and a claim to sanctity as tightly drawn. There were several Scandinavian bishop saints – Eystein of Nidaros (died 1188); Byrnolf of Skara (died 1317) and Nicholas of Linköping (died 1387) – whose claims to sanctity were held to include an element of resistance to tyrannical royal and noble authority, although this was presented as only one element in the full ensemble of episcopal virtues to be expected in a bishop of the 'Becket model'.[14] Otherwise, political saints of the type relatively common in England, venerated wholly or in part for their involvement with, and death in, the course of secular political affairs, appear only rarely in the rest of Europe. Pietro Parenzo, the papal *podestà* of Orvieto, who eventually became the patron saint of the city after his death at the hands of the Ghibellines; Cabrit and Bassa, two obscure Majorcan patriots martyred for their resistance to the troops of Alfonso III of Aragon; and Charles of Blois, duke of Brittany, whose cult undoubtedly owed something (but not everything) to his death in battle against the English-backed Montfortist claimant of the duchy:[15] these provide the only important European counterparts to the well-established tradition of political saints in England. The contrast poses again the questions with which this discussion began. What was it about the English polity that encouraged the emergence of such cults? And what was their place and purpose within English political life?

Several historians have addressed themselves to these questions, though their answers have generally assumed one of two forms. The first is that no explanation is, in fact, required, since the existence of these cults is itself unremarkable, evidence only of 'the tendency of ignorant people to look for . . . a hero in any prominent figure who met a sudden and violent death', for once a cult had started 'simple-minded devotion would ensure its continuance'.[16] While this approach has the merit of emphasising the considerable value that continued to be placed upon violent death – 'the certain agony of martyrdom'[17] – as a sign of sanctity in popular religion, it remains an unsatisfactorily partial explanation, for murdered princes or politicians, however well known, could not automatically expect to be venerated as saints after their death. No cult of Piers Gaveston grew up, despite Edward II's attempts to encourage one,[18] and neither Thomas of Woodstock nor Humphrey of Gloucester attracted any veneration, despite their relative popularity in life. Equally, 'simple-minded' devotion was not, of itself, enough to ensure a cult's continuance. The tomb of Richard, earl of Arundel, condemned to death as a traitor by Richard II in 1397, was the object of a veneration substantial enough to cause the king disquiet, but this enthusiasm proved short-lived; the last reference to Arundel's merits or miracles dates to *c.* 1404.[19] The second, and most widely accepted, explanation advanced concentrates upon the undoubted elements of political manipulation to be found in the promotion of these cults and takes that part of the answer for the whole. The motive behind the devotion to these political saints is, therefore, to be explained in primarily political terms, since such cults represented 'an easy and almost unpunishable way of showing hostility to the king'.[20] A more sophisticated version of the same argument connects the concentration of these 'political' cults in the fourteenth and fifteenth centuries with the contemporary expansion of the political nation; 'with the growing necessity of securing the affections of the commonalty, a new age of political leaders sought to channel and control this enthusiasm' by the skilled manipulation of popular religiosity.[21] This explanation has, at least, a certain empirical value. The alleged activities of Sir Reginald de Montfort and the mayor of Bristol in encouraging the cult of two of Thomas of Lancaster's followers executed there indicates that there were always interest groups quick to recognise the capital to be made from such cults.[22] Nevertheless, the suggested model of political promotion and manipulation, with its implicit assumption that the political and intellectual élite could write at will on the *tabula rasa* of popular devotion, seems at best only a partial explanation. It fails to account for the initial impulse of veneration, which preceded the annexation and 'construction' of these cults by particular interest groups, and was often tenaciously maintained in the face of considerable official discouragement. Nor does it adequately explain the survival and development of some cults and the swift disappearance of others. The fully worked out martyrdom scene, complete with accompanying miracles, offered by Thomas Walsingham in his description of the death of Archbishop Sudbury in 1381, like the report of miracles occurring at the tomb of the Carmelite friar tortured to death by a group of household knights in 1385,[23] provide instances where the initial movement of sympathy and veneration for the clerical victims of violent death was not – despite, in the case of Sudbury, some powerful backing – transformed into an effective cause. In this sense, the canonical tag *non poena sed causa* contains an important sociological truth; since all saints were saints 'for other people', their lives and reputations remodelled to correspond to collective mental representations of the holy,[24] there had to be something in the actions of the victim of violence, or in the circumstances of his death, that appealed to a substantial number of worshippers if his cult was to develop effectively. In order to establish the nature and effectiveness of the appeal exercised by the English political saints, it will be necessary to examine briefly the origins and principal manifestations of their cults, before going on to seek a more satisfactory explanation for their success.

The cult of Simon de Montfort, earl of Leicester, rapidly established itself following his death in battle against the royalist forces at Evesham in August 1265. The Dictum of Kenilworth, promulgated a little over a year later, already speaks of his reputation as a saint and of his reported miracles.[25] Chronicles from every part of the country confirm the widespread belief in his sanctity, frequently adding that reports of many more miracles worked by the new saint had been suppressed for fear of the king.[26] The surviving evidence of this veneration consists of a liturgical office in de Montfort's honour, a collection of his *miracula* produced at Evesham Abbey, and a number of motets and poems in both Latin and Anglo-Norman, celebrating his deeds and his martyrdom.[27] The 196 miracles ascribed to the earl's intercession suggest that devotion to his cause was spread widely across the southern Midlands, with outlying pockets of enthusiasm in Kent and London, and reveal a notably well-connected group of suppliants; de Montfort's miracles were performed on behalf of the countess of Gloucester and the baronial families of Roos, Cantilupe and Peverel, besides several knightly sufferers.[28] Yet although this evidence suggests de Montfort's cult gained rapid and widespread support, enthusiasm for his cause appears to have been short-lived. The last datable cure in his *miracula* took place in August 1279, while the latest of the manuscripts containing material in de Montfort's honour are from the early fourteenth century.[29] When Edward II had 'songs of Simon de Montfort' sung to him at Whorlton Castle in August 1323, it seems more likely that the songs commemorated his life and the justice of his cause than that they saluted him as a saint.[30]

Thomas of Lancaster's cult, though very similar in its origins to de Montfort's, shows some significant differences in its development. Following the earl of Lancaster's execution as a traitor, after a summary trial at Pontefract in July 1322, miracles were soon reported to be occuring at his tomb and the authorities unsuccessfully sought to repress the popular devotion which followed.[31] Within a decade of his death a hagiographic *vita* had been produced, probably at Pontefract,[32] and as in the case of de Montfort, the surviving evidence suggests a widespread and initially popular cult – a liturgical office in Lancaster's honour, and surviving fragments of a second;[33] chronicle reports of his miracles;[34] depictions and *memoriae* of his martyrdom in several mid-fourteenth century psalters and books of hours,[35] as well as evidence for the rapid institutionalisation of the Pontefract pilgrimage.[36] In contrast to the cult of Simon de Montfort, however, devotion to Thomas of Lancaster became a permanent feature of English spiritual life in the later Middle Ages, lasting in a more or less attenuated form until the Reformation. While the initial burst of enthusiasm for the cult may have begun to subside *c.* 1350, the patronage of two powerful noble families, the houses of Bohun and Lancaster, provided sufficient publicity and resources to maintain the shrine as a place of pilgrimage until the end of the fourteenth century, to the extent that in 1390 it was believed, erroneously, that Lancaster had been officially canonised.[37] The advent of the Lancastrian dynasty, determined to promote devotion to their own *Adelsheilige*, inevitably reinvigorated the cult; Henry IV presented vestments depicting the *historia* of Lancaster's martyrdom to St George's chapel, Windsor, in 1401, for example.[38] As a result, there is considerable evidence for Lancaster's continuing popularity as a saint in the fifteenth century: there are references to the existence of a guild of St Thomas at Pontefract itself; new polyphonic settings were written for the existing motets in his honour; his relics continued to be venerated and miracles at his tomb to attract public attention; the anniversary of his death was entered in some English liturgical calendars until well into the sixteenth century.[39]

Different from either of these cults was the fitful veneration that began to gather around the tomb of the murdered Edward II at Gloucester. It is especially difficult to gauge the appeal and success of this cult because, apart from the account of a Gloucester annalist writing at the end of the fourteenth century,[40] the evidence for Edward's veneration is very thin. Two points stand out from that account, however. In contrast to the other 'political' cults, the inception of Edward's cult did not follow immediately on his interment; the prayers and offerings are said to have begun in the time of Abbot Wigmore, who was elected in 1329. As a consequence, the 'oppositional' element in Edward's veneration – the degree to which it can be interpreted as a covert criticism of the regime of Isabella and Mortimer – can only have been slight, since Edward III began his personal rule within eighteen months. Indeed, what distinguishes Edward II's cult from those of either Simon de Montfort or Thomas of Lancaster is the degree to which it was dependent on royal encouragment, whether in the form of the substantial gifts made by Edward III and his family at the shrine in 1343 or in the determined campaign for his great-grandfather's canonisation launched by Richard II *c.* 1385.[41] Apart from these royal initiatives, the evidence for Edward's veneration is slight; no liturgical commemorations are known to survive while the scattered iconographical evidence, such as the depiction of the king, labelled *sanctus Edwardus*, in a Tewkesbury roll-chronicle compiled *c.* 1420, suggests a cult largely confined to the west of England.[42] It seems safest to conclude that the continuing popular debate over Edward's sanctity, to which Ranulf Higden alluded *c.* 1340,[43] had been generally settled to the king's disadvantage some years before Richard II vainly sought to revive enthusiasm for his veneration. It is noticeable that even the Gloucester annalist, writing in the shadow of Richard's campaign for Edward's canonisation, does not accord him the title of saint when describing the offerings at his tomb.

The cult of Richard Scrope, archbishop of York, executed in June 1405 for his rebellion against Henry IV presents no such problems of evidence, though it raises questions of interpretation to which it will be necessary to return. The popular veneration at Scrope's tomb was immediate and, initially, carried on in the face of royal prohibition.[44] The archbishop's subsequent miracles were widely reported and the offerings at his shrine were soon yielding very substantial sums.[45] Fittingly for a clerical martyr, Scrope's death generated a large body of literary material: two separate prose accounts of his trial and execution survive;[46] a Latin poem and a liturgical office in the archbishop's honour were composed soon after his death, and a number of further antiphons and *memoriae* for Scrope survive in contemporary calendars and books of hours.[47] In addition, the inventories of *ex voto* offerings at Scrope's tomb drawn up in 1500 and 1509 make it clear that his cult continued to attract popular devotion.[48] That it did so was certainly due to the continuing regard in which the 'martyr of York' was held, but it also came to owe something to the encouragement of the Yorkist kings, who saw in the archbishop's execution one of the chief demonstrations of the injustice and illegitimacy of Lancastrian rule.[49] It was accordingly at Edward IV's prompting (*regio impulso*) that the dean and chapter of York began to consider the possibility of Scrope's formal canonisation in 1462.[50] The archbishop had always had his enthusiastic devotees among the Minster clergy[51] but it seems likely that, by this date, his cult had begun to surrender some of its earlier prominence. Although there are no precise figures available for oblations at his tomb after 1421, the general level of offerings in the Minster, which had risen with the growth of Scrope's cult (from £31 6s 2d in 1405 to £56 12s 0^{1}/$_{2}$d in 1416 and £54 5s 9^{1}/$_{2}$d in 1419) had fallen back sharply by mid-century, with annual oblations running at about £25 *per annum* during the 1440s and £17 10s 0d during the following decade.[52] The corporate endeavour of the dean and chapter was consequently aimed at establishing the archbishop's cult securely among the many active devotions of the archdiocese[53] rather than according it the special prominence that Edward IV evidently desired. As in the case of Thomas of Lancaster, therefore, a cult that had its origins in a protest against the actions of royal government came to owe a degree of its continued popularity to direct royal sponsorship.

Similar considerations apply, with even greater force, to the cult of Henry VI. Following his death in the Tower and hasty burial at Chertsey Abbey, Henry's tomb soon became a place of pilgrimage, despite the alleged indifference of the monks of Chertsey, who were said to fear the disapproval of Edward IV.[54] Offerings were also being reported before an image of the king in York Minster as early as 1475.[55] It is difficult to assess the true dimensions of Henry's cult before the translation of his body from Chertsey to Windsor in 1484 – at which point it certainly becomes a devotion encouraged by the ruling dynasty – but there are several contemporary sources which ascribe some of Henry's reported miracles to the Chertsey period and the fame of his tomb was already enough to attract pilgrims from as far away as Norwich.[56] Following the 1484 translation, however, there is no doubt about the popularity of Henry's cult, which attracted very considerable numbers of pilgrims, generated a carefully edited collection of 174 miracles performed by the former king, and is commemorated in a considerable body of surviving devotional and liturgical material.[57] There seems good reason to believe that devotion to Henry VI, fuelled by his growing reputation as an effective protector against outbreaks of plague and sweating-sickness, replaced Thomas Becket as the most popular of English cults before the Reformation.[58]

This brief survey raises, at once, one of the principal points to be made about the cults of these political saints; that there is only a limited sense in which their veneration can be said to constitute a 'canonisation of opposition to the Crown'. That there was an element, more or less central, of political protest and defiance in the genesis of these cults seems, with the possible exception of Edward II, to be undeniable. But in four out of the five cases considered above, this oppositional statement came to be overlaid, and largely neutralised, by a degree of royal protection and encouragement that sought to harness the devotion these saints aroused in the interests of the crown. In the case of Thomas of Lancaster, this royal intervention was swift: Edward III began to press for his canonisation as early as 1327.[59] Though in Henry VI's case this royal initiative took a little longer (1471–84) to manifest itself, and in Scrope's the lapse of time was over half a century, it was only in the case of de Montfort's cause that the attitude of the royal authorities remained consistently hostile; Edward I would not allow the office in his honour composed by the Franciscans to be performed in his own lifetime.[60] As a result, to confine discussion of the phenomenon of 'political' saints in later medieval England to the extent to which they represented and encouraged a spirit of resistance to the claims of the crown is to ignore half the question that needs to be answered; which is, the degree to which these same saints contributed to the simultaneous, and generally more successful, enhancement of the spiritual status and claims of the English monarchy. It is in this context that it seems worthwhile to pursue the suggestion that political saints should best be interpreted as an inversion of the *mentalité* of holy monarchy, the claim to a special sacral status advanced with increasing insistence by kings in both England and France. As one of several contemporary but competing representations of the political order, the cult of political saints might be seen as a reaction against the sacral claims of kings which nevertheless continued to depend on the actions and reputation of the monarchy for its appeal and, in the long run, served only to reinforce the ideology it challenged.[61] Though admittedly speculative, this appears a useful hypothesis to pursue for it has, at least, the merit of calling attention to one of the most striking developments in the ideology of the English monarchy in the later Middle Ages; the growing conviction that kings stood in an especially close relationship to God, that they possessed certain distinct spiritual qualities by virtue of their exercise of secular office.

This was not, of course, a phenomenon confined solely to the later Middle Ages. Touching for scrofula, the royal miracle of healing, was performed as far back as Henry II's reign and, if Richard II believed that unique spiritual qualities had been conferred on him by the rite of unction performed at his coronation, Henry III's enthusiasm for the sacral aspects of monarchy 150 years earlier had moved Robert Grosseteste to remind him of the fate of Ozias, king of Judah, who was struck with leprosy for usurping the priestly office.[62] Even the matter-of-fact Edward III had ascribed to him magical powers while his eldest son could, on more than one occasion, be compared to the Son of God.[63] Nevertheless, the late fourteenth and fifteenth centuries appear to mark a new anxiety to emphasise the spiritual claims and powers of the English monarchy, epitomised in the adoption of the title 'most Christian king' and justified by Thomas Polton's argument at the Council of Constance that the English dynasty had the longest association with Christianity of any European ruling house.[64] This emphasis owed a good deal to the anxiety of the Lancastrian dynasty to consolidate their right to the crown, which led them to lay stress upon the divine sanction and approval conferred by their royal ancestry; 'twelve kings of the English successions, martyrs and confessors . . . and the emblems of their sanctity plain for all to see' greeted Henry V on his triumphal entry into London after Agincourt and offered him the sacramental elements of bread and wine, while Henry VI sought the canonisation of Alfred, the first ruler of a united English kingdom.[65] The development of these claims was, however, also testimony to a deeper-seated shift in the public perception of the function and necessity of monarchy fostered by the growing association of heresy with sedition. The Oldcastle rising, the Kentish scare of 1428 and the Perkins rebellion in 1431, as well as the ominous object lesson of contemporary Bohemia, all pointed to the same conclusion; that heresy led inevitably to sedition.[66] By the same token, sedition came increasingly to encompass, and be identified with, heresy. The connection was already immanent in the statue against unauthorised preaching passed, on the initiative of Henry, prince of Wales, in the Long Parliament, which included both Lollard evangelists and Ricardian loyalists within its prohibitions.[67] It was cemented into place by the allegation that Richard, earl of Cambridge, sought the aid of the Lollards for his plot to assassinate the king in 1415.[68] The defence of the Catholic orthodoxy, it was increasingly clear, depended upon the king successfully discharging his duties to maintain the social hierarchy and the public peace; to attack the king was, inevitably, to attack the Christian faith.

In the wake of heresy came a further, and closely related, threat to ecclesiastical and royal authority: sorcery. The association of magical activity – prophecy, divination, necromancy – with the enemies and opponents of the king seems a particular feature of the disturbed political scene between 1397 and 1406, when there was a sudden rash of accusations and counter-charges of reliance on prophecy and magic; as one French observer commented disapprovingly, the English 'very thoroughly believe in prophecies, phantoms and witchcraft, and employ them right willingly'.[69] Once established, the association grew closer throughout the fifteenth century. In 1419 Henry V announced himself to be the intended victim of a magician's plot and required the prayers of his diocesans in order to combat it, while Bishop Stafford of Bath and Wells warned his flock in 1431 that the glorious kingdom of England had twice lost the crown of glory through belief in magic and spells; the startling success of Joan of Arc, unambiguously seen in English sources as a sorceress, provided vivid confirmation of the power of magic to harm the English cause.[70] Accusations of involvement in sorcery and divination became the currency of domestic politics; Henry VI's government sought to win the propaganda war against the Cade rebels in 1450 by presenting their leader as a dabbler in sorcery and consorter with the devil; Jacquetta, duchess of Bedford, had to clear herself of accusations that she had sought the death of the king and his wife by witchcraft in 1470, while similar charges of witchcraft were preferred against the Woodville family by Richard III.[71] This connection between sorcery and

treason was most clearly defined in two famous 'show trials', when Eleanor
Cobham, duchess of Gloucester, was found guilty of imagining the king's death
in 1441 on the grounds that she had sought to know when he would die by
astrological means, and Dr Stacey, Thomas Blake and Thomas Burdet were
condemned as traitors for calculating the nativities of the king and the prince of
Wales in 1477.[72]

There are two points of relevance to the analysis of the phenomenon of
political saints in these much-discussed cases. The first is that those involved
were in both cases adjudged guilty of treason. This is in contrast to the outcome
of earlier cases of a similar type. When the powerful Adam de Stratton,
chamberlain of the Exchequer, was tried for corruption in 1289, the common
talk of his sorcery found no place in the charges against him, while when Walter
Langton, Edward I's treasurer, was accused of sorcery in 1303, the king
continued to accord him his full support. Equally, when the prior of Coventry's
servants were charged with plotting the death of Edward II and the Despensers
by magical means in 1324, the crime was classified as a felony, not a treason.[73]
Secondly, the grounds of the charge of treason in the two fifteenth-century cases
was that the plotters had sought to 'destroy the cordial love' that should always
regulate the relations of a king and his subjects.[74] This is an unusually clear
statement of the implicit assumption behind much ecclesiastical and secular
thinking on the nature of contemporary politics: that the public peace
depended, in the final analysis, upon the maintenance of an ideal of charity
between individuals. The political amity this ideal was intended to effect was,
for instance, proclaimed as a principle of his government on more than one
occasion by Henry IV; in 1400 he pardoned some of the rebels taken in arms
against him in order to 'foster the faith and love of our subjects towards us',
while in 1409 he explained his grant of a general pardon as a means of creating
'the mutual love without which all else is in vain' in order that 'our said lieges
may lift up their hearts with greater joy to remain more truly in faith and love
towards us and our heirs'.[75] How such an ideal of charity should operate in a
properly constituted political society was explained with some precision by the
commons in the 1401 parliament, when they sought to compare a session of
parliament to the sacrifice of the Mass. The point of this elaborate conceit was
that, just as the Mass was envisaged as offering a 'social miracle' to the devout

and contrite, bringing harmony out of discord, so parliament, properly conducted, was the 'political miracle', reconciling the unreconciled and creating anew the body politic, 'by the grace of God all in one faithfully bound together' by the 'good and entire hearts' they bore towards one another. Within this process, it was the king who performed the priestly function, making 'the sacrifice to be offered to God by all Christians' through his preservation and protection of his lay and ecclesiastical subjects.[76] On this view, a king was as crucial to the political salvation of his subjects as a priest to the spiritual salvation of his flock. This was a vision of political relations, idealised but potent, that retained its currency throughout the fifteenth century. Edward IV, whose progress through England in 1471 was accompanied by miracles of divine approbation, justified his tenure of the Crown in the millenial terms of a conflict with, and victory over, 'our great adversary'; Richard III, said by John Rous to reign like Antichrist, was described by Henry VII as 'our adversary, *enemy of nature* and of all public weal'. The disturbance of the political order created by a usurping king was envisaged as a disturbance of the divinely sanctioned natural order as well.[77]

It is within the context of this set of beliefs – that the king was a priest-like figure whose task was to bring about a state of social amity on which the peace and wholeness of the body politic ultimately depended – that the cult of political saints in later medieval England can best be understood. Devotion to such saints was undoubtedly born in an atmosphere of political disorder and their cults contained within themselves, during the early stages of their development, a certain element of protest against the triumph of the unrighteous. Yet if such cults were to survive and prosper, they had to grow beyond their origins and answer the aspirations and concerns articulated in the set of beliefs that grew up around the powers of the monarch in the later Middle Ages, satisfying the desire for reconciliation and re-integration expressed, positively, in the ideal of 'cordial love' and, negatively, in the heavy penalties prescribed for those who destroyed that love. Their success or failure as cults depended, in general terms, on the success or failure with which they did so; if social amity enjoyed 'an intimate relationship with the process of salvation',[78] a saint who could not bring about that social amity could not, in turn, be regarded as a reliable source of salvation. The power of the saints, and their value in political life, was not in preventing disorder or rebellion, for this they manifestly could not do. It was in helping to restore a measure of harmony after the strife was over and in making reconciliation, even on unfavourable terms, easier for the losers by offering a higher, and more objective, constraint to which all could submit without dishonour. As Southern has remarked of the cult of Waltheof, the Anglo-Saxon hero whose tomb was attracting Anglo-Norman devotees by the reign of Henry I, 'the miracles were a common ground on which all men could meet'.[79] The cult of Archbishop Scrope, far from being straightforwardly 'anti-Lancastrian', prospered in precisely the same way; the offerings at his shrine covered the political spectrum, including both the livery badge of Richard II – 'a hart of gold, enamelled with white and green' – and the Lancastrian collar of SS, given by no less a figure than Archbishop Bowet's nephew.[80]

The characteristic development of a political cult along these lines is already foreshadowed in the most famous of them, that of Thomas Becket. The initial reaction of the Canterbury clergy to his murder, preserved in the lections for the anniversary of his martyrdom in the Sarum Breviary, was to emphasise the violence of the act and the political division that it bred – 'the powers of heaven were so disturbed that, as if in vengeance for the spilling of innocent blood, people rose up against people and kingdom against kingdom; even the realm was divided against itself'.[81] Becket's blood called out for vengeance 'more than the blood of the just man Abel, killed at the beginning of the world'.[82] Yet by the time of Becket's translation in 1220 the emphasis of the office written for the occasion – possibly by Stephen Langton[83] – was very different. It avoided the opportunity of restating the divisive claims to ecclesiastical immunity that lay at the root of Becket's martyrdom, concentrating instead on the Levitican idea of a jubilee as a time of repentance and remission and presenting the feast as a time of grace and reconciliation.[84] The author of the office was doing no more than reflect the favoured presentation of Becket's cult at Canterbury. 'What is so remarkable about a saint loving those who love him?' asked Benedict of Peterborough. 'Even the pagans and publicans do that. It is a narrow charity that admits friends and excludes enemies'.[85] It was a cardinal point in Becket's reputation for sanctity that his grace was known to extend to his former enemies, such as Gilbert Foliot and his servants, or the brother of his murderer,

Robert de Broc. It was with the archbishop's help that Henry II's forces captured William the Lion in 1174 and that the king was subsequently able to establish 'so great and perfect a peace' throughout his kingdom.[86] The historical Becket had already given way to the emblematic episcopal martyr, dying for the good of the church but, at the same time, extending his patronage and favour to the whole English people.

Among the political saints discussed in this paper, there is too little evidence for the cult of Edward II to come to any firm conclusions as to how his devotees perceived him, and the case of Simon de Montfort presents some special features, best left to the end of the discussion. For the other three saints, however, it is possible to illustrate in some detail the way their cults developed beyond their immediate origins in an act of political defiance in order to exercise an appeal for a number of different audiences. In the case of Thomas of Lancaster, for instance, several constituents of his sanctity, several claims on the devotion of their audience, are held in tension by the surviving literary and liturgical evidence for his cult. The circumstances of, and reasons for, Lancaster's execution are never ignored; he is presented as a lover of truth and constant fighter for justice, more fearful of offending the divine majesty than its human representative.[87] In the Pontefract *vita*, these claims are given an extended exposition in terms that echo his own propaganda, emphasising the powers and responsibilities of his position as steward of England.[88] But this was only one element in the construction of Lancaster's cult. Besides the carefully crafted reminiscences of the Passion that appear in the *The Brut*'s account of his trial and execution, the most consistent emphasis is laid upon Lancaster's royal birth and knightly virtues. As a royal vessel, born of a royal bed, he will bring about the cure of the kingdom – a claim that seeks an association with, rather than an appropriation of, the thaumaturgic powers of the monarchy.[89] As the flower and gem of knighthood, the knight of the English church, who never held the poor in contempt, Lancaster is portrayed as an emblematic reminder to the nobility of their duty of protection towards the poor and orthodox.[90] Equally, when Lancaster is presented as the secular counterpart of Thomas Becket, it is the Becket of Langton's Translation office, offering salvation and reconciliation to the whole nation, on whom he is modelled; it is for 'the peace and tranquillity of the inhabitants of England' that Earl Thomas 'the champion of plentiful charity' is said to have died.[91] This transformation from partisan figure to national saint, a powerful patron at the court of heaven for the whole English people, was a swift one. As early as 1327 the commons were petitioning for the initiation of his canonisation process 'for the enhancing of the estate of the kingdom', while Edward III's letter to the pope on the same issue describes Thomas's holy blood, fertile and life-giving, flowing through all parts of England like the river of paradise.[92] These were the terms in which his cult continued to be envisaged. One of the fifteenth-century motets in his honour salutes him as the guardian of England (*tutor Angliae*), a peace-maker who brings grace to the hard hearts of sinners and creates concord out of discord.[93]

The evidence for the development of Archbishop Scrope's cult illustrates the same point: that a successful devotion soon grew beyond the circumstances of its origin. The Lancastrian government seems never, in fact, to have ascribed much significance to its potential as a rallying point for dissent. Though John of Lancaster was initially anxious to prevent any concourse of pilgrims at Scrope's tomb, by December 1405 Archbishop Arundel was already taking a more conciliatory line with the Minster clergy, insisting only that they refrain from inducing oblations and devotion on the grounds that these should await the judgement of God and the determination of the Church.[94] When the cult persisted, Henry IV and his advisers accepted it with good grace; the temporary prohibition on offerings at Scrope's tomb had been lifted, in practice, by 1409 and was formally revoked by Henry V early in his reign, while enthusiastic supporters of the dynasty, such as the Kenilworth chronicler John Strecche, nevertheless reported Scrope's miracles and the crowds of pilgrims at York.[95] This was not because the liturgical and devotional material in the archbishop's honour glossed over the circumstances of his death or refrained from passing judgement upon them. Most accounts of his martyrdom emphasise the injustice of his execution without due process of law, while to describe Scrope as a 'new Abel' clearly casts Henry IV in the role of a new Cain, shedding the blood of the righteous man.[96] Yet this aspect of his cult was balanced by several of the other claims for his sanctity advanced by Scrope's advocates, which served to generalise the appeal of his cause beyond the purely political. These included an emphasis on the excellence of Scrope's priestly virtues, as an *exemplum castitatis* whose first recorded miracle was to encourage a sinner to go to confession, and a closely allied association between his cult and the developing devotion of the Five Wounds, fostered by the manner of his death.[97] Comparison with the proto-martyr Stephen, encouraged by Scrope's burial in the chapel of St Stephen in the Minster, provided a narrative model of his death which necessarily involved the archbishop in calling on God to forgive his enemies; Thomas Gascoigne's account of the martyrdom duly has Scrope praying that God will not revenge his death on the king or his servants.[98] When Richard Scrope was further compared to Thomas Becket, therefore, it was the familiar Becket of the liturgy, offering reconciliation to the whole English people, not the Becket of history, to whom reference was made; the convergence of royal and ecclesiastical interests in the intervening centuries had rendered a re-dramatisation of the issues originally in dispute between Henry II and his archbishop increasingly otiose.[99]

The successful transition from a claim to veneration born of a moment of political conflict to an established cult was effected in Scrope's case, as in Thomas of Lancaster's, precisely because devotion to the archbishop was held to offer a means of deliverance from such struggles. The office that salutes Scrope as a new Abel also calls upon the archbishop to dissolve the chains of conflict and re-create the compact of peace, going on to elaborate a parallel between Christ, who died outside the gates of Jerusalem, and Scrope, who died outside the gates of York; it is the task of the archbishop to turn York into a new Sion, an 'abode of peace'.[100] It was for this reason that Edward IV's attempts to re-interpret the Scrope cult in a more partisan and political light met with indifference and, ultimately, failure at York. The dean and chapter gave prolonged consideration to the king's intention to seek the archbishop's canonisation and ended by resolving, instead, to raise the celebration of the Minster's dedication to a double feast and to improve the existing celebrations on the feast of St William.[101] There is significance, as well as prevarication, in their decision. Scrope was valued as a local patron, the 'glory of York', accessible to all who invoked his aid, and faced with seeing him appropriated to act as the supernatural champion of a political faction, the dean and chapter responded by seeking to anchor his cult still more firmly within the spiritual and physical context of the Minster as the mother-church of the archdiocese.

As Edward IV sought, in this way, to exploit the reputation of one political saint for the advantage of his own dynasty, it was natural that he and his advisers should be wary of the growing popular devotion to the last Lancastrian king during the 1470s and should seek to restrain it.[102] Yet Henry VI's claims to sanctity were expressed, from the first, in terms that largely removed them from the arena of political debate. The continuator of the Crowland Chronicle accounted Henry a saint 'by reason of his innocence of life, his love of God and the Church and his patience in adversity'. Writing *c.* 1484, John Blacman produced a more detailed treatment of the king's virtues, portraying him as a saint of the *devotio moderna*, a contemplative and ascetic imitator of Christ, another Job in his sufferings.[103] Above all, Henry appears as the subject of a startling but benign *perepteia*, as the man who lost an earthly kingdom but gained a heavenly one. With the important addition of an emphasis upon the king's powers of healing, these were the terms in which the growing body of liturgical and devotional material in Henry's honour portrayed him as well. The 'prayer of Sixtus IV' uses Henry's life as an *exemplum* of patience and humility in prosperity and adversity, while the emphasis put on the same virtues by Bernard André, Henry VII's chaplain, suggests that this portrayal of Henry as the 'suffering Lamb' was the aspect of his reputation to enjoy the most enthusiastic official sanction.[104] As devotion to the king developed, however, two further elements in the powers and virtues ascribed to him, largely absent from the earlier material in his honour, began to emerge. The first, present also in the cults of Thomas of Lancaster and Richard Scrope, was the store set on Henry's actions as a peacemaker. 'Let there be peace on earth and not war' asks the popular invocation *Rex Henricus, sis amicus*, while one of the English prayers in his honour calls on Henry to 'set this realm in rest'.[105] The same idea was worked out, at greater length and in a secular context, in Petrus Carmelianus' poem on the birth of prince Arthur, in which the task of bringing peace to England's dynastic strife is delegated to Henry by the company of saints.[106] One of the king's early miracles illustrates how his intercession could bring such peace about; the parishioners of Ashby St Leger 'all bound by one chain of charity' at the bidding of their priest, successfully stilled the ravings of a woman possessed by the devil who threatened to disrupt the Mass by their prayers to the king. Besides this image of communities united in charity by the action of the saint,[107] a second and less predictable emphasis was upon Henry's power, upon the assertion of an authority in death that had been denied him in life. 'Those who disparaged you now come before you and adore your footprints' runs the versicle of the office in Henry's honour; an early woodcut of the king as a saint, towering massively above his suppliant subjects, vividly conveys the same idea.[108] Both words and image are reminiscent of the terms in which the *Anglo-Saxon Chronicle* celebrated the emergent cult of Edward the Martyr – 'those who would not bow to his living body now bend humbly before his dead body' – and the perception behind the celebration was very similar.[109] Henry's cult is seen as representing a reassertion of right order in the world, the peaceful triumph of divinely approved monarchical authority over the forces of discord that have temporarily threatened it.

Simon de Montfort's cult provides a significant exception, in several respects, from those examined above. The literary and liturgical material justifies his veneration in appropriately general terms, as a soldier of Christ, fighting for justice and the maintenance of the faith, a 'wall of Israel' for the people and clergy of England. Comparison with Becket's cause and martyrdom is particularly frequent; Thomas is the 'titan of the east', Simon the 'star of the west'.[110] Two features of the songs and prayers in his honour stand out as exceptional, however. One is that many of them were clearly produced very soon after the earl's death at Evesham, since they make reference to the contemporary political scene: de Montfort's office finishes by deploring the faithlessness and lawbreaking that continues throughout the country and calls upon the martyr to confound those who commit such crimes; the poem *Ubi fuit mons est vallis* ends with a similar lament for the destruction done by the *raptores in patria*; the song *Chaunter m'estoit* calls upon God to take care of those of Montfort's followers who are still in prison.[111] This helps to locate the context in which such material was produced, dating it to the period of violent social and tenurial disruption between Evesham and the Dictum of Kenilworth, when Henry III's government was seeking to implement a policy of absolute forfeiture against the Montfortians.[112] As a consequence, de Montfort's cult was valued by his devotees chiefly as a weapon in a continuing struggle, rather than as a means of reconciliation once the struggle was over, and the devotional material it generated preserved and perpetuated the divisions of the earl's secular career instead of seeking to transcend them. His office includes, for instance, two verses recording and celebrating the punishment of an 'ignoble esquire' who derided the nascent cult; one of his miracles describes a monk of Peterborough, doubtful of his status as a saint, confronted by the earl in a dream and faced with the choice of death or eating a raw piglet. The saint's reply to Margaret Maunsell, who enquired what would become of those who were his enemies during his lifetime, indicates the unconditional nature of the capitulation he demanded from his former opponents: 'some have repented, some will repent, and some have died a bad death without penitence'.[113]

There is significance in the contrast between the ordeal-miracle reported in de Montfort's *miracula* and the several deliverance miracles of Henry VI. A Derbyshire nobleman, giving a feast for his neighbours, encounters two persistent detractors of the earl; calling on Christ to prove that de Montfort had died for 'truth and justice in the land', he thrusts his hand into a cauldron of boiling water and it remains unharmed.[114] The miracle is used as a means of coercing agreement, of distinguishing unequivocally between right and wrong. In delivering a prisoner from gaol, and saving two others from the gallows, Henry VI acts, on the other hand, in conformity to an Augustinian tradition of indifference to the facts of guilt or innocence that provides a deliverance, not only from gaol, but from the divisive necessity of making a final judgement at all.[115] His action is typical of the ability of a successful cult to develop a more than factional appeal by offering the powers of its saint as protector, healer and intercessor to all those who invoked him. De Montfort's cult, alone of those examined in this paper, failed to reach this stage of development and remained enmeshed in the political circumstances of its inception. In consequence, once the immediate political and personal needs the cult had satisfied began to disappear, as the reconciliation of the majority of the Disinherited with Edward I took gradual effect,[116] so too did the belief in his sanctity. After 1280, evidence for de Montfort's veneration as a saint is hard to find, though his commemoration as a virtuous political leader remained common well into the fourteenth century.[117]

Political saints were, then, no different from the other saints venerated in later medieval England in being valued 'not primarily as exemplars or soul-friends, but as powerful helpers and healers in time of need'.[118] For their devotees, the virtues and vicissitudes of their earthly careers were of secondary importance when compared to the promise of assistance held out by their miracles. What set them apart from other saints was that their helping and healing characteristically extended beyond the individual to the community, seeking to effect the recreation of concord in a disordered body politic by the reintegration of the defeated and marginalised. Though fissile and disordered, later medieval English society was also rich in the resources of compromise and conciliation, not the least of which was this power of the saints. In reaching this conclusion there is always a danger of mistaking rhetoric for reality. In certain circumstances, the proclamation of harmony could become the assertion of a still-disputed hegemony, which only served to remove the conflict from one arena to another. The clerical promoters of the cult of Henry VI were quick to point out, for instance, that the sacral powers of a dead but legitimate king were greater than those of a living usurper.[119] Yet even in such cases, the existence of the rhetoric was itself of importance; it affirmed an ideal of political conduct to which all parties were anxious to appear to subscribe. If the conflicting claims embodied in the death of a political saint continued to be fought out in symbolic fashion, the subsequent cult nevertheless canalised and contained the most immediately destructive effects of the struggle. And once established, no cult could be maintained by pious aspiration alone; if the terms in which Thomas of Lancaster, Richard Scrope or Henry VI were presented had appeared irrelevant to their devotees, their cults would have lasted no longer than Simon de Montfort's. This continued popular support for the cults of political saints – in origin, cults of martyrs venerated at the place of their death, the oldest and most traditional type of devotion – was recognised by contemporaries to be significant, for it provided a means by which the popular and clerical conceptions of sanctity, in general increasingly divergent by the later Middle Ages, could be reconciled and the norms of canonical expectation internalised within the world of popular piety. It was for this reason that successive kings and their advisers concluded that such cults were better tolerated than suppressed. Far from being a threat to royal authority, they provided an important point of contact with a diverse popular audience, a potentially significant resource in the constant dialogue of rulers and ruled by which a polity as varied and sophisticated as later medieval England had necessarily to be governed.

Notes

1. E.M. Forster, *A Passage to India* (Harmondsworth, 1970), pp. 249–50.

2. A. Vauchez, *La sainteté en Occident aux dernières siècles du Moyen Age* (Bibliothèque des Écoles Françaises d'Athènes et de Rome, CCXLI, 1988), pp. 71–98, 449–489; A.M. Kleinberg, 'Proving Sanctity: Selection and Authentication of Saints in the Later Middle Ages', *Viator*, XX (1989), pp. 183–205.

3. E.W. Kemp, *Canonization and Authority in the Western Church* (Oxford, 1948), pp. 116–22, 176–7.

4. N. Orme, 'Two Saint-Bishops of Exeter. James Berkley and Edmund Lacy', *Analecta Bollandiana*, CIV (1986), pp. 403–18; N. Tanner, *The Church in Late Medieval Norwich* (P.I.M.S. Studies and Texts, LXVI, 1984), pp. 89–90.

5. J.R. Shinners, 'The Veneration of Saints at Norwich Cathedral in the Fourteenth Century' *Norfolk Archaeology*, XL (1988), pp. 137–9.

6. K. Walsh, *Richard Fitzralph in Oxford, Avignon and Armagh* (Oxford, 1981), pp. 455–61.

7. J. Hughes, *Pastors and Visionaries. Religion and Secular Life in Late Medieval Yorkshire* (Woodbridge, 1988), pp. 302–5.

8. P. Grosjean, 'Thomas de la Hale. Moine et martyr à Douvres en 1295', *Analecta Bollandiana*, LXII (1954), pp. 167–91; A.G. Little, *The Grey Friars in Oxford* (Oxford Historical Society, XX, 1892), p. 174; L. Boyle, *A Survey of the Vatican Archives and its Medieval Holdings* (P.I.M.S. Subsidia Medievalia, I, 1972), pp. 143–4. For the text of Richard II's petition for Thomas de la Hale's canonisation, c.1380, see C.U.L. Ms Dd 53 f. 38.

9. R.M. Wooley, *The Officium and Miracula of Richard Rolle of Hampole* (1919).

10. *Chronica Monasterii de Melsa*, E.A. Bond (ed.) (3 vols, R.S., 1866–8), III, pp. 194–5; Tanner, *Church in Norwich*, pp. 221–3; W. Sparrow Simpson, 'Master John Schorne', *Records of Buckinghamshire*, III (1870), pp. 354–69.

11. *Historiae Rhythmicae: Liturgisches Reimoffizien des Mittelalters*, G.M. Dreves (ed.), II (Analecta Hymnica Medii Aevii, 13, Leipzig, 1892), p. 7; 'Miracula Simonis de Montfort', *The Chronicle of William de Rishanger*, J.O. Halliwell (ed.) (Camden Society, 1st series XV, 1840), p. 104; N. Rogers, 'The Cult of Prince Edward at Tewkesbury', *Transactions of the Bristol and Gloucester Archaeological Society*, CI (1983), pp. 187–9; M.R. James, *A Descriptive Catalogue of Manuscripts in the Fitzwilliam Museum, Cambridge* (Cambridge 1895), p. 121.

12. *The Ecclesiastical History of Orderic Vitalis*, M. Chibnall (ed.) (6 vols, Oxford, 1969–80), II, pp. 346–51; B.J. Levy, 'Waltheof, "Earl" de Huntingdon et de Northampton: la naissance d'un héros anglo-normand', *Cahiers de civilisation médiévale* XVII (1975), pp. 183–96; 'De Morte et Sepultura Henrici Regis Junioris', *Radulphi de Coggeshall Chronicon Anglicanum*, J. Stevenson (ed.) (R.S., 1875), pp. 265–73; *Chronicles of the Reigns of Stephen, Henry II, and Richard I*, R. Howlett (ed.) (4 vols, R.S., 1884–9), II, pp. 471–3.

13. S.J. Ridyard, *The Royal Saints of Anglo-Saxon England* (Cambridge, 1989), pp. 234–52; D.W. Rollason, *Saints and Relics in Anglo-Saxon England* (Oxford, 1989), pp. 115–29, 133–44.

14. Vauchez, *La sainteté en Occident*, pp. 202–3.

15. V. Natalini, *S. Pietro Parenzo* (Rome, 1936), pp. 76–133; *Bibliotheca Hagiographica Latina Antiquae et Mediae Aetatis* (Brussels, 1898–9), p. 234; A. Vauchez, 'Canonisation et politique au XIVe siècle', *Religion et société dans l'Occident mediévale* (Turin, 1980), pp. 237–60.

16. J. Sumption, *Pilgrimage. An Image of Medieval Religion* (1975), p. 282; J.R. Maddicott, *Thomas of Lancaster* (Oxford, 1970), p. 329.

17. Gregory of Tours, *Life of the Fathers*, E. James (ed.) (Liverpool, 1985), p. 60.

18. *Proceedings of the Commissioners for the Public Records of the Kingdom*, June 1832–August 1833, I (1833), p. 502; H.M. Colvin, R. Allen Brown and A.J. Taylor, and others, *The History of the King's Works*, (6 vols, 1963), I, p. 258.

19. John de Trokelowe and anonymous, 'Annales Ricardi Secundi et Henrici Quarti', in *Chronica et Annales*, H.T. Riley (ed.) (R.S., 1866), pp. 216–9; *Chronicon Adae de Usk*, E.M. Thompson (ed.) (2nd edn, 1904), p. 15; J.M. Theilmann, 'Political Canonization and Political Symbolism in Medieval England', *Journal of British Studies* XXIX (1990), pp. 261–3.

20. J.C. Russell, 'The Canonization of Opposition to the Crown in Angevin England', *Haskins Anniversary Essays*, C.H. Taylor (ed.) (New York, 1929), pp. 279–90 (quotation at p. 286). Russell's pioneering discussion has remained influential in many more recent analyses: e.g., Vauchez, *La sainteté*, p. 200; *Saints and their Cults*, S. Wilson (ed.) (Cambridge, 1983), pp. 34–5; J.R. Bray, 'Concepts of Sainthood in Fourteenth-Century England', *B.J.R.L.* LXVI (1983), p. 68; R.N. Swanson, *Church and Society in Late Medieval England* (Oxford, 1989), pp. 99–101, 288.

21. J.W. McKenna, 'Popular Canonization as Political Propaganda: the Cult of Archbishop Scrope', *Speculum*, XLV (1970), pp. 608–23 (quotation at p. 609); idem, 'Piety and Propaganda: the Cult of Henry VI', *Chaucer and Middle English Studies in Honour of Rossell Hope Robbins*, B. Rowland (ed.) (1974), pp. 72–88.

22. N.M. Fryde, *The Tyranny and Fall of Edward II* (Cambridge, 1979), pp. 152–3.

23. *Thomas Walsingham Historia Anglicana*, H.T. Riley (ed.) (2 vols, R.S., 1863–4), I, pp. 459–62; II, p. 114; *The Westminster Chronicle 1381–1394*, L.C. Hector and B.F. Harvey (eds.) (Oxford, 1982), p. 80. For further consideration of 'shrines that failed', B. Ward, *Miracles and the Medieval Mind* (1982), pp. 127–31.

24. P. Delooz, 'Pour une étude sociologique de la sainteté canonisée dans l'Eglise catholique', *Archives de sociologie des religions*, XIII (1962), pp. 22–3.

25. W. Stubbs, *Select Charters and other Illustrations of English Constitutional History* (9th edn, 1913), p. 409.

26. *The Chronicle of Bury St. Edmunds*, 1212–1301, A. Gransden (ed.) (1964), p. 33; 'Continuatio Willelmi de Newburgh', *Chronicles of Stephen, Henry II and Richard I*, II, p. 548; *Chronica Monasterii de Melsa*, II, p. 131; *The Historical Works of Gervase of Canterbury*, W. Stubbs (ed.) (2 vols, R.S., 1879–80), II, p. 243. For further evidence of de Montfort's reputation at Canterbury, Historical Manuscripts Commission, *Fifth Report* (1876), pp. 454–5.

27. G.W. Prothero, *The Life of Simon de Montfort* (1877), pp. 388–91; *Chronicle of William de Rishanger*, pp. 67–110; *Historiae Rhythmicae*, II, p. 7; P.M. Lefferts, 'Two English Motets on Simon de Montfort', *Early Music History*, I (1981), pp. 203–25; F.W. Maitland, 'A Song on the Death of Simon de Montfort', *E.H.R.* XI (1896), pp. 314–8; *Anglo–Norman Political Songs*, I.S.T. Aspin (ed.) (Anglo-Norman Text Society, XI, 1953), pp. 12–35.

28. R. Finucane, *Miracles and Pilgrims: Popular Beliefs in Medieval England* (1977), pp. 135, 169–70.

29. *Chronicle of William de Rishanger*, p. 108; *Anglo–Norman Political Songs*, pp. 24–5; H. Shields, 'The

Lament for Simon de Montfort: an Unnoticed Text of the French Poem', *Medium Aevum*, XLI (1972), pp. 202–7.

30. P.R.O. Exchequer, Accounts Various, E.101/379/17 f. 1ᵛ.

31. *Calendar of Inquisitions Miscellaneous* (7 vols, H.M.S.O., 1916–68), II, no. 2103, pp. 528–9; *Historical Papers and Letters from the Northern Registers*, J. Raine (ed.) (R.S., 1873), pp. 323–6.

32. *Anecdota ex Codicibus Hagiographicis Johannis Gielemans* (Société des Bollandistes, Brussels, 1895), pp. 92–100.

33. *The Political Songs of England, from the Reign of John to that of Edward II*, T. Wright (ed.) (Camden Society, old series VI, 1840), pp. 268–72; C. Page, 'The Rhymed Office for St. Thomas of Lancaster: Poetry, Politics and Liturgy in Fourteenth-Century England', *Leeds Studies in English*, XIV (1983), pp. 135–6.

34. *Flores Historiarum*, H.R. Luard (ed.) (3 vols, R.S., 1890), III, p. 314; *Polychronicon Ranulphi Higden*, C. Babington and J.R. Lumby (eds.) (9 vols, R.S., 1865–6), VIII, p. 314; *Croniques de London*, G.J. Aungier (ed.) (Camden Society, old series XXVIII, 1844), p. 46; *The Brut*, F.W.D. Brie (ed.), (2 vols, E.E.T.S. original series CXXXI, CXXXVI, 1906–8), I, pp. 228–31; V.H. Galbraith, 'Extracts from the Historia Aurea and a French Brut', *E.H.R.* XLIII (1928), pp. 215–6; *The Anonimalle Chronicle, 1307 to 1334*, W.R. Childs and J. Taylor (eds.) (Yorkshire Archaeological Society, CXLVII, 1987), pp. 112–14.

35. Bodl. L. Ms Douce 231 f. 1; N.R. Ker, *Medieval Manuscripts in British Libraries*, III (Oxford, 1983), p. 518; E.G. Millar, *The Luttrell Psalter* (1932), p. 28; M.R. James, *Catalogue of Manuscripts in the Library of Clare College, Cambridge* (Cambridge, 1905), pp. 11–13; J.T. Micklethwaite, 'Antiquities and Works of Art Exhibited', *Archaeological Journal*, XXXVI (1879), pp. 103–4.

36. *C.I.P.M.* 1352–1361, p. 178; H. Tait, 'Pilgrim-Signs and Thomas, Earl of Lancaster', *British Museum Quarterly*, XX (1955–6), pp. 39–47.

37. *Letters from Northern Registers*, p. 385; *Calendar of Papal Registers, Petitions 1342–1419*, pp. 271–2; *John of Gaunt's Register 1372–1376*, S. Armitage-Smith (ed.) (Camden Soc., 3rd series XX–XXI, 1911), nos. 297, 949; *Testamenta Vetusta*, N.H. Nicholas (ed.) (1826), p. 68; Walsingham, *Historia Anglicana*, II, p. 191. For further evidence of Bohun patronage of Lancaster's cult, J. Edwards, 'The Cult of "St." Thomas of Lancaster and its Iconography', *Yorkshire Archaeological Journal*, LXIV (1992), pp. 112–3; A. Gransden, *Historical Writing in England* (2 vols, 1982), II, p. 74.

38. M.F. Bond, *The Inventories of St. George's Chapel 1384–1667* (Windsor, 1947), pp. 44–5.

39. *Testamenta Eboracensia*, J. Raine (ed.) (6 vols, Surtees Society, 1836–1902), I, p. 281; Borthwick I.H.R., Probate Register 2 f. 537; *Fifteenth Century Liturgical Music*, Andrew Hughes (ed.) (Early English Church Music, VIII, 1964), pp. 10–11; A.F. Johnston and M. Rogerson, *Records of Early English Drama: York* (2 vols, Toronto and Manchester, 1979), II, pp. 637, 858–9; *Abbreviata Chronica*, J.J. Smith (ed.) (Cambridge Antiquarian Society Publications, I, 1840–6), p. 10; Ker, *Medieval Manuscripts in British Libraries*, II, pp. 5, 10; M.R. James, *Catalogue of Manuscripts in the Library of King's College, Cambridge* (Cambridge, 1895), p. 50; M.L. Colker, *Trinity College Library, Dublin. Descriptive Catalogue of the Medieval and Renaissance Latin Manuscripts* (Aldershot, 1991), p. 958; *William Worcestre Itineraries*, J.H. Harvey (ed.) (Oxford, 1969), p. 81.

40. *Historia et Cartularium Monasterii Sancti Petri Gloucestriae*, W.H. Hart (ed.) (3 vols, R.S., 1863–7), I, pp. 44–6.

41. Ibid., pp. 47–8; *Westminster Chronicle*, pp. 158, 436–9; *The Diplomatic Correspondence of Richard II*, E. Perroy (ed.) (Camden Society, 3rd series XLVIII, 1933), p. 210. Note that the record evidence suggests that Edward III's offering was originally made at the high altar, and then transferred to the shrine of Edward II by the monks; W.M. Ormrod, 'The Personal Piety of Edward III', *Speculum*, LXIV (1989), pp. 860, 870–1.

42. Bodl. L. Ms Lat. Misc. b 2 (R); J. Evans, *English Art, 1307–1461* (Oxford, 1949), pp. 164–5; F.E. Hutchinson, *The Medieval Stained Glass of All Souls College* (1949), pp. 47–8.

43. *Polychronicon Ranulphi Higden*, VIII, p. 326. For the likely date of the composition of this passage, J. Taylor, 'The Development of the Polychronicon Continuation', *E.H.R.* LXXVI (1961), pp. 22–3. The comments to the same effect in *Chronicles of the Reigns of Edward I and Edward II*, W. Stubbs (ed.) (2 vols, R.S., 1882–3), II, p. 290, *Annales Monastici*, H.R. Luard (ed.) (5 vols, R.S., 1864–9), IV, p. 348 and *Chronica Monasterii de Melsa*, II, p. 355 are all directly derived from Higden.

44. *The Fabric Rolls of York Minster*, J. Raine (ed.) (Surtees Society, XXXV, 1859), p. 196; *York Memorandum Book*, M. Sellers (ed.) (2 vols, Surtees Society, 1912–15), I, pp. 236–8.

45. *Eulogium Historiarum sive Temporis*, F.S. Haydon (ed.) (3 vols, R.S., 1858), III, pp. 405, 421; C.L. Kingsford, *English Historical Literature in the Fifteenth Century* (Oxford, 1913), pp. 282, 314; Trokelowe and anonymous, 'Annales', p. 410; *Chronicon Adae de Usk*, p. 99; Raine, *Fabric Rolls*, pp. 32, 37.

46. *The Historians of the Church of York and its Archbishops*, J. Raine (ed.) (3 vols, R.S., 1879–94), II, pp. 306–11; III, pp. 288–91. For the authorship and relationship of these accounts, W.A. Pronger, 'Thomas Gascoigne', *E.H.R.* LIII (1938), pp. 607–10, which remains preferable to the conjecture of S.K. Wright, 'The Provenance and Manuscript Tradition of the Martyrium Ricardi Archiepiscopi', *Manuscripta*, XXVIII (1984), pp. 92–102.

47. Bodl. L. Ms Lat. Liturg. F 2, ff. 146^V–147; Y.M.L. Ms XVI K. 6 f. 27^V, Add. Ms 2 ff. 100^V–101^r, Add. Ms 54, p. 3, Add. Ms 67 ff. 102^{r-v}; *Political Poems and Songs relating to English History*, T. Wright (ed.) (2 vols, R.S., 1859–61), II, pp. 114–18; *Historiae Rhythmicae*, VII, p. 317; M.R. James, *A Descriptive Catalogue of Manuscripts in the Library of St. John's College, Cambridge* (Cambridge, 1913), pp. 162–5; *idem*, *A Descriptive Catalogue of Manuscripts in the Library of Sidney Sussex College, Cambridge* (Cambridge, 1895), pp. 44–5; *Hymns to the Virgin and Christ*, F.J. Furnivall (ed.) (E.E.T.S., original series XXIV, 1867), p. 128.

48. Raine, *Fabric Rolls*, pp. 225–7.

49. *Political Poems and Songs*, II, p. 267; *C.C.R. 1468–71*, II, 188–90.

50. Y.M.L. M 2/1 (f), ff. 70–72^V.

51. E.g., the request of Thomas Rothwell, chaplain, that his executors have made a wax image 'in the likeness of a canon', worth 4 marks, to be offered to the blessed Richard Scrope: Y.M.L. L 2/4 f. 332^V.

52. Y.M.L. E 3/6–8, 12–23.

53. E.g., the practice of requiring penitents to make offerings at a circuit of shrines, which included the tombs of Scrope and St William at York, St Wilfrid at Ripon and St John at Beverley: Borthwick I.H.R. D/C, A. B. 1 ff. 118^V, 193.

54. *Henrici VI Angliae Regis Miracula Postuma*, P. Grosjean (ed.) (Société des Bollandistes, Subsidia Hagiographica, XXII, 1935), pp. 182*, 112.

55. Raine, *Fabric Rolls*, p. 82 (though this roll is best dated 1475–6, not 1473). Note, too, the

sudden rise in offerings in the Minster which takes place between 1473 (£10 4s. 10d.) and 1475/6 (£49 16s. 6d.): Y.M.L. E 3/26–7.

56. R. Lovatt, 'A Collector of Apocryphal Anecdotes: John Blacman Revisited', in *Property and Politics: Essays in Later Medieval English History*, A.J. Pollard (ed.) (Gloucester, 1984), pp. 177–9.

57. *Henrici VI Angliae Regis Miracula*; W. Maskell, *Monumenta Ritualia Ecclesiae Anglicanae* (2nd edn, 3 vols, Oxford, 1882), III, pp. 367–71; *Trevelyan Papers*, J.P. Collier and others (eds.) (3 vols, Camden Soc., old series LXVII, LXXXIV, CV, 1857–72), I, pp. 53–60; *Henry the Sixth: A Reprint of John Blacman's Memoir*, M.R. James (ed.) (Cambridge, 1919), pp. 12–14, 50–1; F.A. Gasquet, *The Religious Life of Henry VI* (1923), pp. 128–9; *The Miracles of Henry VI*, R. Knox and S. Leslie (eds.) (Cambridge, 1923), pp. 5, 11; M.R. James, *A Descriptive Catalogue of Manuscripts in the Fitzwilliam Museum* (Cambridge, 1895), pp. 138–9; *idem*, *A Descriptive Catalogue of the Manuscripts in the Library of Lambeth Palace. The Medieval Manuscripts* (Cambridge, 1932), pp. 747–50.

58. B. Spencer, 'King Henry of Windsor and the London Pilgrim', *Collectanea Londiniensia: Studies in London Archaeology and History presented to Ralph Merrifield*, J. Bird, H. Clapman and J. Clark (eds.) (London and Middlesex Archaeological Society, Special Papers, II, 1978), pp. 283–9. Note, too, the steep decline in the offerings made at the tomb of St Thomas after c. 1420: C.E. Woodruff, 'The financial aspect of the cult of St. Thomas of Canterbury, as recorded by a study of the monastic records', *Archaeologia Cantiana*, XLIV (1932), pp. 22–4.

59. *Foedera, Conventiones, Litterae*, T. Rymer (ed.) (new edn, 4 vols in 7, Record Commission, 1816–69), II (ii), p. 695.

60. *Chronica de Mailros (The Melrose Chronicle)*, J. Stevenson (ed.) (Edinburgh, 1835), p. 212.

61. G. Duby, 'Ideologies in Social History', *Constructing the Past*, J. Le Goff and P. Nora (eds.) (Cambridge, 1985), pp. 152–6.

62. M. Bloch, *The Royal Touch: Sacred Monarchy and Scrofula in England and France* (1973), pp. 21–7; H.G. Wright, 'The Protestation of Richard II in the Tower in September, 1399', *B.J.R.L.* XXIII (1939), pp. 157–9; M.T. Clanchy, 'Did Henry III have a Policy?', *History*, LIII (1968), p. 213.

63. *Adami Murimuthensis Chronica sui Temporis*, T. Hog (ed.), (English Historical Society, VIII, 1846), p. 226; R. Barber, *Edward, Prince of Wales and Aquitaine* (Woodbridge, 1978), pp. 213–14; *Political Poems and Songs*, I, p. 97.

64. J.W. McKenna, 'How God became an Englishman', *Tudor Rule and Revolution*, D.J. Guth and J.W. McKenna (eds.) (Cambridge, 1982), pp. 25–43; C.M.D. Crowder, *Unity, Heresy and Reform, 1378–1460* (1977), pp. 118–20. For the prior claim of the French monarchy to be the 'most Christian Kings', C. Beaune, *The Birth of an Ideology. Myths and Symbols of Nation in Late-Medieval France* (Berkeley, 1991), pp. 172–93.

65. *Gesta Henrici Quinti: The Deeds of Henry the Fifth*, F. Taylor and J.S. Roskell (eds.) (Oxford, 1975), pp. 106–8; *Memorials of the Reign of Henry VI: Official Correspondence of Thomas Bekynton, Secretary to Henry VI, and Bishop of Bath and Wells*, G. Williams (ed.) (2 vols, R.S., LVI, 1872), I, pp. 118–19.

66. M. Aston, *Lollards and Reformers: Images and Literacy in Late Medieval Religion* (1984), pp. 1–47.

67. *R.P.* III, pp. 583–4.

68. T.B. Pugh, *Henry V and the Southampton Plot* (Southampton Records Series, XXX, 1988), p. 169.

69. J. Creton, *Histoire du Roy d'Angleterre Richard*, J.T. Webb (ed. and trans.), *Archaeologia*, XX (1824), p. 170.

70. *The Register of Henry Chichele, Archbishop of Canterbury, 1414–1443*, E.F. Jacob (ed.) (4 vols, Canterbury and York Society, XLII, XLV–XLVII, 1937–47), IV, pp. 206–7; *The Register of John Stafford, Bishop of Bath and Wells, 1425–1443*, T.S. Holmes (ed.) (2 vols, Somerset Record Society, XXXI, XXXII, 1915–16), I, pp. 104–8; W.T. Waugh, 'Joan of Arc in English Sources of the Fifteenth Century', in *Historical Essays in Honour of James Tait*, J.G. Edwards, V.H. Galbraith, E.F. Jacob (eds.) (Manchester, 1933), pp. 388–91.

71. Historical Manuscripts Commission, *Fifth Report* (1876), p. 455; *R.P.* VI, pp. 232, 240–2.

72. R.A. Griffiths, 'The Trial of Eleanor Cobham: An Episode in the Fall of Duke Humphrey of Gloucester', *B.J.R.L.* LI (1968–9), pp. 381–99; M. Hicks, *False, Fleeting, Perjur'd Clarence* (revised edn, Bangor, 1992), pp. 119–22.

73. Bartholomew de Cotton, *Historia Anglicana*, H.R. Luard (ed.) (R.S., XVI, 1859), pp. 171–2, 180; *Calendar of Papal Registers, Papal Letters* (15 vols, H.M.S.O., 1893–1960), I, p. 607; A. Beardwood, 'The Trial of Walter Langton, Bishop of Lichfield, 1307–12', *Transactions of the American Philosophical Society*, LIV. iii (1964), pp. 7–8; *Select Cases in the Court of King's Bench*, G.O. Sayles (ed.) (7 vols, Selden Society, 1936–71), IV, pp. 154–7.

74. J.G. Bellamy, *The Law of Treason in England in the Later Middle Ages* (Cambridge, 1970), pp. 127–8.

75. P.R.O. Exchequer, Pleas of the Hall, E.37/28 m. 1; Sayles, *Select Cases in the Court of King's Bench*, VII, pp. 174–5.

76. R.P. III, p. 466. For the 'social miracle' of the Mass, J. Bossy, 'The Mass as a Social Institution, 1200–1700', *P.P.* C (1983), pp. 29–61 and, for subsequent discussion and elaboration, M. Rubin, *Corpus Christi. The Eucharist in Late Medieval Culture* (Cambridge, 1991), pp. 2, 265–7 and E. Duffy, *The Stripping of the Altars. Traditional Religion in England, c. 1400–c. 1580* (New Haven, 1992), pp. 91–130.

77. *Historie of the Arrivall of Edward IV in England and the Finall Recoverie of his Kingdomes from Henry VI, A.D. 1471*, J. Bruce (ed.) (Camden Society, old series I, 1838), pp. 13–14; Rymer, *Foedera*, XI, pp. 709–11; *Joannis Rossi Antiquarii Warwicensis Historia Regum Angliae*, T. Hearne (ed.) (Oxford, 1716), p. 218; *York Civic Records*, A. Raine and others (eds.) (9 vols, Yorkshire Archaeological Society, XCVIII, 1939–78), I, p. 25.

78. J. Bossy, 'Some Elementary Forms of Durkheim', *P.P.* XCIX (1982), p. 12.

79. R.W. Southern, *Medieval Humanism and other Studies* (Oxford, 1970), p. 137.

80. Raine, *Fabric Rolls*, pp. 226, 235.

81. *Breviarium ad Usum Insignis Ecclesiae Sarum*, F. Proctor and C. Wordsworth (eds.) (3 vols, Cambridge, 1879–86), I, cols. ccxlvii–cclxi.

82. *Materials for the History of Thomas Becket, Archbishop of Canterbury*, J.C. Robertson and J.B. Sheppard (eds.) (7 vols, R.S., LXVII, 1875–85), II, p. 29.

83. A. Duggan, 'The Cult of St. Thomas Becket in the Thirteenth Century', in *St. Thomas Cantilupe, Bishop of Hereford. Essays in His Honour*, M. Jancey (ed.) (Hereford, 1982), pp. 37–41.

84. *Breviarium ad Usum Insignis Ecclesiae Sarum*, III, pp. 445–51.

85. *Materials for the History of Thomas Becket,* II, p. 128.

86. Ibid., I, pp. 251–2; II, pp. 149–50; III, pp. 546–8.

87. All Souls College, MS 182 ff. 73–4.

88. *Anecdota . . . Johannis Gielemans*, p. 96; L.W. Vernon Harcourt, *His Grace the Steward and Trial by Peers* (1907), pp. 138–69.

89. *The Brut*, I, pp. 221–4; *The Political Songs of England*, p. 269.

90. *The Political Songs of England*, p. 270; *Historiae Rhythmicae*, II, p. 7; Micklethwaite, *Arch. J.* XXXVI (1879), p. 104.

91. *Political Songs of England*, pp. 268, 272; Edwards, *Yorks. Arch. J.* LXIV, pp. 118–21. For the close association of the cults of Becket and Lancaster in the fifteenth century, R. Foreville, *Le Jubilé de Saint Thomas Becket: du XIIIe au XVe siècles (1220–1470)* (Paris, 1958), pp. 111, 129.

92. *R.P.* II, p. 7; *Foedera*, II. ii, p. 695.

93. *Historiae Rhythmicae*, VII, p. 321.

94. Raine, *Fabric Rolls*, pp. 193–5.

95. Ibid., pp. 198–200 (which conflates a number of separate decisions of the chapter; Y.M.L. H 2/1 ff. 19^V, 25^V, 58^V); *The Chronicle of John Hardyng*, H. Ellis (ed.) (1812), p. 372; B.L. Add. Ms 35295, f. 265.

96. Bodl. L. MS Lat. Liturg. F 2, f. 147.

97. Y.M.L. Add. Ms 54, p. 3; Raine, *Historians of the Church of York*, II, p. 309; T. Gascoigne, *Loci e Libro Veritatum*, J.E.T. Rogers (ed.) (Oxford, 1881), p. 227; *Hymns to the Virgin and Christ*, p. 128; R.W. Pfaff, *New Liturgical Feasts in Later Medieval England* (Oxford, 1970), p. 86.

98. *Political Poems and Songs*, II, p. 115; Raine, *Historians of the Church of York*, II, p. 307.

99. Y.M.L. Add. Ms 2 f. 101^r; Add. Ms 54, p. 3; *Political Poems and Songs*, II, p. 116; R.W. Southern, *Western Society and the Church in the Middle Ages* (1970), pp. 51–2.

100. Bodl. L. Ms Lat. Liturg. F 2, f. 147.

101. Y.M.L. M 2/1 (f), ff. 70–72^r.

102. *The Records of the Northern Convocation*, G.W. Kitchin (ed.) (Surtees Soc., CXIII, 1907), pp. 349–51; *Acts of the Court of the Mercer's Company 1453–1527*, L. Lyell and F.D. Watney (eds.) (Cambridge, 1936), p. 139.

103. *The Crowland Chronicle Continuations 1459–1486*, N. Pronay and J. Cox (eds.) (1986), pp. 128–30; James, *Henry the Sixth*, pp. 4, 6, 18–22; R. Lovatt, 'John Blacman: Biographer of Henry VI', in *The Writing of History in the Middle Ages: Essays presented to R.W. Southern*, R.H.C. Davis and J.M. Wallace–Hadrill (eds.) (Oxford, 1981), pp. 440–5.

104. Maskell, *Monumenta Ritualia*, p. 370; Collier, *Trevelyan Papers*, p. 58; Bodl. L. Ms Gough Liturg. 19 f. 32^V; *Historia Regis Henrici Septimi a Bernardo Andrea Tholosate Conscripta*, J. Gairdner (ed.) (R.S., X. 1858), pp. 21–3.

105. Bodl. L. Ms Jones 46 ff. 117^V–18; Ms Gough Liturg. 7 f. 119; James, *Henry VI*, p. 50.

106. B.L. Add. Mss 33736 ff. 4–6.

107. *Henrici VI Regis Angliae Miracula*, pp. 19–21; note also pp. 141–3, 176–8.

108. Maskell, *Monumenta Ritualia*, p. 371; C. Dodgson, 'English Devotional Woodcuts of the Late Fifteenth Century', *Walpole Society*, XVII (1928–9), pp. 104–8 and plate XXXVII.

109. *English Historical Documents, c.500–1042*, D. Whitelock (ed.) (2nd edn, 1979), pp. 230–1.

110. Lefferts, *Early Music History*, I, pp. 222–3; Prothero, *Simon de Montfort*, p. 389; Maitland, *E.H.R.* XI, p. 317.

111. Prothero, *Simon de Montfort*, pp. 390–1; Maitland, *E.H.R.* XI, p. 318; *Anglo-Norman Political Songs*, p. 32.

112. C.H. Knowles, 'The Resettlement of England after the Barons' War, 1264–67', *T.R.H.S.* 5th series XXXII (1982), pp. 25–7.

113. Prothero, *Simon de Montfort*, p. 390; *Chronicle of William de Rishanger*, pp. 81–2, 99–100.

114. *Chronicle of William de Rishanger*, p. 85.

115. *Henrici VI Regis Angliae Miracula*, pp. 41–4, 106–12, 185–90; E. James, '*Beati pacifici:* Bishops and the Law in Sixth-Century Gaul', *Disputes and Settlements. Law and Human Relations in the West*, J. Bossy (ed.) (Cambridge, 1983), pp. 33–5.

116. Knowles, *T.R.H.S.* 5th series XXXII, pp. 37–41.

117. E.g., *Vita Edwardi Secundi*, N. Denholm-Young (ed.) (1957), p. 18, where de Montfort is described as having died for the cause of justice but is only 'the noble man'. Note, too, the use of de Montfort's struggle as a piece of anti-English polemic in Scotland. An early sixteenth-century Scottish source preserves the story that two horsemen appeared before the sacrist of Glastonbury on the eve of Bannockburn, saying that they were on their way to deal vengeance for the unjust death of Simon de Montfort; Ker, *Medieval Manuscripts in British Libraries*, II, p. 523.

118. Duffy, *The Stripping of the Altars*, p. 178.

119. *Henrici VI Regis Angliae Miracula*, pp. 122–3.

5

HENRY IV AND EUROPE: A DYNASTY'S SEARCH FOR RECOGNITION

Anthony Tuck

The Lancastrian revolution of 1399 was greeted in France with hostility and distaste. The contemporary French chroniclers are unanimous in reporting events in England from a pro-Ricardian standpoint and in condemning Henry Bolingbroke as a usurper.[1] Their stance reflected the French court's attitude to Henry: letters in which Henry undertook to observe the 1396 truce between England and France were glossed by a French royal clerk '*littere Henrici Lancastrie dicentis se esse regem Anglie*'. Early in 1400, when the two sides sent envoys to negotiate at Calais, the bishop of Chartres for the French side was instructed not to call Henry king of England during the negotiations, while it was reported to a Great Council in England in February 1400 that envoys sent to France had been refused access to Charles VI. Even a year after Henry's accession the French were still unwilling to recognise Henry's title to the throne: the instructions to the French envoy sent to England in September 1400 refer to '*cellui qui se dit roy d'Engleterre*'.[2]

The reasons for the hostility of the court in Paris and its unwillingness to recognise Henry as king of England are not hard to find. There was perhaps some sense that usurpation was in itself a crime, but it might be unwise to lay too much stress on this issue. Charles V had aided and abetted the Trastamara usurpation in Spain,[3] and some months after the Lancastrian revolution in England the deposition of Wenceslas in Germany and his replacement by Rupert of Wittelsbach the Elector Palatine did not arouse the same feelings of hostility and revulsion in Paris as events in England.[4] The duke of Burgundy's strategy of peace with England seemed, from the standpoint of the Paris court, to be threatened by Henry's usurpation. Furthermore, had it survived, the

THE WITTELSBACH FAMILY

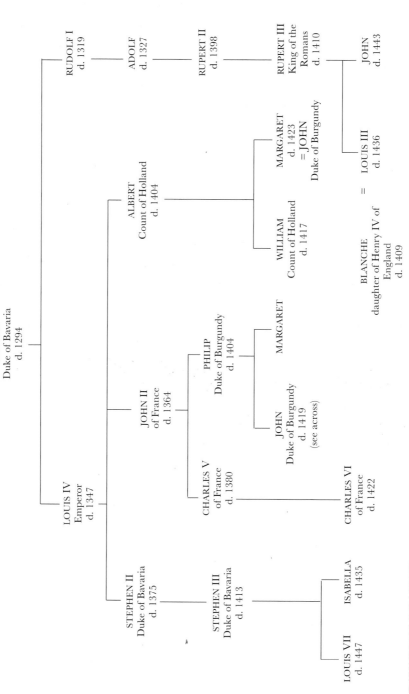

LOUIS II
Duke of Bavaria
d. 1294

RUDOLF I
d. 1319

ADOLF
d. 1327

RUPERT II
d. 1398

RUPERT III
King of the
Romans
d. 1410

LOUIS IV
Emperor
d. 1347

JOHN II
of France
d. 1364

ALBERT
Count of Holland
d. 1404

MARGARET
d. 1423
= JOHN
Duke of Burgundy

JOHN
d. 1443

STEPHEN II
Duke of Bavaria
d. 1375

CHARLES V
of France
d. 1380

PHILIP
Duke of Burgundy
d. 1404

WILLIAM
Count of Holland
d. 1417

LOUIS III
d. 1436

STEPHEN III
Duke of Bavaria
d. 1413

JOHN
Duke of Burgundy
d. 1419
(see across)

MARGARET

CHARLES VI
of France
d. 1422

BLANCHE
daughter of Henry IV of
England
d. 1409

=

LOUIS VII
d. 1447

ISABELLA
d. 1435

BAVARIAN BRANCH

RHENISH BRANCH

alliance which Burgundy's rival the duke of Orléans made with Henry in 1399 might have threatened Burgundy's position in French politics.[5] Equally significant, perhaps, was the position of Richard II's young queen Isabella, the daughter of Charles VI. Her position in England after Richard's downfall was almost that of a hostage. Henry may have hoped for a marriage between her and his own eldest son, the future Henry V, but the French court refused to consider any such proposal until Isabella was returned to France. Indeed, there was some suspicion in France that Henry might seek to arrange a marriage for her presumably to the prince of Wales while she was still in England, and French ambassadors to England were instructed in September 1400 to insist that Isabella should be returned to her father '*franche et quitte de tout mariage*'.[6] The negotiations over the return of the queen herself and her dowry dragged on for nearly two years in circumstances which seemed to contemporaries in France to be demeaning to Isabella and insulting to the French royal family. In 1402, when the monk of St Denis asked the seven French knights who had challenged seven English knights to a joust why they showed such animosity towards the English, they replied that they had conceived an implacable hatred of the English because of the murder of their king and the 'indecent expulsion' of the queen, the daughter of the king of France. However, they went on to make the significant point that they dare not make open war on the English for fear of violating the truce, and so they looked for an honourable pretext to avenge 'these intolerable injuries'.[7]

Such bellicose noises – which the seven knights were not alone in making – served to conceal some anxiety in both England and France that the deposition of Richard II might lead to the unwanted renewal of Anglo-French warfare. For their part, the dukes of Burgundy and Berry feared that Henry might be pushed into war by the commons: Berry wrote to Burgundy shortly after hearing of Richard's downfall saying that the duke of Lancaster would govern by the voice of the commons of England, and that the commons of England wanted war. He went on to advise Burgundy to ensure that the frontiers were properly garrisoned.[8] Berry's opinion was shared – or reflected – by Juvénal des Ursins, who reported that when Charles VI heard the news from England '*il en fut bien desplaisant, et cognut-on bien que toutes alliances et tresves estoient rompues, et qu'on estoit revenue a la guerre*'.[9] The view that the English were an inherently warlike people was not limited to alarmist circles in Paris. Froissart had implied as much when he put into the mouth of the duke of Gloucester in 1391 the sentiment that the comfort and station in life of the poor knights and esquires of England depended on war, and the same opinion of the English was held as far afield as Italy and Castile. A sycophantic Veronese, writing to Rupert, king of the Romans in March 1402, congratulated him on the forthcoming marriage of his son Ludwig to Henry IV's daughter Blanche, and pointed out the value of an alliance with the English, whom he described as '*bellicosissimum genus*'. The Castilian author of the chronicle *El Victorial*, Don Pero Niño, observed that the 1396 truce with France had been unpopular in England, 'because they do not wish to have peace with any nation'.[10] In England too there was fear that war with France might follow Henry's usurpation, and Henry took steps to defend Calais and the south coast of England itself. Coastal castles were placed in a state of readiness, commissions of array were issued, and the captain of Calais was instructed to be vigilant in face of French troop movements in the region.[11]

If both sides feared war, however, neither side wanted it. Henry made his pacific intentions clear at the very outset of his reign when he sent the bishop of Durham and the earl of Worcester to Paris to seek confirmation of the truce and to negotiate marriage alliances between the Lancastrian and Valois families.[12] Both sides agreed to extend the truce, and Françoise Lehoux, the biographer of the duke of Berry, has argued that Charles VI never had any intention of making war on England itself on behalf of the deposed Richard II, but saw the Lancastrian usurpation merely as a useful opportunity to stir up trouble in Guienne.[13] This is probably a correct analysis: with queen Isabella virtually a hostage in England open warfare would jeopardise her chances of making a safe and honourable return to France, and, perhaps more significantly, the duke of Burgundy's interests in Flanders and the safety of Anglo-Flemish commerce would both be damaged by any renewal of hostilities. Pressure on Guienne, by contrast, was relatively risk-free, and would have little impact on Anglo-Flemish commerce. Charles VI sent a clear signal of his intentions over Guienne when he created his eldest son duke of Guienne in January 1402 and required him to do homage for the duchy.[14] The grant of Perigord to the duke of Orléans in 1399 and his subsequent alliance with the count of Foix, who defected from his English allegiance in 1401, increased the threat to Henry IV in Guienne, and after the return of Queen Isabella, when French policy towards England could afford to become more uninhibited, Orléans stepped up military pressure on the duchy.[15]

Guienne was not the only place where the French might apply pressure on Henry while at the same time seeking to maintain the truce with England. The Scots too saw Henry as a usurper, and more perhaps than the French appreciated the weakness of his position. Walter Bower referred to Henry as king '*de facto*,' and in a reflection on his usurpation quoted the Revelations of St Bridget on the fate of those 'who obtain possessions by cheating and then unjustly hold on to what they have taken'.[16] Robert III was initially disinclined to recognise Henry as king: in letters to him on 6 October and 2 November 1399 he addressed him as '*nostre tresame et treschier cousyn, le Duk de Lancastre, Counte de Derby, et Seneschal d'Engleterre*', though in the following March he used the address '*nostre treschier cousin d'Engleterre*'.[17] The Scots had not been party to the twenty-eight year Anglo-French truce of 1396, and the Anglo-Scottish truce was simply extended for six months or a year at a time in the last years of Richard II's reign.[18] In the opening months of his reign, Henry saw the renewed war with Scotland as perhaps an even more serious threat than the risk of a breakdown of the truce with France. The possibility that the Scots were more openly hostile than the French to Henry in 1400 receives some support from the instructions given to French ambassadors bound for Scotland in the winter of 1400–1. Robert III was evidently unhappy ('*prenoit ombrage*') about French negotiations with 'Henry of Lancaster who calls himself king of England', presumably over the renewal of the truce. The ambassadors were therefore instructed to inform king Robert that Charles VI had to negotiate with Henry in order to obtain the return of Isabella, and that the truce was real, not personal: in other words, it was not merely an agreement between Charles and Richard II, but between '*lour royaumes, terres, seigneuries et subgiez*'.[19] Henry, however, was anxious that the truce with Scotland should be renewed, and his correspondence with Robert III over the winter of 1399–1400 dwelt on arrangements for doing so. A meeting of the Great Council in February 1400 discussed the real fear that the Scots might invade England '*par l'aide de ceux de France*'.[20] The king's council seems to have believed that the Scots would be less willing than the French to maintain the truce, and in 1400 they perhaps had less incentive to do so. The prevarication of the Scots over renewal of the truce, together with the defection to England of George Dunbar, earl of March, prompted Henry to invade Scotland in August 1400 in a campaign which achieved little and lasted only a fortnight. If the campaign had been intended to drive a wedge between the Scots and the French it was unsuccessful, and the French encouraged the Scots to harry English shipping during 1401 and 1402. The Percies' decisive victory over the Scots at Homildon Hill on 14 September 1402, however, brought this phase of warfare to an end. Grant has argued that Homildon Hill 'marks an important step towards eventual Anglo-Scottish disengagement'.[21] In the short run, it certainly discouraged the Scots from further aggression against England at the instigation of the French: although French pressure on Guienne continued and even intensified over the following years, pressure on Henry's northern border diminished sharply as a result of the successful military action of 1402.

Even though neither England nor France had any wish to renew open war, there is no doubt of the implacable nature of French hostility to the Lancastrian regime in the opening years of the fifteenth century. Henry IV therefore needed to establish his position and find support in western Christendom just as he did at home; and in doing so he might find the French court a more dangerous opponent than the rump of the Ricardians or the Percies in England. In his negotiations with other European rulers, Henry had a number of advantages. His personal reputation stood high, not least because of the contacts he had made during his crusade in 1394 and even, to some degree, during his exile in 1399. McFarlane drew attention to his meetings with German rulers, including the king of the Romans Wenceslas in 1394. Indeed, McFarlane suggested that Henry's stay with the drunken Wenceslas must have been an uproarious occasion.[22] It may have been, but as with Berry's and Bourbon's encounter with the massively hungover king at Rheims in 1398, the meeting may also have served to persuade Henry that the slothful and inebriate Wenceslas was not a ruler with whom one could do business.[23] Henry, furthermore, had been a widower since 1394, and his own remarriage was an important card in his hand. There were those who saw him as an attractive prospect: Lucia Visconti, daughter of the ruler of Milan, had apparently been proposed as a bride for Henry sometime during John of Gaunt's lifetime, and had declared in 1399 that although Henry was at that time out of favour with the king of England, 'if she was certain to have (him) for her husband, she would wait for him as long as she could, to the very end of her life, even if she knew that she would die three days after the marriage'.[24] Furthermore, as Goodman has reminded us in his recent biography of John of Gaunt, the House of Lancaster had an international role in the late fourteenth century. Henry's sister was queen of Portugal, and his half-sister queen of Castile.[25] Such family ties might prove important in Henry's diplomacy, and, as we shall see, the court in Paris was well aware of the impact that these links might have on Castile's relationship with England. In addition to this Henry had, unlike his predecessor, his own family of four sons and two daughters whose potential value in diplomacy he sought to exploit within weeks of his accession in 1399.

On the other hand, it is important not to overemphasise the importance of ties of kinship. In England, both Henry IV and Henry V used marriage alliances to strengthen links between the crown and leading noble families, and the Beauforts played a major part in these arrangements.[26] But in Henry's dealings with continental rulers, family ties did not generally override considerations of national interest, as we shall see in the case of Castile, and the marriage alliances that Henry negotiated followed rather than created a perception of mutual interest. In establishing his relationship with other European rulers, the king's own astuteness and, to a significant degree, the mistakes and hesitations in Paris, explain his success in ensuring that hostility and non-recognition were confined to the French in the years after 1400.

For Charles VI, faced with the possibility of renewed Anglo-French hostility after 1399, it was essential to ensure that the Franco-Castilian alliance would remain effective despite the tie of kindred between Castile and the new dynasty in England. In 1394, when Enrique III had attained his majority, he had formally renewed the alliance with France,[27] and according to the Monk of St Denis when war with England looked a possibility after the deposition of Richard II the French sought naval assistance from Castile. Enrique prevaricated, however, and promised to send ships only in the following year.[28] The French historian of the Franco-Castilian alliance doubted whether the monk was correct about this. He preferred to accept the evidence of the Castilian chronicler Don Pero Niño, who played a leading part in the naval warfare of these years, that Enrique was quite happy to send help to Charles VI.[29] On the other hand the monk of St Denis may well have been reflecting suspicions in Paris that Enrique, influenced by his English wife, took an unenthusiastic view of his obligation to France, and this belief was given some substance when in July 1400 letters from the queen of Castile to Henry IV were intercepted by the French and found to contain a reference to Henry as king of England and France.[30] This was no doubt a tactless mistake rather than a harbinger of a change in Castile's diplomatic stance, but Enrique had no wish to become committed to full-scale war with England, not least because of the damage it might do to Castilian commerce in the Channel, and in 1402 the English seneschal of the Landes in Gascony received a letter from Enrique stressing the importance of Anglo-Castilian friendship.[31] None the less, as we know from Don Pero Niño, Castilian galleys were called in aid by the French when they stepped up pressure on Aquitaine, and they engaged in raids on the south-western peninsula of England.[32] The Castilian nobility would not support any change in Castile's relationship with France, and the French alliance was an essential prop for the Trastamara dynasty. Goodman has argued that the Treaty of Bayonne in 1388, for all its window-dressing with a marriage alliance, was 'an admission of the failure of Lancastrian policy' towards Castile. English influence in Castile in the first decade of the fifteenth century seems to have been minimal, and French fears groundless.[33]

The alliance between England and Portugal held firm, however, though even here, despite the close family links between the two dynasties – and their common origin in coups d'état – Henry had to work hard to maintain good relations. In a move unprecedented where foreign royalty were concerned, Henry appointed King João of Portugal to the order of the garter. The king of Denmark was soon to receive the same honour, and their appointments are evidence of the importance Henry attached to such symbols and ceremonies in obtaining international recognition for his dynasty.[34] Both Henry and his sister the queen of Portugal brought pressure to bear on the earl of Arundel in 1404 to marry Beatriz, an illegitimate daughter of the Portuguese king. The Portuguese described Arundel as '*do sangue Real da Inglaterra,*' which was perhaps stretching a point, and they seem to have been most anxious for a prestigious marriage for the newly legitimised offspring of João and Donna Agnes Perez. Arundel, however, proved a reluctant suitor, and though the marriage took place it was accompanied by unseemly wrangles between the king and the earl over money.[35]

Henry's own marriage, to Joan dowager duchess of Brittany, brought him little diplomatic advantage, for the duke of Burgundy moved fast to forestall any re-establishment of English influence in the duchy. Since the death of John IV of Brittany in November 1399, the French had feared that the English would use the minority of his son to regain some ascendancy there and even establish bases in the duchy. Henry's marriage to Joan served only to intensify these fears about English intentions, and to forestall any threat from the English, Burgundy moved swiftly to establish French troops in the duchy. Perhaps French fears were exaggerated: the marriage in 1397 of John IV's son and heir John, count of Montfort, to Joan, one of Charles VI's daughters, and Montfort's subsequent presence at the French court, made it unlikely that English influence in Brittany would be revived after John IV's death. If Henry had hoped by his marriage to re-establish a pro-English party in the duchy he had little success.[36]

In northern Europe, however, the situation was very different, and events there turned much more to Henry's advantage. In August 1400 growing hostility within Germany to Wenceslas IV, king of the Romans and Bohemia, culminated in a formal proclamation of his deposition, and Rupert of Wittelsbach, the Count Palatine, was elected king of the Romans in his stead.[37] In less than a year two European monarchs had been deposed by their subjects; both had been the subject of a series of charges against them, though the charges against Wenceslas dwelt on his sloth and untrustworthiness rather than his tyranny, and both depositions raised important legal issues in the minds of contemporaries.[38] The parallels between the two depositions are perhaps worth fuller investigation, though they should not be pressed too far, not least because of the major constitutional differences between England and the Empire, and because Wenceslas still remained king of his inherited realm, Bohemia. Both depositions presented diplomatic difficulties for the French. If the issue with England had been refusal to recognise Henry as king, and fear that war might break out, the problem with the Empire was whether to recognise Rupert or Wenceslas, and the issue now fatally divided the French court. Both Rupert and Wenceslas were anxious for French support and recognition, and were soon to send embassies to Paris in the hope of obtaining it.[39] Each had some grounds for optimism: the duke of Burgundy was related to by marriage to the Wittelsbachs, and Stephen, duke of Bavaria, another Wittelsbach partisan of Rupert, was the queen of France's father.[40] On the other hand Wenceslas could – and did – argue that the alliance between France and the Luxemburg dynasty went back over a hundred years, and had been renewed in 1398 in a ceremony at Rheims.[41] This ceremony, furthermore, had been followed by a treaty between Wenceslas and the duke of Orléans in which the two agreed to the marriage of Orléans's son with Wenceslas's niece the daughter of Prokop, Margrave of Moravia.[42]

The Franco-Imperial meeting at Rheims and the subsequent treaty with Orléans, however, proved one source of the friction which developed in Paris in 14001 over recognition of the rival kings of the Romans, and which paved the way for the Anglo-Imperial marriage of 1402. Another source was the different approach which the French and the Germans took to the problem of the schism. Although Wenceslas had followed his father Charles IV in recognising Urban VI, diplomatic pressure from France and from some of the princes within the Empire had served to diminish Wenceslas's commitment to Urban and his successor Boniface IX.[43] Indeed, as Harvey has pointed out, one of the counts against Wenceslas at the time of his deposition was his willingness to bow to French pressure and support the policy of withdrawal of obedience from Boniface.[44] Rupert on the other hand sought to retain the support of the German church by continuing to recognise Boniface, yet the price of French support against Wenceslas might well be a more flexible stance on the schism. To this end, early in 1401 he proposed an imperial Diet to discuss the issue, which would be held the following June.[45]

A little before this, in October 1400, both Rupert and Wenceslas sent envoys to Paris, who were heard separately by the French court: but the French lords could not reach agreement. Orléans vigorously supported Wenceslas, and was reportedly so incensed by his deposition that he began preparations for a military expedition to reinstate him. He was only dissuaded by heavy Wittelsbach pressure on the queen of France.[46] Burgundy and Berry, on the other hand, seem to have been sympathetic to Rupert's claims, but an embassy which they sent to the electors, and which apparently stressed the French approach to the ending of the schism, failed to reach any agreement, and French policy towards the Empire remained in limbo.[47]

As the negotiations between Rupert and the French ran into the ground, Rupert turned to England. On 9 January 1401 he issued a commission to treat for a marriage between his eldest son Louis and Blanche, Henry IV's eldest daughter, and in the following month Henry appointed his envoys to treat with the king of the Romans.[48] The negotiations went ahead with remarkable speed, and a marriage treaty was drawn up on 7 March 1401. It was confirmed on 12 August. Both sides seem to have been anxious for the negotiations to succeed. Henry was also anxious to appear sympathetic to Rupert's plans for ending the schism, and the anti-French tone of some English writing on the schism at this time suggest a concern on the part of Henry IV's council to support Rupert's plan to call a diet to bring about a solution to the schism.[49] For Henry, however, a more immediate problem was the provision of the dowry for Blanche. Under the terms of the marriage treaty, this was set at the substantial sum of 40,000 nobles (£13,333 6s 8d), and Henry was to have great difficulty in raising such a large amount. He was, of course, able to levy the traditional feudal aid '*pur fille marier*',[50] but the proceeds from this came in slowly and were in any case insufficient to fulfil Henry's obligation over the dowry and to pay the other expenses of her marriage. At least three letters survive in which Henry sought loans from his subjects to defray the costs of the marriage,[51] and he found it difficult to obtain full cooperation from the council. In May 1402 he wrote to the council complaining that money collected to pay the dowry of Blanche and the expenses of her marriage had been used for other purposes, and requiring that payment should now be given priority over all other expenditure. This was followed, a few weeks later, by the payment to Blanche's treasurer of £5,333 6s 8d in part payment of her dowry. Part of the dowry remained outstanding at Blanche's death in 1409, and Henry's obligation was not finally discharged until 1446.[52]

Henry came under some pressure from Rupert and Louis to pay the dowry promptly, and Henry's dealings with his council suggested that he was both embarassed and annoyed at the dilatoriness over collecting and paying the money.[53] The king of the Romans, however, was interested in more than money from Henry. His principal preoccupation in 1401 and 1402 was his expedition to Italy, which would necessitate bringing Milan to heel. Its ruler had been created a duke by Wenceslas, yet progress into Italy depended crucially on Milanese goodwill.[54] To this end, Rupert sought military assistance from England. In February 1402 he wrote to Henry asking for 2,000 archers to be sent to participate in the Milanese expedition. These archers were to be paid for by Henry, for Rupert, so the letter said, found it too difficult to provide for them.[55] To encourage Henry to accede to Rupert's request, the German ambassadors to England were instructed to warn Henry that the duke of Orléans was trying to gather support in Germany for a military campaign against England, though there is little reason to suppose that this was true.[56] Wylie suggested that Henry was quite willing to agree to Rupert's request, but before any practical steps were taken to recruit and despatch the archers Rupert wrote to Henry on 24 April 1402 saying that they were no longer needed because he was returning to Germany.[57] It is perhaps fortunate that Rupert's request never came to anything, for it is difficult to believe that the council – let alone the commons – would have been happy about it. There are, perhaps, parallels with Richard II's proposed expedition to Lombardy in 1397, which the commons were reluctant to finance and which never took place.[58] Three days after Rupert wrote the letter countermanding the request for military assistance, Henry empowered envoys to treat for an alliance with Rupert.[59] It does not appear, however, that such an alliance was ever concluded. Weizsacker printed what he claimed was the text of the alliance in *Deutsche Reichstagsakten*, and some French historians have accepted his view that an alliance was agreed, but the document – John Prophete's collection of documents from the Privy Seal office in Harley MS 31 – reads more like an English diplomatic draft. It is remarkably similar in content to the draft of an alliance between Henry and the king of Denmark, and it may be safer to conclude that the marriage alliance between the two families was not extended into a more general alliance.[60]

Nevertheless, the Anglo-Imperial *rapprochement* was watched with concern in Paris. Rupert maintained a conciliatory approach towards France, not least because he hoped the French court would put pressure on the count of Savoy to recognise him as king of the Romans and facilitate his passage southwards to Italy. In May 1401 Rupert sent his secretary, Master Albrecht, to Paris with instructions to probe French intentions over Savoy, but also to say, if the French raised the question of the marriage between Louis and Blanche of England, that Rupert would rather have had a marriage alliance with the French royal house *'lieber dann mit iman anders'*, but that the French themselves had not been willing to enter into negotiations.[61] In view of the divisions in the French court about recognising Rupert, which have already been discussed, this was not an unreasonable statement, but later the same year Rupert expressed willingness to consider a French marriage for his younger son John. This does not seem to have gone down particularly well in Paris, not least because it was accompanied by an insistence on Rupert's part that he would only observe strict neutrality between France and England if Charles VI undertook to forbid his subjects to give aid to Rupert's enemies in the Empire, a demand that was probably directed principally at the duke of Orléans.[62]

To some extent, therefore, the divisions and irresoluteness of the French court in the face of the German political crisis played into Henry's hands, and encouraged Rupert to look to England when in other circumstances he might have looked to France. Both the monk of St Denis and Juvénal des Ursins stress the part played by the duke of Orléans in the arguments over Germany, and although Orléans had a treaty relationship with Wenceslas his main motive seems to have been his rivalry with the duke of Burgundy in the struggle for influence over Charles VI.[63] Even at the outset of his reign, Henry IV was the beneficiary, at least in his diplomacy, of the domestic divisions and rivalries in France.

A similar point can be made about the Anglo-Danish marriage alliance for which negotiations began in the spring of 1401. The emergence in the 1390s of a united Scandinavian monarchy, however insecurely based, was a development of some general significance for the European realms, not least because of the close and often acrimonious relations that existed between the Scandinavian rulers and the Hanse.[64] From the standpoint of English commercial interests in northern Europe an alliance with Eric of Denmark and by implication therefore with his great-aunt Margaret, who was the real power behind the Kalmar union, might have important advantages. Queen Margaret, however, like Rupert. seems to have looked first of all to France. According to the monk of St Denis, Margaret sent envoys to France in 1400 seeking to negotiate a marriage between a French princess and Eric, the designated heir to the crowns of

Denmark, Norway and Sweden. Margaret's envoys were instructed to say to the French that Eric honoured the family of the fleur de lys above all Christians, but the French were not impressed by such flattery.[65] The monk says that Charles VI's uncles, put off by the unjust treatment of Queen Isabella in England, were ill-disposed towards more foreign marriages. Eventually the duke of Bourbon offered his only daughter Isabella, when she reached marriageable age.[66] Whatever the truth of this – and it does not seem entirely convincing – the Danish envoys returned from France empty-handed, and in the following year Margaret opened negotiations with Henry IV for a double marriage treaty between Eric and Henry's younger daughter Philippa and between the prince of Wales and Eric's sister Katerina.[67] English enthusiasm for a marriage alliance with Denmark seems however to have been muted. The proposal for a marriage between the prince of Wales and Katerina made little or no progress, and the council may have raised objections to the marriage of Philippa and Eric, perhaps on financial grounds. In April 1402 Henry wrote to the council pointing out that their draft reply to a letter from the king of Denmark about his proposed marriage to Philippa 'must give the king of Denmark good cause to refuse the marriage altogether,' and Henry, who was as anxious for this marriage to take place as he had been for the marriage of Blanche and Louis, advised them to take into account the most recent letters from the Danish king and devise 'a more acceptable reply'.[68] According to Walsingham it took the impressive advocacy of Archbishop Eystein of Oslo and continued pressure from other Danish envoys to persuade the council to agree to the marriage, and then only on the understanding that the king of Denmark would not seek '*dotem vel divitias, sed solum corpus virginis nominatae*'.[69] Perhaps this concession clinched the matter as far as the English council was concerned. The marriage did not actually take place until October 1406, but the two parties seem to have reached substantial agreement by November 1402.[70]

Neither the Germans nor the Danes seem to have had any reservations about Henry's position as king of England, and their dealings with Henry suggest that they had every reason to suppose that Henry's tenure of his throne was secure. In one document Rupert went so far as to refer to Henry as king of England and France,[71] a form of address never adopted by the king of Denmark, and probably, like its Castilian counterpart, a tactless mistake. Indeed, it was evidently Henry who had reservations about Rupert's position rather than the other way round, for in a set of diplomatic instructions issued in 1402 Rupert provided an answer to an expected question from the English ambassadors to Germany about the extent to which the Electors were really committed to Rupert's cause.[72] If the French court had been more astute and united in its response to overtures from the king of the Romans and the queen of Denmark, Henry's relationship with those two rulers would not have developed as successfully as it did. Henry, by contrast, seems to have acted with speed and determination, and was able to bring his council into line when they appeared to be hesitating. If Margaret's and Rupert's approaches to France had met with a favourable response, Henry would have been isolated and the determination on the part of the French in 1400 and 1401 not to recognise him as king of England might have been taken up elsewhere in Europe, with incalculable consequences for his kingship. For the French, the presence in England of Queen Isabella probably inhibited a more overtly bellicose stance towards England, though the interests of the duke of Burgundy also played a part. Most scholars have observed, however, that after the return of Queen Isabella to France French hostility towards England was stepped up, and both Ford and Pistono, in a series of important articles, have explored the relationship between 'piracy and policy' in the Channel in the years after 1402.[73] As with the Anglo-Scottish war at sea between 1400 and 1402, so now with hostilities in the Channel it is difficult to draw a clear distinction between unofficial piracy and officially encouraged attacks on English and French shipping. For Henry, as for the duke of Burgundy, it was important to try as far as possible to limit the damage to Anglo-Flemish trade both from piracy and from more formal hostilities, and the same point needed to be made in respect of Anglo-Castilian trade, though this issue has not yet been examined in the same detail as Anglo-Flemish trade. In the event. Henry was keep open his lines to the burgesses of Flanders, and reach a commercial agreement over the winter of 1406–7 with John the Fearless which, as Harriss has observed, was to endure and was to have important 'political implications for future Anglo-French relations'.[74]

In his study of Henry IV in *Lancastrian Kings and Lollard Knights*, McFarlane reminded us of the importance attached to international recognition of the new regime in 1399.[75] In February 1400, Henry despatched envoys to the papal curia and to the courts of Castile, Aragon and Portugal, formally announcing his accession.[76] Yet formal announcements in themselves could do little to confer international recognition on Henry's regime. The recognition which was expressed in the marriages of his daughters to the king of the Romans and the king of Denmark, and the effective containment of French hostility to the new regime arose from Henry's own astute and opportunistic diplomacy, and his ability to take advantage of the divisions and rivalries which impeded the French court's approach to key diplomatic issues in 1400 and 1401. If his familiy ties in Europe were less useful than he might have hoped, and if the council's occasional reluctance to go along with his plans is evidence of the financial constraints that underlay much of Henry's policy both in England and abroad, the king's own energy, thoroughness and determination do much to explain the speedy acceptance of the House of Lancaster amongst the dynasties of Europe.

Notes

1. *Chronique de la Traison et Mort de Richart Deux Roy Dengleterre*, B. Williams (ed.) (London 1846); J. Creton, 'Metrical History of the Deposition of King Richard the Second', J. Webb (ed. and trans.), *Archaeologia*, XX (1825); *Chronique du Religieux de Saint-Denys 1380–1422*, M.L. Bellaguet (ed.) (6 vols, Paris 1840). For discussion. see J.J.N. Palmer, 'The Authorship, Date and Historical Value of the French Chronicles of the Lancastrian Revolution', *B.J.R.L.* (1979); *Chronicles of the Revolution 13971400: The Reign of Richard II*, C. Given-Wilson (trans. and ed.) (Manchester 1993), especially pp. 7–10. Dr Given-Wilson makes the important point that 'There is nothing to suggest that either the *Traison* or the "Metrical History" was known in England before about 1470': ibid. p. 8.

2. *Chronique du Religieux de Saint-Denys*, II, pp. 7446; *La chronique d'Enguerran de Monstrelet*, L. Douët-D'Arcq (ed.) (6 vols, Paris, 1857–62), I, pp. 534, note 1; *Foedera, Conventiones, Litterae*, T. Rymer (ed.) (20 vols, London 1704–35), VIII, p. 125: L. Douët-D'Arcq, *Choix de pièces inédites relatives au règne de Charles VI* (2 vols, Paris 1863–4), I, p. 193.

3. See, for example, P.E. Russell, *The English Intervention in Spain and Portugal in the Time of Edward III and Richard II* (Oxford, 1955), pp. 139–40, 174, 186–203; G. Daumet, *Étude sur l'Alliance de la France et de la Castille au XIVe et au XVe siècles* (Bibliothèque de l'École des Hautes Études, CXVIII, Paris, 1898).

4. H. Moranvillé, 'Relations de Charles VI avec l'Allemagne en 1400', *Bibliothèque de l'École des Chartes*, XLVII (1886), pp. 489–511; F. Lehoux, *Jean de France, duc de Berry* (3 vols, Paris 1966–8), II, pp. 435–8.

5. Douët D'Arcq, *Choix de Pièces*, I, pp. 157–60; Lehoux, *Jean de France*, p. 416: J.J.N. Palmer. *England France and Christendom, 1377–1399* (London 1972), pp. 224–6.

6. *Foedera*, VIII, p. 108 (commission dated 29 November 1399 for English envoys to treat for

marriage between Henry Prince of Wales, his brothers and sisters, and the children of the king of France or his uncles). For the French reaction. see C.P. Cooper, *Report on Rymer's Foedera: Appendices A–E* (H.M.S.O., 1869). appendix D, p. 68, no. 1. See also J.H. Wylie, *History of England under Henry IV* (4 vols, London 1884), I, pp. 86–7.

7.   *Chronique du Religieux de Saint-Denys*, III, pp. 302, 546: J.L. Kirby. *Henry IV of England* (London, 1970), pp. 119–22; Wylie, *Henry IV*, I, pp. 129–31, 205–11.

8.   Cited in Lehoux, *Jean de France*, II, pp. 420–1.

9.   J. Juvénal des Ursins, *Histoire de Charles VI, 1380–1422*, Michaud and Poujoulat (eds.) (Paris, 1884), p. 418.

10.   E. Martène and U. Durand, *Thesaurus Novus Anecdotorum* (5 vols, Paris, 1717, reprinted Farnborough, 1965), I, p. 1699: J. Froissart, *Oeuvres*, K. de Lettenkove (ed.) (25 vols, Brussels 186777), XIV, p. 314: *El Vitorial: Cronica de Don Pero Niño*, J. de Mata Carriazo (ed.) (Madrid, 1940), p.182.

11.   *Foedera*, VIII, pp. 120, 123, 125–7: *C.P.R. 1399–1401*, pp. 209–14, 216–17: *C.C.R. 1399–1402*, pp. 123, 138.

12.   *Foedera*, VIII, pp. 108–9; Chronique du Religieux de SaintDenys, II, pp. 7446: Lehoux. Jean de France, p. 422.

13.   *Foedera*, VIII, p. 124; Lehoux, *Jean de France*, p. 422

14.   *Report on Foedera*, appendix D, p. 71, no. 23.

15.   M.G.A. Vale, *English Gascony 1399–1453* (Oxford, 1970), pp. 46–9: see also, for some of the more symbolic aspects of Orléans' pressure, Wylie, *Henry IV*, I, pp. 322–36.

16.   Walter Bower, *Scotichronicon*, D.E.R. Watt (ed.) (8 vols, Aberdeen, 1987), VIII, pp. 20, 30.

17.   *Royal and Historical Letters during the Reign of Henry IV*, F.C. Hingeston (ed.) (R.S., 1860), pp. 4, 8, 25.

18.   *Foedera*, VIII, pp. 17–18, 35–6, 45.

19.   *Report on Foedera,* appendix D, p. 69, no. 12. The complete instructions are printed in Douët D'Arcq, *Choix de Pièces*, I, pp. 187–93.

20.   *Royal and Historical Letters*, I, pp. 4, 8, 20; *Foedera*, VIII, pp. 125–8.

21.   Wylie, *Henry IV*, I, pp. 119–40; R. Nicholson, *Scotland: The Later Middle Ages* (Edinburgh, 1974), pp. 222–3: A. Grant, *Independence and Nationhood: Scotland 1306–1469* (London 1984, p. 45.

22.   K.B. McFarlane, *Lancastrian Kings and Lollard Knights* (Oxford, 1972), p. 39.

23.   *Chronique du Religieux de Saint-Denys*, II, pp. 564–70. According to the monk, Wenceslas called off a dinner engagement with Bourbon and Berry because he was recovering from an orgy of eating and drinking.

24.   *Calendar of State Papers, Milan, I, 1385–1618* (H.M.S.O., 1912), no. 2, pp. 1–2.

25.   A. Goodman, *John of Gaunt* (1992), especially chapter 9.

26.   G.L. Harriss, *Cardinal Beaufort* (Oxford, 1988), p. 70

27.   Daumet, *Étude sur l'Alliance*, p. 62

28.   *Chronique du Religieux de Saint-Denys*, III, pp. 158, 160.

29.   Daumet, *Étude sur l'Alliance*, pp. 66–7; *El Vitorial: Cronica de Don Pero Niño*, pp. 184–7.

30.   L. Suarez Fernandez, *Navegación y Comercio en el Golfo de Vizcaya* (Madrid, 1959), p. 83, note 3; *Foedera* VIII, p. 155.

31. Suarez Fernandez, *Navegación*, p. 84 note 4.

32. *El Vitorial: Crónica de Don Pero Niño*, pp. 184–7.

33. A. Goodman, 'England and Iberia in the Middle Ages', in *England and her Neighbours, 1066–1453: Essays in Honour of Pierre Chaplais*, M. Jones and M. Vale (eds.) (1989), especially p. 87.

34. G.F. Beltz, *Memorials of the Order of the Garter* (1841), pp. liv, clvi.

35. The correspondence between Henry IV and the Portuguese court is printed in *Royal and Historical Letters*, II, pp. 83–102. For some discussion, see *Collectanea Topographica et Genealogica*, I (1834), pp. 80–90.

36. M. Jones, *Ducal Brittany 1364–1399* (Oxford, 1970), pp. 134–42: Wylie, *Henry IV*, I, pp. 306–12; *Chronique du Religieux de Saint-Denys*, III, pp. 40–2.

37. *Deutsche Reichstagsakten*, J. Weizsäcker and others (eds.) (16 vols, Munich and Gotha, 1867–1928), III, pp. 254–64, 266–71.

38. F.R.H. du Boulay, *Germany in the Later Middle Ages* (London, 1983), pp. 46, 227; G.E. Caspary, 'The Deposition of Richard II and Canon Law', *Proceedings of the Second International Congress of Canon Law* (Rome, 1965), pp. 189–206.

39. Lehoux, *Jean de France*, II, pp. 436–7.

40. See the table on p. 108.

41. *Chronique du Religieux de Saint-Denys*, II, pp. 762–6.

42. Douët D'Arcq, *Choix de Pièces*, I, pp. 140–2; *Chronique du Religieux de Saint-Denys*, II, pp. 564–70.

43. N. Valois, 'Le Grand Schisme en Allemagne de 1378 a 1380', *Romische Quartalschrift* VIII (1893), pp. 107–64. My forthcoming article on Richard II and the House of Luxemburg in *Richard II*, A. Goodman and J. Gillespie (eds.), deals with some aspects of this problem.

44. M.M. Harvey, *Solutions to the Schism* (St. Ottilien, 1983), p. 114.

45. Harvey, *Solutions*, pp. 113–24.

46. *Chronique du Religieux de Saint-Denys*, II, p. 770. The queen's father, Stephen duke of Bavaria, was one of the envoys who visited Paris in October 1400.

47. Juvénal des Ursins, *Histoire*, p. 419; *Chronique du Religieux de Saint-Denys*, II, p. 762–6. See R. Vaughan, *Philip the Bold* (London, 1962), pp. 54–6 for a brief discussion of the duke of Burgundy's role in the negotiations.

48. *Foedera*, VIII, pp. 170–2, 176–7.

49. *Foedera*, VIII, pp. 179–81; Harvey. *Solutions*, pp. 117–24: W. Holtzmann. "Die englische Heirat Pfalzgraf Ludwigs III". *Zeitschrift fur die Geschichte des Oberrheins*, XLIII (1930), pp. 1–38.

50. *Foedera*, VIII, pp. 232–3.

51. M.D. Legge, *Anglo-Norman Letters and Petitions* (Oxford, 1941), no. 380: P.R.O. E.28/8.

52. *Proceedings and Ordinances of the Privy Council, 1386–1542*, N.H. Nicolas (ed.) (7 vols, Record Commission, 1834–7), I, pp. 184–5; *Foedera*, VIII, pp. 200–2; *Deutsche Reichstagsakten*, V, no. 295: Holtzmann, 'Englische Heirat', pp. 37–8.

53. *Proceedings of the Privy Council* , pp. 184–5: *Calendar of Signet Letters Henry IV*, no. 71, p. 35.

54. Lehoux, *Jean de France*, II, pp. 450–2.

55. *Deutsche Reichstagsakten*, V, no. 295.

56. Ibid.

57. Wylie, *Henry IV*, I, p. 203: *Deutsche Reichstagsakten*, V, no. 258

58.   *R.P.* III, p. 338.

59.   *Foedera*, VIII, pp. 253–4.

60.   *Deutsche Reichstagsakten*, V, no. 257; B.L. Harley MS 431, fo.26: Lehoux, *Jean de France*, II, p. 517.

61.   *Deutsche Reichstagsakten*, IV, no. 297; Lehoux, *Jean de France*, II, pp. 450–1.

62.   *Deutsche Reichstagsakten*, V, no. 157; Lehoux, *Jean de France*, II, pp. 451–2.

63.   *Chronique du Religieux de Saint-Denys*, II, pp. 764–6; Juvénal des Ursins, *Histoire*, pp. 419–20. Des Ursins argues that Berry and Burgundy were displeased when Orléans made an alliance with the duke of Gelders, which might be construed as an anti-Burgundian move. See Moranvillé, *Bibliothèque de l'École des Chartes*, XLVII, p. 499.

64.   A. Tuck, 'Some Evidence for Anglo-Scandinavian Relations at the End of the Fourteenth Century', *Mediaeval Scandinavia*, V (1972), pp. 75–88.

65.   *Chronique du Religieux de Saint-Denys*, II, p. 768

66.   Ibid.

67.   *Foedera*, VIII, pp. 257–61, 165–7: *Diplomatarium Norvegicum*, A. Bugge (ed.) (22 vols, Oslo, 1914), XIX, pp. 747, 751, 753, 761.

68.   *Calendar of Signet Letters*, no. 70, p. 35; *Royal and Historical Letters*, I, pp. 97–9: *Diplomatarium Norvegicum*, XIX, p. 753.

69.   John de Trokelowe and Henry de Blaneforde, 'Annales Henrici Quarti', in *Chronica et Annales*, H.T. Riley (ed.) (R.S., 1866), p. 412.

70.   Correspondence between the English and Danish courts about the marriage is printed in *Royal and Historical Letters*, I, pp. 80–1, 97–8, 117–30, 406–11.

71.   *Deutsche Reichstagsakten*, V, no. 258.

72.   *Deutsche Reichstagsakten*, V, no. 294.

73.   S.F. Pistono, 'The Accession of Henry IV: Effects on Anglo-Flemish Relations 1399–1402', *Tijdschrift voor Geschiedenis*, LXXXIX (1976), pp. 465–74; C.J. Ford, 'Piracy and Policy: The Crisis in the Channel, 1400–1403", *T.R.H.S.* 5th series, XXIX (1979), pp. 63–78.

74.   Harriss, *Cardinal Beaufort*, pp. 23–6.

75.   McFarlane, *Lancastrian Kings*, p. 39.

76.   Trokelowe and Blaneforde, 'Annales Henrici Quarti', p.320: *Proceedings of the Privy Council*, I, p. 111; Wylie, *Henry IV*, I, p. 90.

6

MAGNATES AND THEIR AFFINITIES IN THE PARLIAMENTS OF 1386–1421

Linda Clark

HISTORY OF PARLIAMENT

It is thought right necessarie . . . that my lord have at this tyme in the parlement suche persones as longe unto him.
Eleanor, duchess of Norfolk, writing to John Paston, 8 June 1455 [1]

I cannot claim, as Richmond does, to have total recall of the first time I read McFarlane's essay on 'Parliament and Bastard Feudalism', even though, like most historians of the fifteenth century who came after, I was profoundly influenced by it.[2] At the core of McFarlane's seminal article was an exploration of the involvement of members of the aristocracy in the East Anglian elections of the mid-fifteenth century, based on the vivid correspondence of the Pastons, and concluding that in this part of the country, at any rate, management was already a necessary art for those who wished to influence elections. The great lords by no means controlled the suffrage; the opinion of the gentlemen of the shires counted for much. As he rightly pointed out, what was true of that politically turbulent period might not necessarily have applied in earlier, or more stable times.[3] But earlier periods, including the one covered by the *History of Parliament* volumes recently published, are not blessed with any collections of personal letters providing comparable material; we need to deduce what happened at elections from other, often entirely circumstantial evidence. This inevitably leads to differences of interpretation. Illsley, looking at parliamentary returns in the reign of Edward I, disagreed with Riess's opinion that the shire elections were dominated and controlled by the great men of the county, who nominated the knights for election to parliament and then presented them to the county court for approval, since Riess had relied heavily on 'irregular' returns which he treated as evidence of the rule, rather than the exception, in electoral procedure. Illsley concluded that the county court was dominated in the thirteenth century by the local gentry rather than by the magnates. By contrast, Payling has argued on the basis of returns of 1297 and 1322, and less convincingly from a shrieval election of 1338, that in the early fourteenth century men of baronial rank, acting through their attorneys or stewards, exerted a powerful influence over the electoral process, as they did over other business of the county courts. He goes so far as to suggest that the *only* men then involved in the election process were a small number of leading county suitors.[4] As he pointed out, if this was indeed the case, the legislation for electoral reform in the early fifteenth century would suggest that representation became a matter of concern to a much wider section of the county community at some uncertain stage in the intervening period. However, if there was such a change it is difficult to pinpoint when it occurred and to avoid making the convenient assumption that it happened simultaneously right across the country.

There were places where the magnates' stewards or attorneys apparently long continued to make their presence felt at the elections. At least, they were named with their official titles on the indentures which after the statute of 1406 had to be sent into Chancery in response to the writs of summons. This was so in Yorkshire, where on many occasions in the first half of the fifteenth century the archbishop of York was represented in the county court by an attorney, as too were the earls of Westmorland and Northumberland and the Earl Marshal; and also in Devon, where an impressive array of officials habitually gathered at Exeter Castle for the elections, including the steward of the county's most influential nobleman, the Courtenay earl of Devon. Even so, the returns state clearly that the elections remained subject to the 'assent and consent' of the whole county court, and this cannot simply be dismissed as an empty formula. Retainers of the Nevilles and Percies were sometimes returned to parliament for Yorkshire, but there is nothing to suggest they were forced on an unwilling electorate (and more often than not the successful candidates were attached to the house of Lancaster, apparently unrepresented by attorneys in the court). And although altogether no fewer than forty-two Devonian MPs elected between 1377 and 1421 were connected with the earls of Devon, and at least five were their kinsmen, there is nothing to suggest that the elections there went contrary to the wishes of the local gentry.[5]

In other counties the participation of agents of the magnates is not stated directly on the indentures of return: where stewards of baronial landowners did attend the county courts for the parliamentary elections, they were not described as such in the official record. In Warwickshire, for example, Thomas Crewe, the chief steward of Richard Beauchamp, earl of Warwick, was named (without his office being mentioned) at the head of the list of attestors to the indentures of 1407, 1411, May 1413, and November 1414; and others of the Beauchamp affinity were also recorded at the hustings. The predominance of men of this affinity at the shire court is particularly notable, given that the number of named attestors sometimes fell below seven and rarely exceeded a dozen.[6] Likewise, in Suffolk the second earl of Suffolk's interests at the elections were promoted on the spot by his stewards and councillors, but, again, they were not so called on the indentures.[7]

There were three places where magnates, by virtue of unusual powers accorded them, might actually exert direct control over the elections: these were Westmorland, Worcestershire and Lancashire. In Westmorland the shrievalty was an hereditary office held by the lords Clifford, who appointed nominees acceptable to the crown as their deputies, and these men, often members of the Cliffords' retinue, conducted the elections in their name. At least fourteen of the MPs sitting between 1386 and 1421 were attached to this important baronial family as tenants, trustees, annuitants or estate staff, and on possibly twelve occasions this factor may have had a direct bearing on the outcome of the elections.[8] Similarly, in Worcestershire the shrievalty was held in fee by the earls of Warwick. No doubt they left the actual conduct of elections to the deputy sheriffs, who were their nominees, but the electoral indentures were nearly always drawn up in the earl's name, and on one occasion, in 1420, this formula concealed the fact that the then deputy sheriff, John Weston, had returned himself. It is perhaps not surprising to discover that a very high proportion of the knights of the shire for Worcestershire between 1386 and 1421 were closely connected with one or other of the two earls of the period, Earl Thomas (d.1401) and his son Richard (d.1439). At least one member of Earl Thomas's affinity was returned for Worcestershire to every parliament meeting between

1385 and January 1397; and between 1404 and December 1421 no fewer than fourteen men closely associated with Earl Richard followed suit, filling twenty-four out of a recorded twenty-eight seats. Indeed, in at least fourteen of the thirty-two parliaments of the period *both* members for Worcestershire are known to have belonged to the Beauchamp affinity. To realize the significance of these statistics, we need only look at the elections of September 1397, when, unusually, a royal appointee was sheriff, since Earl Thomas was in prison awaiting trial for treason against Richard II. Then, the two members elected came from an entirely different stable; they were Sir John Russell, personally known to the king as master of the horse and a prominent member of the council, and Richard Ruyhale, a lawyer who had recently strengthened his contacts with Thomas, Lord Despenser, one of the eight counter-appellants employed by the king in this parliament to secure the condemnation of Warwick and his erstwhile allies.[9]

As in Westmorland and Worcestershire, so too, albeit on a grander scale, in Lancashire. The grant of *jura regalia* in the county palatine to John of Gaunt in 1377 not only gave him the right to return to every parliament two knights 'for the community of the county', but also enabled him to appoint the local sheriff, escheator, justices of the peace and other officials, who would otherwise have been chosen by the crown. There were also many important administrative posts on the duchy of Lancaster estates in the palatinate. Given that almost all the leading members of the local community during the late fourteenth century were either employed by Gaunt or else belonged to his large and well-paid retinue, it is unlikely that in order to secure the return of such men to parliament he ever needed to dictate to the county court at election time. Furthermore, because of the indirect transmission – through Gaunt and his chancellor – of the parliamentary writs of summons, there was ample scope for the duke's personal intervention in favour of one retainer rather than another. Indeed, in 1378 and again in October 1383 he himself returned the names of his followers without any reference to the county court.[10]

Nevertheless, except for the participation of magnates' stewards and attorneys and the influence of deputy sheriffs or, as in Lancashire, the sheriff, the parliamentary returns themselves reveal no hint of an interest on the part of the aristocracy in the outcome of elections. Where other sources, unusually, do provide evidence of controversy, they simply relate to the wrong-doing of sheriffs. Indeed, the commons' petition for electoral reform in 1406 focused on returns *'faitz d'affection des visconts'*, making no mention of interference by lords; nor did this figure as a cause for grievance in the preambles to the statutes passed in 1410, 1413 and 1430.[11] Interference by sheriffs was not restricted to the county elections. In 1384 the sheriff of Dorset substituted the name of one burgess of Shaftesbury for another, against the wishes of the mayor and townsmen, and in the following year the sheriff of Devon, for personal gain, returned a stranger for Barnstaple. But the most serious instance occurred, in January 1404, when the sheriff of Rutland attempted to secure a place for his own candidate by altering the county return, a false return which stirred the commons to demand immediate disciplinary action.[12]

In none of these cases is there the slightest indication that any baronial interest lay behind the sheriff's arbitrary action. Nor was it, apparently, to any individual magnate's advantage that these particular candidates should be promoted or others set aside. The 1420s witnessed increasing incidents of disruption at elections, again to all appearances with members of the gentry, not the nobility, acting as prime movers. In 1427 the sheriff of Nottinghamshire dispensed altogether with the troublesome business of holding an election and simply returned two of his friends; and in Warwickshire a mob of townsmen from Warwick led by Sir William Peyto successfully persuaded the under-sheriff to substitute his name for John Mallory's on the electoral indenture. Worse was to come in 1429, when at least three county elections were affected. In Cumberland the sheriff replaced one of the elected representatives with a nominee of his own choice. In Buckinghamshire and Huntingdonshire Sir Thomas Waweton (the former Speaker) made a bid to influence the outcome – in Buckinghamshire, as sheriff, by drawing up a second, false set of indentures, and in Huntingdonshire by invading the county court with a gang brought in from outside.[13]

These inadequately documented events have been interpreted to fit preconceived ideas about the balance of power in each locality. Carpenter was convinced that the initial return of John Mallory for Warwickshire in 1427 was a direct challenge to the lordship of Richard, earl of Warwick, then overseas in France, by Warwick's rival, Joan, Lady Beauchamp of Abergavenny, in alliance with John Mowbray, duke of Norfolk. In her view, 'an election was an acid test of a magnate's local worth', so when the county court elected a candidate inimical to the earl, its decision had to be forcibly overturned by his men, headed by his retainer Peyto. The latter was 'acting on behalf of the absent earl, to ensure that the county bowed to his will'.[14] There is something to be said for this interpretation. Although the earls of Warwick did not hold the shrievalty of Warwickshire in fee, as they did that of Worcestershire, their *caput honoris* was in the county, and over the years they may have come to take domination of its parliamentary representation for granted. Members of Earl Thomas's affinity occupied no fewer than seventeen of the twenty-six seats available between 1386 and 1401, and no fewer than fourteen of the seventeen men returned between 1404 and 1421 are known to have been awarded annuities charged on Earl Richard's lands, or to have been engaged as members of his council and officers on his estates. Several MPs served the latter earl as feoffees, legal advisers or executors. Furthermore, at least one Beauchamp retainer was elected by Warwickshire to every parliament between 1422 and 1439 (when Earl Richard died).[15] Yet it is unrealistic to assert that in 1427 and on other occasions when the earl was overseas he maintained the same personal interest in local politics as he may have done while at home. Surely his overriding concern must have been directed to the progress of the military campaign, and difficulties in communication are bound to have precluded any spontaneous response to rapidly changing political circumstances. Similarly, it has been argued (albeit inconclusively) that the stormy events of the Huntingdonshire election of 1429 were a direct consequence of a violent quarrel between John, earl of Huntingdon, and the duke of Norfolk, which had come to a head in the previous year.[16] However, the only unambiguous evidence of direct intervention by a magnate in an election at this time does not concern the representation of a shire at all, nor was the prime mover a layman. We learn from the records of Canterbury that John Langdon, bishop of Rochester, successfully persuaded the sheriff of Kent to override the citizens' choice by returning one of his own servants in place of a nominee already dispatched by them to Westminster.[17]

Save for the bishop of Rochester's arbitrary action in 1429, Henry, Lord Grey of Codnor's intervention at Derby in 1433 is the first recorded instance of a nobleman's active involvement in the electoral process. On that occasion Grey arrived for the county elections with a force of 200 men, only to be outmatched on the following day by two local landowners, Sir Richard Vernon and Sir John Curson, who got themselves returned to parliament in open defiance of their powerful neighbour.[18] Before then, our interpretation of events depends largely on guesswork. How far back can we find ready acceptance of the notion that lords should not have a say in elections to the commons? If we can believe John, Lord Tiptoft's version of the events at the Cambridgeshire election of 1439, when Sir James Ormond attempted to impose his candidates on an unwilling assembly, Tiptoft occupied the moral high ground throughout, valiantly seeking to preserve order, as was his duty as a justice of the peace, and all the while 'supportyng and comfortyng the commones to make free eleccion'.[19] He clearly wished Cardinal Beaufort and his fellow members of the council to believe that he himself would never have dreamed of attempting to influence the outcome.[20]

Whereas the parliamentary representation of eight out of the thirty-seven counties, including Devon, Worcestershire and Lancashire, was apparently dominated by a particular seignorial affinity, in roughly the same number of shires the palpable strength of the gentry communities and the absence of resident magnates left little scope for outside intervention. Indeed, save perhaps at times of political crisis, it looks as if in most counties the electoral process was controlled by influential local gentlemen, whose discussions both before and during the meeting of the county court were possibly coordinated by the sheriffs. The latter, not necessarily against the wishes of the rest, were sometimes tempted to return themselves, although this had become an increasingly rare phenomenon after it was forbidden by ordinance in 1372.[21] They were more likely to return kinsmen. For example, during the forty years after 1397 the representation of the county of Cornwall was to a certain extent controlled by the Arundells of Lanherne and their close relations, the most blatant instance occurring in 1419 when the steward of the duchy, Sir John Arundell, as sheriff, returned his sons, John and Thomas, both still in their twenties.[22] Elsewhere, sheriffs returned their brothers,[23] uncles,[24] and sons,[25] and other cases involved the election of their in-laws, stepsons, nephews and cousins. Similarly, sheriffs intruded their own deputies, as happened in the autumn of 1397 at Warwick, and in 1419 at Portsmouth.[26]

As many of the biographies in the volumes of the *History of Parliament* suggest, the outcome of elections frequently depended on the decisions of certain prominent individuals from among the gentry, whose influence made itself felt both in counties and certain boroughs. Clearly outstanding in this respect were Sir Thomas Erpingham in East Anglia,[27] Sir William Sturmy and Sir Walter Hungerford in the boroughs and county of Wiltshire,[28] the two Sir Thomas Brookes (father and son) in Lyme Regis and to a lesser extent in Somerset and Devon,[29] Sir John Tiptoft in Huntingdonshire,[30] and Thomas Chaucer in Taunton, Wallingford and the upper Thames valley.[31] Even in Warwickshire, where the earls of Warwick might have expected to rule the roost, matters did not always go entirely their way. Sir William Bagot, who owed his early political rise and his growing influence in the county largely to the patronage of Earl Thomas, came to dominate the representation of the shire in the 1390s, even monopolizing a seat when he and his erstwhile lord no longer saw eye to eye. Indeed, his election to parliament in January 1397, for the ninth consecutive time, occurred while he was on bail awaiting trial for many crimes, including homicide and an alleged assault on one of the earl's most favoured retainers, for which he had been indicted in a court presided over by the earl himself.[32] Nicholas Blundell, who sat for Lancashire in 1414, could refer to Sir John Stanley, a contemporary member of the commons, as his 'sovereign master', so we should be careful not to exaggerate the role played by magnates in determining the composition of the lower house to the extent that we lose sight of the ubiquitous involvement of the higher gentry.[33]

Yet the inescapable fact remains that the men selected as knights of the shire were quite often retainers of members of the parliamentary peerage at some point in their careers. In an exercise full of obvious pitfalls, I tried to count how many of the 3,173 MPs biographed in the Roskell volumes of the *History* had known links with magnates, both lay and ecclesiastical, close enough to cast doubt upon their political independence. I excluded, of course, any such relationships which could not conceivably have been relevant in the context of the particular parliaments which these men attended. At an inevitably rough count I found that only 456 MPs – just fourteen per cent of the total – fell into this category. We are dealing with a small minority of MPs. For the majority, relationships with members of the nobility were irrelevant to their careers and to their elections to parliament. This said, however, we should note that 361 members of the group were knights of the shire, and they equalled thirty-nine per cent of the total of 929 knights returned between 1386 and 1421. This, moreover, must be an underestimate – perhaps even a considerable one, since it depends almost entirely on the chance survival of estate papers or fortuitous enrolments on the patent rolls. So it is far from impossible that retainers of magnates dominated the representation of the counties.

However, to state the obvious, relations between magnates and shire knights varied in strength. The knights included those who received annuities for past and future services, indentured retainers either contracted for life or recruited for a single military campaign, and those paid a fee for their legal advice. Simply listing MPs who were in some way baronial dependents is an exercise of limited value unless the nature of the relationship in each case can be explored, but ties between members of the lords and commons were sometimes very close indeed. At least 125 of the MPs of the period 1386–1421 were related to members of the parliamentary peerage, fourteen of them being the sons of men who had sat in the upper house, and others the siblings of more recently ennobled lords and bishops. Brothers of the archbishops of Canterbury and York, and the bishops of Exeter, London, Bangor and Rochester all secured seats in the commons, as did uncles of the earls of Suffolk and Devon.[34] Connections by marriage were by no means rare, especially with members of the lesser nobility. But not all of these links can have been relevant to individual parliamentary careers; in fact it is possible in only thirty-three cases that kinship with someone sitting in the lords can have meant anything at all in this particular context. And although ties of blood and kinship by marriage made for a different type of relationship from that of lord and feed man, we should not necessarily assume that harmony and identity of purpose prevailed between close kin. To take an extreme example where the opposite was the case, Sir Ralph Botreaux, member for Cornwall, was accused of plotting the death of his nephew, William, Lord Botreaux, by the use of necromancy.[35]

Interestingly enough, one of the subjects causing strong differences of opinion between lords and commons was that of liveries. For some forty years after 1377 the commons fought for legislation against maintenance, and called for the abolition of badges despite considerable opposition from the lords. Saul has suggested that the members did this because they were concerned by the threat to their status represented by the growing aspirations of their inferiors.[36] This may have been true of some of the shire knights. But by no means all of them were retained by lords, and the majority of members – those who sat for towns and cities – lived lives largely untouched by 'bastard feudalism'. In fact, of the 2,244 parliamentary burgesses sitting between 1386 and 1421 only ninety-five are known to have had close links with magnates, these few being either retained or employed by them in the capacity of estate staff or lawyers. They, a mere three per cent of all the burgess MPs, filled less than one per cent of all the seats accounted for in the period. Of course, merchants from the larger urban centres, such as London, also had contact with members of the nobility, several of them supplying noble households and military retinues with consumable goods, offering loan facilities or mortgages, and acting as brokers for ransom payments. The resulting web of debt and credit, obligation and dependency, led to highly complex relations of a different order from the relatively straightforward bonds of lord and retainer.[37]

Even in the small towns there are few indications of the ' pocket boroughs' to come. For the most part men from the local community, closely involved in its affairs and well aware of the issues affecting their fellow burgesses, were elected. They knew they would have to face their constituents on their return home from Westminster, possibly with unwelcome news about taxation, and in a small town personal recriminations might be daunting. On only extremely rare occasions did one of the ninety-eight boroughs return someone connected with a local magnate, and only in certain manorial boroughs, such as Warwick and the Devonshire towns of Totnes and Plympton Earl, does it seem likely that the lord of the manor, or rather his estate staff, ever directly influenced the outcome of elections.[38] Of course, elsewhere it may have been becoming hard to resist external pressures: the citizens of Canterbury were naturally reluctant to lose the friendship of the bishop of Rochester by protesting too strongly at his intervention in 1429, even though they clearly begrudged the extra expense this had caused them.[39]

Nevertheless, we should not leap to the conclusion that, in the rare cases when retainers or estate staff secured borough seats in the commons the initiative invariably came from outside and above. It could easily happen the other way around; that a borough chose a certain individual because he was in close contact with a particular lord and might be able to influence him on the community's behalf.[40] Such seems to have been the case with John Hacon, the master mariner whom the burgesses of Great Yarmouth sent to six parliaments in the ten years from 1383. Hacon had already been retained by John of Gaunt, with an annuity of £10, and his fellow townsmen no doubt hoped he might be instrumental in gaining the duke's help in their epic struggle to retain control over Kirkley Road, in the face of vociferous opposition in the commons. Hacon appears to have been the link between the duke's council and the group in the lower house promoting Yarmouth's cause, which ultimately proved successful, although not until after considerable debate.[41]

The knights and burgesses could still be thought of as separate groups in the early fifteenth century, and we should be wary of attributing too great a solidarity to their ranks. The interests of the gentry and the burgesses did not necessarily coincide. Perhaps the recorded differences between the lords and commons over the grant of subsidies in 1407 and of tunnage and poundage in 1425, as well as the unexplained delays in grants on other occasions, should be properly viewed as conflicts between lords and parliamentary burgesses, and in particular the merchants among the latter.[42]

Whatever the links between magnates and MPs, we are not much nearer finding out what happened in practice, when the two houses of parliament assembled. Once elected to parliament, can we assume that the members dutifully followed guidelines set by their noble patrons or kinsmen? We should heed McFarlane's warning against 'the habit of assuming a simplicity of behaviour and of motive in medieval politicians', much as it facilitates our task to put MPs into convenient compartments.[43] How numerous in fact were those criticized in the poem 'Richard the Redeless' who 'were hired men and would not take any step for fear of their masters', who 'had already been taken into the confidence of the council, and knew well how matters would have to end or the assembly would rue it', or who 'were so afraid of great men that they forsook well-doing'?[44] The satirist was drawing attention to the different types of MP whose personal concerns may have led them to forget the interests of the people they were representing, and we should note that in his view subservience of members to lords was not the overriding cause of malaise in the parliament of 1397–8, to which he was specifically alluding. What is significant, however, is his assumption that parliament was usually guided by a very few highly articulate individuals.[45] Undoubtedly, a small number of MPs could and often did control the house, and if they had links with a political faction or powerful individuals in the lords much might he achieved to the latter's advantage. Evidently, on occasion, careful management of the house, orchestrated by the Speaker, made numerical superiority an irrelevance.

If we can accept the inference of contemporary accounts and the rolls of parliament themselves, the shire representatives, although heavily outnumbered by the burgesses, dominated the proceedings. Their links with the nobility were evidently significant at times of political crisis. In the Good Parliament of 1376, for instance, Sir William Wingfield, sitting for Suffolk for the first time, played a prominent part in the attack on ministerial corruption by providing evidence for the impeachment of John, Lord Neville of Raby. Working in close concert with Michael, Lord de la Pole, his kinsman by marriage, he gave telling testimony to add to the weight of evidence against the accused.[46] According to Thomas Walsingham, John of Gaunt interfered in elections to the next parliament, due to meet in January 1377, to ensure its rejection of the enactments of its predecessor. His alleged intention was to have nominees of his own arbitrarily substituted for shire knights of the Good Parliament, thus replacing the men who had been active in the cause of reform. Possibly as a result of his intervention, no more than nine knights were re-elected. Yet the Lancastrian presence in this complaisant parliament was only slightly greater than it had been among the commons who, in the preceding parliament, had given the duke such a rough time. It looks as if Gaunt's political objective was achieved not so much by weight of numbers as through the leadership of Sir Thomas Hungerford, now elected Speaker. He, as chief steward of the duchy of Lancaster south of the Trent and holder of several other offices by Gaunt's appointment, was a prominent member of the duke's council, and a forceful enough character, so it was reported, to prevent anyone from saying anything in the house which might displease his lord.[47] Recent studies on John of Gaunt have concluded that he did not recruit an affinity specifically for use as a political force in national affairs.[48] Even so, there were a number of counties besides Lancashire where his influence was pervasive. In Derbyshire, for example, the majority of the shire knights received some kind of fee, annuity or gifts from the duke, and some were heavily dependent upon this source of revenue, which often totalled in excess of £40 or £50 a year. They were committed supporters of the house of Lancaster and this, in John of Gaunt's lifetime, made them a formidable contingent in the lower house. Looking at the picture overall, in the eleven parliaments summoned between 1386 and September 1397 Gaunt's men in the commons averaged a dozen, and on occasion there were up to seventeen identified retainers of his gathered there. We may assume that some, at least, were primed beforehand regarding the duke's political attitude, although the evidence is never clear-cut.[49]

Like Gaunt in 1377, the five Lords Appellant of 1387–8 may have successfully dominated the proceedings of the Merciless Parliament by the careful briefing of a few selected MPs. Although only 34 of the 259 members of the commons can now be identified as closely linked with these noblemen, they included certain outstanding individuals who were doubtless fiercely partisan: notably, Sir Nicholas Lilling, the earl of Warwick's most highly trusted councillor and constant companion; Thomas Coggeshall, on whom the duke of Gloucester depended in a variety of ways; and, perhaps most important, Sir William Bagot, whose ties with three of the Appellants, Warwick, Mowbray and Bolingbroke, enabled him to play a complex and influential part in their counsels. We know from an eyewitness account that the Appellants entered the White Hall at Westminster 'arm in arm, wearing cloth of gold', which prompts an interesting question about the apparel donned by their retainers, meeting first in this general assembly and then with their fellow members of the commons.[50] Livery advertised in a visually striking way the bond between lord and man. If, say, Thomas Coggeshall stood at the lectern to address his fellows wearing Thomas of Woodstock's livery, they would assume that he was either acting as the duke's mouthpiece, or at least that what he said had his lord's approval.

A similar state of affairs prevailed in 1399, when a parliament formally summoned by Richard II met and ratified his deposition, and then, just a few days later, reassembled as Henry IV's first parliament. There had been next to no support at the elections for anyone associated with the Ricardian court party. Furthermore, at least twenty-three of the members had been retained by Henry of Bolingbroke or his father, and eighteen more had been closely attached to the leading Lords Appellant of 1387–8. But this did not provide numerical superiority. Once more, what counted was the identity of the Speaker, John Doreward, formerly a retainer of the murdered duke of Gloucester, who guided the proceedings to suit the new regime: significantly, he and six of his fellow commoners were made members of the new king's council during the session. The key figures in the assembly included Sir Walter Blount, who enjoyed an income of nearly £150 a year by grant of Bolingbroke and John of Gaunt; Sir John Pelham, whose devotion to Henry had already earned him 100 marks a year and was eventually to provide him with a massive £800 more; and several others who had joined Bolingbroke on his journey south from Ravenspur.[51]

Again, we may point to the existence of a cohesive 'faction', if not a party, in the commons of 1410. Eleven out of the 121 Members known were retainers of the prince of Wales, Henry of Monmouth, some being officials on his estates and recipients of substantial annuities amounting to £50 by his gift. They included such prominent figures as John Wynter, his receiver-general, Sir John St John, a veteran of his campaigns in South Wales, and William Stourton, the steward of the principality, as well as Sir Andrew Butler, Henry's deputy as constable of Dover castle and warden of the Cinque Ports. Significantly, too, ten more of the members had close personal links with Bishop Henry Beaufort and his influential cousin, Thomas Chaucer. The latter, re-elected Speaker of the house the day after parliament opened, was doubtless primed to direct the proceedings in line with conciliar policy as now established by his kinsmen and the prince. It looks very much as if Chaucer had been involved in a certain amount of electoral manipulation to secure the presence in the house of people on whom he himself could rely, notably the representatives for Taunton and the outsiders elected for Lyme Regis and Wareham. Even so, this may not have been a simple matter. There were serious disturbances at Taunton about the time of the elections, and in Oxfordshire, Chaucer's own constituency, the unusually large number of people witnessing the indenture suggests that the election was contested. And, despite Chaucer's efforts, the prince and his allies found themselves unable to command at will the cooperation of the commons, who made no financial provision whatsoever for national defence during a turbulent first session.[52]

As this clearly illustrates, magnates who were government ministers and members of the king's council appreciated the need for able spokesmen in the lower house. Thomas Fitzalan, earl of Arundel, immediately appointed treasurer of the exchequer at Henry V's accession, could look in the first parliament of the reign to the support of at least eleven of his retainers, among them his under-treasurer and his deputy-constable of Dover Castle, and in the parliament of November 1414 he was backed among others by both shire knights for Sussex and both those for Shropshire. In fact, Fitzalan's men monopolized the Shropshire seats in all the parliaments convened before his death in 1415, and it is worthy of remark that after he died not only were there complete and immediate changes in the pattern of representation there and in Sussex, but petitions supported by the commons were promptly brought in parliament complaining about his perversion of justice, his unlawful seizure of land, and the wrong doings of his over-powerful followers.[53] When, during the absences of Henry V in France, one or other of the king's younger brothers was deputed to preside over parliaments at Westminster – the duke of Bedford doing so in 1415, 1417, 1419 and December 1421, and the duke of Gloucester in 1420 – they, too, must have welcomed the presence in the commons of men whom they could trust. Bedford, for instance, was no doubt ably helped in 1415 by the Speaker, Sir Richard Redmayne, his feudal tenant and councillor, although following news of the king's triumph at Agincourt the commons were in any case disposed to be generous and gave him no trouble.[54]

The presence of a nobleman's retainers in the lower house might sometimes have proved crucial in carrying through changes in foreign policy. For instance, in January 1380 taxation was granted by the commons on the understanding that the money would be exclusively applied to finance an expedition to Brittany commanded by Thomas of Woodstock; and in the assembly of November following it was stressed that the new poll tax was expressly to be used to 'refresh' the leaders of this expedition, and honour the military covenants between the king and the earl. It was surely not coincidental that the Speaker in both parliaments was one of Woodstock's henchmen, Sir John Gildesburgh, who in the summer in between the parliamentary sessions was among those appointed to act as receivers of the subsidies allocated for the expeditionary force.[55] Yet the lords could not automatically depend upon financial backing for their schemes, as is evident from debates in the parliaments of October 1382 and February 1383. Two new military projects –

John of Gaunt's in Spain and Bishop Despenser's in Flanders – were in competition. While the lords firmly supported Lancaster's scheme, the commons obviously preferred the bishop's, and despite recourse, at the commons request, to consultation with a committee of ten peers (including both Lancaster and Despenser), the two houses failed to reach agreement. The ensuing debate triggered impassioned exchanges in which the brothers Sir Peter and Sir Philip Courtenay, sitting in the commons, were most vociferous in opposing Gaunt's policy, and their eloquence eventually won the day.[56]

By the end of the fourteenth century private individuals had begun to address petitions directly to 'the commons in parliament', asking them to request the king 'to ordain by authority of parliament' a specified remedy. By lending its support, the lower house thus assumed the role of an intermediary, whose formal assent might be taken for granted, and whose backing ensured that the petition in question would be dealt with sooner. A telling illustration of the complexity of relations between the lords and commons is provided by evidence that in the early fifteenth century members of the nobility frequently made use of this device. Although the process whereby particular common petitions won adoption in the lower house remains obscure, there can be little doubt that magnates' retainers acted as sponsors, perhaps enlisting the help of the Speaker.[57] William, Lord Clinton, chose to address his petition in the parliament of December 1421 to 'les honurables et tres sages communes', and was successful, despite the presence in the house of his opponent at law, Sir Richard Stanhope, himself not lacking in influence.[58] Reynold, Lord Grey of Ruthin, twice asked the commons to sponsor petitions in the parliament of 1401, and in the next parliament he had to rely on his friends in both houses to act for him in absentia, after he was taken captive in Wales by Owen Glendower, who demanded an extortionate 10,000 marks as the price for sparing his life.[59] It is perhaps surprising to find that on a number of occasions during the reigns of Henry IV and Henry V even the king's close kinsmen considered it advantageous to enlist the help of the commons to ensure a satisfactory hearing for their petitions. In October 1404 the commons asked the king to consider the good service done by his cousin, the duke of York, when lieutenant in Guienne, and his parlous state after selling off plate to pay his soldiers. In the house were Roger Flore and Sir Thomas Oudeby, both sitting for Rutland, and William

Worfton, representing Wiltshire, who, being all closely connected with the duke, doubtless supported the request.[60] The Beauforts quite often made similar use of their contacts in the lower house: in the years 1401 to 1421 no fewer than eight common petitions were presented on their behalf.[61] As by no means all of the returns for the parliaments of these years now survive, the full personnel of the lower house is no longer identifiable, but it is nevertheless clear that the Beauforts could always rely on the support of at least three prominent members of the commons, and on some occasions their known associates there numbered more than ten. The activities of their cousin, Thomas Chaucer, and of Richard Wyot, the steward of Bishop Beaufort's estates, hint that some electioneering went on to secure this end.[62]

Much less evidence, circumstantial or otherwise, survives to give us an idea of how support for the Percys and the Nevilles, rivals for political hegemony in the north of England, might have been organized in the house, but if need arose both noble families could find friends to put their case. When Henry Percy, earl of Northumberland, arrived at Westminster for the parliament of 1402, fresh from his crushing defeat of the Scots at Homildon Hill, he was greatly disturbed by Henry IV's orders that none of the important captives taken on the field were to be ransomed or released. Sharing his concern was one of the shire knights for Cumberland, John Skelton, who had captured the Scottish commander, Murdoch, earl of Fife, from whose ransom he had expected to make a substantial profit. Both Skelton and John Mitford, member for Northumberland and legal counsel to the earl, must have given their whole-hearted backing to a request, made by the commons to the king, that Percy should be shown special favour because of his victory.[63] The earl of Northumberland proved to be in even greater need of friends at Westminster when parliament met there in January 1404, following the abortive rebellion of his son and heir, Hotspur, the latter's defeat and death at the battle of Shrewsbury, and his own imprisonment without trial. It is perhaps surprising that notwithstanding the political climate the commons were ready to take the initiative on his behalf. The Speaker, Sir Arnold Savage, asked the king that the earl be allowed to appear in parliament to answer for his alleged crimes, and if it were found that he had committed any trespass against the crown that the king would of his special grace pardon him. The commons insisted that if no '*enblemessment*' were proved he should be reinstated in his forfeited lands. Henry IV, with poorly concealed ill humour, adjourned parliament and rode to Windsor where he grudgingly pardoned Northumberland, who then came with him to Westminster '*bien araie et de bonne chere*'. 'By judgement of the parliament' he was then delivered and excused of all treasons, felonies and trespasses, and took his seat in the lords. In a speech he thanked his peers for their correct judgement, and members of the lower house '*de lour bons coers et diligence faitz et monstrez*', and a witness to the events noted the earl's heartfelt appreciation of the support of those he called 'my frendes the comuns'. But the latter were not necessarily being partisan. Rather, their concern seems to have been for the establishment of a balance of power in the north, for they asked the king that '*pleine unite et concorde se purroient faire par entre les conts de Northumb' et Westmorland*', wherupon the earls were made to shake hands and embrace. They further requested that the earls, on their return home, would encourage their tenants, servants and familiars to live peaceably together.[64]

Most great landowners had a personal interest in parliamentary business at some point in their lives, and recruited among their chief advisers men well-versed in parliamentary procedure and used to taking a prominent role in the business of the lower house. When, in 1425, the claim of John Mowbray, the Earl Marshal, for precedence over the earl of Warwick came before the lords, detailed evidence was presented by the former Speaker Roger Hunt, who had already been sitting on Mowbray's council for at least ten years.[65] As in this, so in less well-documented cases, a considerable amount of discussion and strategic planning must have gone on behind the scenes in baronial councils. We are told that while parliaments were being held, John of Gaunt's council, like the king's, met in afforced session to settle legal difficulties, examine recalcitrant ministers, and call in overdue debts.[66] It is hardly conceivable that it did not also consider questions of policy, and the protection if not active promotion of the lord's interests, as they were likely to be affected by matters under debate in the two houses; and probable that councillors there present would be fully briefed regarding lines of argument to pursue in the commons. Not infrequently, a lord's advisers had more experience of parliaments than he had himself. Their contribution to discussions before and during parliamentary sessions doubtless often proved invaluable.

Such discussions behind the scenes may have assumed even greater importance if the nobleman in question was unable or unwilling to attend parliamentary sessions in person. As Roskell has amply demonstrated, the attendance in parliament of members of the house of lords was sometimes very poor, especially if they were not directly involved in government as members of the king's council. In some cases these absentee lords may have been content to be 'represented' at the assembly by their retainers, who could report back to them what had taken place. Of course, this might be done quite legitimately by lords unable to attend because of illness or owing to military or ambassadorial commitments elsewhere. To take one example: after he became blind, Edward Courtenay, earl of Devon, regularly appointed proxies to take his place in parliament, in 1406 formally nominating his cousin, Sir Hugh Luttrell, who had already been elected as a shire knight.[67] If a magnate was serving overseas and accordingly never received a writ of summons, this option of appointing a proxy was not open to him, but even so he might still wish to have at least one of his retainers in the commons to ensure that his interests, in a personal and political sense, were being well looked after. When John Mowbray, the Earl Marshal, was away in France with Henry V, his most highly paid councillor, John Lancaster, sat in four parliaments as a shire knight for Norfolk. Lancaster was no doubt aware that, whatever his brief from the county community, he also had a duty to perform as the earl's attorney-general and the guardian of his son and heir. Mowbray was most likely kept informed of events at home, but the initiative and responsibility for decisions must of necessity have rested with Lancaster and his fellow members of the earl's council.[68]

Then too, retainers clearly had a role to play in parliament when the head of the noble house they served was a minor. At least three of the most influential of the councillors of the late Richard Fitzalan, earl of Arundel, were present in the lower house in 1399 to press on behalf of his son and heir, Thomas, that the judgement of Richard II's last parliament against his father should be reversed. Likewise, in 1426 the Speaker, Sir Richard Vernon, used his influence to good effect on behalf of the young earl of Westmorland, whose petition for an increased allowance passed successfully. As a mesne tenant of the Nevilles and farmer of one of their more profitable manors, Vernon had a direct interest in this item of parliamentary business, and he was in fact then officially ordered to provide the new earl with some of the revenues freshly assigned to him. Also in the young man's interests, another member, Sir Peter Tilliol, petitioned with fellow executors of his father, the late Earl Ralph, for the correction of an error in an exchequer process, whereby the crown had been able to claim £100 a year from the estates of the deceased.[69]

Dowagers, who like minors technically went unrepresented in parliament, also found champions in the lower house. Joan de Bohun, countess of Hereford, invariably had a number of friends in the commons, among them her trusted counsellor Sir William Marney, to whom she married her great-niece; and her grand-daughter Anne, countess of Stafford, did not lack for supporters and advisers in the parliament of May 1421 when the division of the former de Bohun estates between her and Henry V was fully debated and eventually ratified. Although, as a special concession, Anne herself was permitted to attend part of the proceedings, she doubtless depended on the chief steward of her estates, John Tyrell, to advocate her cause in the lower house. At least nine of the shire knights returned for Essex between 1399 and 1421 were of the affinity of one or other of these two countesses, occupying twenty of the thirty-four seats available.[70] In 1402 Isabel, relict of William le Scrope, earl of Wiltshire, put in an impassioned plea for help, claiming that the forfeiture of le Scrope's estates had left her all but destitute. Her father, Sir Maurice Russell, then sitting for Gloucestershire, was most probably the member largely instrumental in securing a promise from the king, granted by the advice of the lords and at the special prayer of the commons, of an annuity of £100 a year for the rest of her life. Of course, the widowed Beatrice, countess of Arundel, being Portuguese-born, had no such close relations on hand to be her advocates. When petitioning the king in the parliament of May 1421 for her full entitlement to dower, she had to depend on a number of her employees, but most of all on the eloquence of William Ryman, her late husband's executor and confidante, whose wife had nursed the earl in his last illness.[71]

McFarlane challenged the highly influential writings of Richardson and Sayles and of Cam, finding the idea that the commons were subservient to the lords quite unacceptable. The key to further understanding of the relationship between the two houses was, he thought, a study of the individuals who sat in parliament, and he strongly endorsed the detailed biographical approach then, in the late 1930s, being undertaken by Roskell. No doubt the biographies now published in the *History of Parliament* will, as he predicted, 'render generalization difficult, if not impossible for a time', until their contents can be properly absorbed, but, as he expected, a more enterprising House of Commons than it was then fashionable to assume has indeed emerged.[72] Yet while biographies of independently minded individuals help to refute Richardson's claim that the commons were 'credulous and willing to be led' and were 'inspired and sustained' in any dealings in 'high politics' by the lords, we should remain alert to regional variations. Aristocratic influence was apparently rather greater in some areas than in others. We need to take into account the differences in personality, and involvement in politics of individual lords (not to mention of individual MPs such as Thomas Chaucer, who were clearly extremely forceful); the fact that evidence survives adequately for the affinities of some magnates, not at all for others; to accept that when it was politically expedient certain lords could and probably did secure the return of their most prominent retainers, but that they may not have felt the need to do so on anything like a regular basis. The impression of the strength of a gentry élite in some counties and of the dominance of the noble affinity in others is equally valid; nor should the staunch independence of certain urban communities be overlooked while undue stress is laid on the relative dependency of smaller manorial boroughs on their lords' favour.[73]

What these volumes reveal above all is the interdependence of lords and commons, and the need for management, whether orchestrated behind the scenes or directed centre-stage by articulate Speakers. The links between lords and knights made working together easier, but there were still difficulties in controlling the lower house. This was, no doubt, because the boroughs also fielded able spokesmen, among them many experienced lawyers, and merchants with a strong financial base could provide a powerful lobby when circumstances required. Furthermore, the weight of numbers was on the side of the townsmen. Relations between members of the two houses were highly complex, and a lord who dominated in his own country might be a mere cipher elsewhere. As a cautionary tale, I will end with the story of John Tregoose, a Cornish lawyer whose links with the chief justice, Sir Robert Tresilian, led to his persecution by Thomas Beauchamp, earl of Warwick, after Tresilian had been put to death by

Warwick and his fellow Appellants in the Merciless Parliament. In 1392, the earl, alleging that Tregoose was a bondman from his manor of Carnanton, had him seized on the Thames near Westminster Palace and hauled off to Warwick Castle, to be held prisoner. But Tregoose had powerful friends, at whose instigation the administration of the Beauchamp estates in Cornwall was disrupted, orders were sent to the sheriff to confiscate the earl's chattels, and Warwick was forced to release the captive and promise a fair hearing of his free status before the King's Bench. Tregoose then waylaid the Cornish jurors called before the judges at Derby, and persuaded them to turn back at Crediton, thus, as the earl complained to the parliament of 1394, forcing him to make the long journey to attend a court at Saltash, some 160 leagues away from his seat at Warwick, although he was ill at the time. Earl Thomas was outwitted at every turn and the lawyer triumphed.[74] I leave it to you to decide whether, when attending parliament as a member for the four Cornish boroughs he represented in turn, Tregoose would have meekly kowtowed to the lords.

Notes

1. *Paston L. & P.* II, p. 117. I am most grateful to Professor J.S. Roskell and Dr Carole Rawcliffe for their invaluable comments on drafts of this paper.

2. C.F. Richmond, 'After McFarlane', *History*, LXVIII (1983), pp. 57–60; K.B. McFarlane, 'Parliament and Bastard Feudalism', first printed in *T.R.H.S.* 4th series, XXVI (1944), pp. 53–79, then in McFarlane, *England*, pp. 1–21.

3. McFarlane, *England*, p. 4.

4. J.S. Illsley, 'Parliamentary Elections in the reign of Edward I', *B.I.H.R.* XLIX (1976), p. 31; L. Riess, *History of the English Electoral Law in the Middle Ages* (Cambridge 1940), pp. 52–4; S.J. Payling, 'The Widening Franchise: Parliamentary Elections in Lancastrian Nottinghamshire', *England in the Fifteenth Century: Proceedings of the 1986 Harlaxton Symposium*, D. Williams (ed.) (Woodbridge, 1987), pp. 172–3. Palmer concluded that 'it was, thus, the body of seneschals and bailiffs who normally elected the knights of the shire': R.C. Palmer, *The County Courts of Medieval England 1150–1350*, (Princeton, 1982), pp. 293–4.

5. *Commons 1386–1421*, I, pp. 339–40, 734.

6. Ibid. I, p. 669.

7. Ibid. I, p. 618.

8. Ibid. I, pp. 674–5, 677.

9. Ibid. I, pp. 722–4.

10. Ibid. I, p. 465.

11. *R.P.* III, pp. 601, 641; IV, p.8; *S.R.* II, pp. 162, 170.

12. *Commons 1386–1421*, I, pp. 343, 379, 573; P.R.O., Chancery, Writs and Returns of Members to Parliament, C.219/8/10, 13; *R.P.* III, p. 530.

13. *Commons 1386–1421*, I, pp. 277, 449, 554; III, pp. 673, 777; IV, p. 67; P.R.O., C.219/13/3, 5, 14/1; J.S. Roskell, *The Commons in the Parliament of 1422* (Manchester, 1954), pp. 16–17.

14. Carpenter, *Locality*, pp. 383–7.

15. *Commons 1386–1421*, I, pp. 667–9.

16. Roskell, *Commons*, pp. 18–20 a view not taken by R.E. Archer, 'The Mowbrays, Earls of Nottingham and Dukes of Norfolk, to 1432', (unpub. D. Phil. thesis, Oxford Univ. 1984), pp. 258–62, and in *Commons 1386–1421*, IV, pp. 791–2.

17. *Commons 1386–1421*, I, p. 459; Canterbury Cathedral, City and Diocesan R.O. city accounts, FA 1, f. 198.

18. *Commons 1386–1421*, I, p. 333; IV, pp. 714–15; S.M. Wright, *Derbyshire Gentry in the Fifteenth Century* (Derbyshire Record Society, VIII, 1983), p. 114.

19. *Commons 1386–1421*, IV, p. 627; R. Virgoe, 'The Cambridgeshire Election of 1439', *B.I.H.R.* XLVI (1973), pp. 96–101.

20. Members of the parliamentary peerage had always been exempted from contributing to the wages of the shire knights: L.C. Latham, 'Collection of the Wages of the Knights of the Shire in the Fourteenth and Fifteenth Centuries', *E.H.R.* XLVIII (1933), p. 458; S.B. Chrimes, 'The Liability of Lords for Payment of Wages of Knights of the Shire', *E.H.R.* XLIX (1934), pp. 306–8. It may well have been generally assumed from this that they should therefore have no direct say in the choice of MPs.

21. *Commons 1386–1421*, I, pp. 179–81.

22. Ibid. I, p. 294; II, pp. 58–63. Five years earlier Sir John had presided over John's election as shire knight for Devon, when he was barely twenty-two years old and completely inexperienced in local government.

23. Sir Henry Neville officiated as sheriff of Leicestershire in 1401 when his brother, Sir John, was elected after an absence from the commons of nigh on twenty years; and William Brokesby occupied the shrievalty of the same county at the time of his brother Bartholomew's first election to parliament in 1410: ibid. II, pp. 371–4; III, pp. 819–21. Another example is the return of Sir John Leek for Nottinghamshire in 1399 by his brother William: ibid. III, pp. 583–5, 586–7.

24. In Staffordshire in 1404, for example, Sir Humphrey Stafford returned his uncle Ralph: ibid. IV, pp. 439–42, 444–5.

25. Sir Thomas Radcliffe was returned for Lancashire by his father in May 1421 and again in 1423: ibid. IV, pp. 165–7.

26. Ibid. III, pp. 474–5; IV, pp. 337–8.

27. Ibid. I, pp. 511, 617; T.E. John, 'Sir Thomas Erpingham', *Norfolk Archaeology*, XXXV (1973), pp. 96–109.

28. *Commons 1386–1421*, I, pp. 687, 692, 699–700, 702, 707–8, 711; III, p. 452; IV, p. 523.

29. Ibid. I, p. 372; II, p. 379.

30. Ibid. I, p. 447.

31. Ibid. I, pp. 270–2, 595–7; II, pp. 531–2.

32. Ibid. II, pp. 99–101; P.R.O., King's Bench, Ancient Indictments, KB.9/176 m. 12 *et seq*; Coram Rege Rolls, KB.27/541 *rex rot.* 26.

33. *Commons 1386–1421*, II, pp. 266–7.

34. For brothers of the archbishop of Canterbury, see Robert and William Chichele (ibid. II, pp. 560–4), the archbishop of York, Sir John le Scrope (ibid. IV, pp. 323–6), the bishop of Exeter, Sir William Brantingham (ibid. II, pp. 338–41), the bishop of London, Robert Clifford (ibid. II, pp. 590–2), the bishop of Bangor, Richard Clitheroe II (ibid. II, pp. 602–3), and the bishop of Rochester, Thomas Langdon (ibid. III, pp. 556–7). For uncles of the earls of Devon and Suffolk, see Sir Hugh and Sir Philip Courtenay and Sir Edmund de la Pole (ibid. II, pp. 668–73; IV, pp. 96–9). Thomas Stafford was the nephew and heir of Bishop Edmund Stafford of Exeter, Thomas Wykeham was the great-nephew and heir of Bishop William Wykeham of Winchester, and (in what must have been a unique relationship) Robert Lowther was the son-in-law of Bishop William Strickland of Carlisle (ibid. III, pp. 639–41; IV, pp. 446–7, 920–2).

35. Ibid. II, pp. 313–14.

36. N. Saul, 'The Commons and the Abolition of Badges', *Parliamentary History*, IX (1990), pp. 302–15.

37. See e.g. Drew Barantyn (*Commons 1386–1421*, II, pp. 117–18) and John Woodcock (ibid. IV, pp. 896–8).

38. Ibid. I, pp. 354, 361, 670–2. Stafford is another possibility, but less clear cut: ibid. I, pp. 610–12.

39. Ibid. I, pp. 459, 461.

40. An argument used in discussing a later period by R. Horrox in 'Urban Patronage and Patrons in the Fifteenth Century', *Patronage, the Crown and the Provinces in Later Medieval England*, R.A. Griffiths (ed.) (Gloucester, 1981), pp. 145–66.

41. *Commons 1386–1421*, I, pp. 521–2, 524; III, pp. 259–60.

42. *R.P.* III, p. 611; *Commons 1386–1421*, I, pp. 92–3, 133; *Historical Collections of a Citizen of London in the Fifteenth Century*, J. Gairdner (ed.) (Camden Society, new series, XVII, 1876), p. 157. As McFarlane noted, the merchant class was very active in lobbying the commons in their interests all through the period, and in 1429 the representatives of Bishop's Lynn informed their local assembly that the citizens of London, York, Bristol, Hull and other towns proposed to labour the knights for a restriction of the subsidy: McFarlane, *Nobility*, p. 294, correcting M. McKisack, who translated '*proponunt laborare militibus comitatum pro restrictione subsidee*' as the burgesses working together with the knights: *The Parliamentary Representation of the English Boroughs during the Middle Ages* (1932), p. 131 and n. 3.

43. McFarlane, *Nobility*, pp. 280–1.

44. *Mum and the Sothsegger*, M. Day and R. Steele (eds.) (E.E.T.S. original series, CXCIX, 1936), pp. 25–6, as translated in *English Historical Documents, IV: 1327–1485*, A.R. Myers (ed.) (1969), p. 454. I have called it 'Richard the Redeless' not simply in imitation of McFarlane, but following D. Embree, 'Richard the Redeless and Mum and the Sothsegger, A Case of Mistaken Identity', *Notes and Queries*, CCXX (1975), pp. 4–12.

45. See A. Gross, 'Langland's Rats: A Moralist's View of Parliament', *Parliamentary History*, IX (1990), pp. 286–301, which develops the arguments of H.M. Cam, The Relation of English

Members of Parliament to their Constituencies in the Fourteenth Century: A Neglected Text', *Liberties and Communities in Medieval England* (Cambridge 1944), pp. 227–8, 231–2.

46. *Commons 1386–1421*, IV, pp. 876–7.

47. *Chronicon Angliae 1328–1388*, E.M. Thompson (ed.) (R.S., 1874), p. 112; *Commons 1386–1421*, I, p. 49; III, p. 445.

48. S.K. Walker, *The Lancastrian Affinity 1361–1399* (Oxford, 1990), p. 239; A. Goodman, 'John of Gaunt: Paradigm of the Late Fourteenth Century Crisis', *T.R.H.S.* 5th series, XXXVII (1987), pp. 133–48, especially pp. 135–6.

49. For instance, what interpretation should we place on Lancaster's dealings with Sir Maurice Berkeley of Uley? In 1391 the duke arbitrated in a property dispute which went in favour of Berkeley's opponent. Perhaps as compensation, he then named Berkeley as one of his bachelors, retaining him for life in peace and war, and awarding him an annuity of £20. Sir Maurice had already been elected to represent Gloucestershire in the parliament which was due to assemble the very next day, but can we deduce from this that he would have supported the policies of his new lord if called upon to do so? See *Commons 1386–1421*, II, pp. 201–2.

50. *Commons 1386–1421*, I, pp. 185–91; T. Favent, *Historia Mirabilis Parliamenti*, M. McKisack (ed.) (Camden Miscellany XIV, Camden Society, 3rd series, XXXVII, 1926), p. 14. Appearances counted for much, which was why the counter-appellants deliberately aped the Appellants of 1388 when they appeared in parliament in September 1397. On this occasion the commons made oral requests to the king to attest the loyalty of Henry of Bolingbroke and Thomas Mowbray, the two youngest Appellants who were now believed to have exercised a moderating influence in 1388, and Bolingbroke sought full pardon for his part in the '*riotes, troubles et malfaits*'. In the commons he had the support of three of his own retainers and ten of his father's. Those sporting the 'SS' collar as a symbol of their relationship with the house of Lancaster would have stood out in the assembly as a distinct group, sharing something, perhaps much, in common. The other surviving uncle of the king, Edmund of Langley, duke of York, also gained the voice of the commons, who asked that his innocence as a member of the commission of 1386 be attested. We know that at least six of his retainers were present. *Commons 1386–1421*, I, pp. 84, 197–208; R.P. III, pp. 353, 367.

51. *Commons 1386–1421*, I, pp. 209–17.

52. Ibid. I, pp. 218–24, 595–6.

53. Ibid. I, pp. 577, 646–7; R.P. IV, pp. 78, 82, 87–8.

54. *R.P.* IV, pp. 62, 111–13, 116, 123, 151–3; *Commons 1386–1421*, I, pp. 22–3; IV, p. 186.

55. *Commons 1386–1421*, I, p. 126; III, pp. 185–7.

56. Ibid. I, pp. 106–7; II, p. 671; *Westminster Chronicle 1381–1394*, L.C. Hector and B.F. Harvey (eds.) (Oxford, 1982), p. 36.

57. *Commons 1386–1421*, I, pp. 77–9, 82–3; A.R. Myers, *Crown, Household and Parliament in Fifteenth Century England*, C.H. Clough (ed.) (1985), pp. 14, 17–18.

58. *R.P.* IV, pp. 151–3. Clinton's dispute with Stanhope was not apparently related to the matter in hand: ibid. IV, p. 165; *Commons 1386–1421*, IV, pp. 453–4.

59. Grey's supporters in the commons, most notably Reynold Ragon, sitting for Bedfordshire, and Sir Gerard Braybrooke, one of the shire knights for Essex, petitioned the king to allow the hostage's friends to raise loans in order to meet Glendower's demands, and within a matter of days

Braybrooke, in conjunction with his father and his uncle, the bishop of London, secured a royal licence enabling them to sell off some of Grey's estates if need be: *R.P.* III, pp. 480, 487; *Commons 1386–1421*, II, p. 348.

60.   *R.P.* III, p. 553; *Commons 1386–1421*, III, pp. 91–2, 884–5; IV, pp. 899–900 (Worfton's connexion was with the duke's late father).

61.   *R.P.* III, pp. 460, 483, 488, 534, 550; IV, pp. 17, 111–13, 132–5. Bishop Beaufort's course of action in 1421 directly stemmed from the commons' refusal to grant taxation: G.L. Harriss, *Cardinal Beaufort* (Oxford, 1988), pp. 1079.

62.   *Commons 1386–1421*, I, pp. 222, 228, 235; II, 524–32; IV, pp. 931–3.

63.   Ibid. III, p. 745; IV, p. 378.

64.   C.M. Fraser, 'Some Durham Documents relating to the Hilary Parliament of 1404', *B.I.H.R.* XXIV (1961), pp. 192–9; *R.P.* III, pp. 524–5.

65.   C. Rawcliffe, 'Baronial Councils in the Later Middle Ages' , in *Patronage, Pedigree and Power in Later Medieval England*, C. Ross (ed .) (Gloucester, 1979), p. 95; *Commons 1386–1421*, III, pp. 457–8.

66.   Walker, *Lancastrian Affinity*, p. 237.

67.   J.S. Roskell, 'The Problem of Attendance of the Lords in Medieval Parliaments', *B.I.H.R.* XXIX (1956), pp. 153–204; *Commons 1386–1421*, I, pp. 27–39; III, p. 658; P.R.O. Special Collections, Parliamentary Proxies, S.C.10/52/18. For Sir William Bagot reporting to the countess of Derby what was happening in the Cambridge parliament of 1388, see P.R.O. Duchy of Lancaster, Various Accounts, D.L.28/1/2.

68.   *Commons 1386–1421*, III, pp. 548–51. Similarly, Richard Sterysacre, another of Mowbray's attorneys and councillors, and one, indeed, whose entire career was devoted to service to the earl and his family, took a seat in the house in 1420: ibid. IV, pp. 472–3. While sitting in the parliament of 1423, William Yerde did his best for *his* lord, John Holand, earl of Huntingdon, who was then a prisoner of war in France, actively helping to obtain Huntingdon's release by promoting a petition for parliamentary authority for an exchange of high-ranking prisoners with the French: ibid. IV, p. 936; *R.P.* IV, p. 247.

69.   *R.P.* III, pp. 435–6, 469–70; *C.P.R. 1422–9*, p. 334; *Commons 1386–1421*, IV, pp. 617, 714. The Fitzalan retainers in the parliament of 1399 were John Burley I (*Commons 1386–1421*, II, pp. 430–1), Sir Payn Tiptoft (ibid. IV, pp. 628–30), and Thomas Young I (ibid. IV, pp. 938–9). Retainers of the late duke of Gloucester, the late earl of Arundel and the earl of Warwick proved less successful on their own account when they petitioned that the ransoms and fines '*torcenoursement prys*' from them by Richard II be refunded '*en oevre de charitee*': *R.P.* III, p. 440. The house of Stafford suffered from three long minorities in the late fourteenth and early fifteenth centuries, yet even when the young earls themselves were unable to direct their own affairs their kinsmen and retainers were often returned to parliament. For example, Sir Nicholas Stafford, a cousin of the second earl, Hugh (*d.* 1386), who headed the latter's council and subsequently directed the administration of the family estates, sat in nine parliaments between January 1377 and November 1390: *Commons 1386–1421*, I, p. 604; IV, pp. 442–4. Similarly, Sir Hugh Cheyne sat in parliament five times during the minority of Roger Mortimer, earl of March, having witnessed his father's will in 1380 and then been appointed to administer it; and on becoming a life member of the earl's council in 1397 he promised that if his lord died first he would continue to advise his heirs. He was to be returned

again during the minority of Earl Roger's heir: ibid. II, pp. 545–7; G.A. Holmes, *Estates of the Nobility in Fourteenth Century England* (Cambridge, 1957), p. 130.

70. *Commons 1386–1421*, I, pp. 393–4; III, pp. 693–5; *R.P.* IV, pp. 135–40.

71. *R.P.* III, pp. 483–4; IV, p. 130; *Commons 1386–1421*, IV, pp. 252, 268–70. On other occasions the commons supported petitions made on behalf of the duchess of Ireland and successive countesses of Kent, who were no doubt reassured by the presence in the house of certain of their personal advisers: *R.P.* III, pp. 432, 460, 535; IV, pp. 143–5. See also the assistance given to the widowed countess of March by the Speaker Sir Thomas Waweton in the parliament of 1425: *Commons 1386–1421*, IV, pp. 790–1.

72. McFarlane, *Nobility*, pp. 2967. Such was McFarlane's commitment to the idea of a full biographical study of the members of parliament that in 1953 he accepted an invitation from the Editorial Board of the *History of Parliament* to take responsibility for the section devoted to the reign of Edward III, and he promised, with the misguided optimism shared by all the *History*'s early editors, that although other commitments would prevent him from signing a contract before 1960 the work would be completed in the following five years. From the beginning, however, there were differences of opinion with the 'modernists' over McFarlane's insistence that his volumes should contain, besides biographies of members of the commons, those of spiritual and temporal peers and of persons who attended parliaments by virtue of a special summons. Perhaps his earlier criticisms of Sir John Neale, who, he considered, had 'rewritten the prologue to suit his play', lay behind clashes which caused him to decline invitations to attend meetings of the Board in 1955 and 1956, to accept that of July 1957 'without any great hope that the time will be well spent', and then to withdraw from the project: History of Parliament archives, boxes N24, N27.

73. A point made by P.R. Coss in 'Bastard Feudalism Revised', *P.P.* CXXV (1989), pp. 57–8.

74. *R.P.* III, p. 326; *Commons 1386–1421*, IV, pp. 643–4.

7

WAS THERE POPULAR POLITICS IN FIFTEENTH-CENTURY ENGLAND?

I.M.W. Harvey

The political history of fifteenth-century England has always, from the fifteenth century onwards, been primarily aristocratic and upper class in its focus. It has been concerned with the governors rather than the governed. If in recent decades more emphasis has been laid on the broader-based county communities who existed below the magnates, these gentry have been revealed as themselves members of the same ruling élite, and rather more active as agents of government than their social superiors. Looking at statistics emphasizes just how small an élite it was. According to the rough guide offered by taxation returns made in 1436, there were 51 lay peers, 183 greater knights, 750 lesser knights, 1,200 esquires, 1,600 men with incomes of £10 to £19 a year from land and 3,400 with incomes between £5 and £9, which put them on the border between yeomen and gentlemen.[1] All told, these figures come to a total of 7,184. Even when members of households and ecclesiastics are included in the calculation the proportion cannot be more than two per cent of the total population of England (which may be hazarded as standing at somewhere around two million). The figures cannot be exact, but the overall picture is unambiguous: the political society of the realm was formed by a tiny minority of the population. It is worth asking the question, even if the answer is as compressed as this one, what part, if any, was played in national politics by the remaining ninety-eight per cent of the population.

For present purposes 'popular politics' is not understood to mean popular political goals or a set of agenda distinct from those of the ruling class. By that definition there was no popular politics in fifteenth-century England. With very few exceptions, the disaffected commons of the realm sought reform in the shape of new governors, not radical new policies; in the way things were done more than what was done. For the vast majority, ideas about government were

not formulated in theoretical terms but took the form of certain long-held
assumptions about the personal nature of government that probably appeared
to them to be common sense: politics was to do with lordship and loyalty. These
were assumptions centred, of course, upon the person of the king. The realm as
a whole was his, so all men held their land ultimately of the king; but those of
his humble tenants who held directly of him, on land known as 'ancient
demesne', regarded themselves as especially privileged and protected, through
the mystique of a close association with the Crown.[2] The French were 'the
king's enemies' and the central courts administered 'the king's peace'. To
commit treason was to commit a crime against the king; in 1450 the cry of
'traitor' condemned several of the king's ministers to popular execution.
Schoolboys learning Latin were set to translate English tags about the happiness
of the realm in which the king was feared and loved and the necessity of a king's
love for his subjects.[3] Other general beliefs were that the king should ideally live
off his own sources of income and should be guided by his natural counsellors,
that is, by the top rank of the hereditary nobility and not by court favourites
elevated beyond their natural rank. All these were old and familiar political
assumptions. However, more can be said about popular politics in the fifteenth
century than to note its traditional attitudes, and 'popular politics' here will
centre upon political influence. By this definition popular politics not only
existed but grew in importance in the fifteenth century. During this period the
common people can be seen growing some political muscle, evidently not
because there were new theories but because of new circumstances, economic,
social and political. They began to act as if they thought they mattered in
politics, as if they were part of the political commonweal. This edging into the
political arena, by the very people whom their monarchs might have hoped to
have been able to discount, forms the theme of this discussion.

The common voice made itself heard in politics by various means. First, to
look at the crudest method, there was the direct intervention of the mob, which
occurred with increasing frequency in the second half of the century. In 1400
great crowds of peasants in Essex lynched Richard II's half-brother John, earl of
Huntingdon, in revenge for Huntingdon's part in the death of Thomas, duke of
Gloucester.[4] Similar popular executions made by crowds taking justice into their
own hands occurred in 1450 when the hated courtiers of Henry VI, Adam

Moleyns, bishop of Chichester, and William Ayscough, bishop of Salisbury, were, in two separate incidents, dragged from buildings by furious crowds and publicly put to death. Such outbreaks of collective violence became markedly more frequent during the ensuing period of civil war. In 1460 the earl of Warwick spared a potential prisoner, Lord Scales, and let him go free from the Tower only to see him slaughtered by Thames watermen; in 1463 the commons of Northamptonshire made an attempt upon the life of the duke of Somerset; and the earl of Salisbury's death after the battle of Wakefield when he had been imprisoned in Pontefract castle came about, as one chronicler put it, because 'the commune peple of the cuntre, whyche loued hym nat, took hym owte of the castelle by violence and smote of his hed'.[5] A further example is the murder in 1469 of the earl of Devon by the common people of Bridgwater in Somerset. McFarlane, who noted these popular interventions during the Wars of the Roses, had doubts about the discrimination of the common people and questioned how gullible they were in the face of political persuasion.[6] The point to note here, however, is that none of these brutal incidents was an act of indiscriminate violence: individuals were targeted for specific reasons by an apparently informed public. The Thames boatmen hated Lord Scales for having bombarded their city, and the commons of Northamptonshire had just measure of the treacherous duke of Somerset; the chronicler Gregory could only lament their failure to put the duke to death 'for the saving of his life at that time caused many a man's death soon after'.[7] Such incidents make clear the two features of fifteenth-century life mentioned above: popular concern with persons rather than abstractions and an increasing willingness on the part of the common people to take matters into their own hands.

More surprising, perhaps, considering the government's disdain for those it governed, is the degree to which the common people entered the political sphere with their requests and grievances. They could not vote for their MP but they were not to be prevented from petitioning parliament.[8] In 1421 the fishermen of the Thames petitioned parliament asking that the waters of the Thames should be better preserved, whilst the inhabitants of Oxfordshire, Berkshire and Buckinghamshire wished for some drastic action to be taken to remedy the nuisance they suffered from violent and disorderly Oxford students. In 1461 the tenants of the bishop of Winchester's manor of East Meon were involved in a dispute with the bishop. They sent a deputation to parliament to present a petition complaining of the new customs and services demanded of them. It was more usual, however, for individuals or local groups with petitions to ask their MP to present their petitions on their behalf rather than doing so in person. A problem for the ordinary subject was that not only were petitions increasingly being delayed or ignored but also the extent of bribery meant that petitioning could be an expensive business. Parliament, then, was not an entirely closed channel for those with something personal or local to voice but it was not a highly effective one. It could not deal at all with general discontent at political malaise such as was felt during the late 1440s. Frustration at a lack of constitutional power in the face of widespread government corruption drove thousands of the inhabitants of south-east England to rise up in 1450 and follow those who were petitioning the king for reform.

Even more surprising than their petitioning, however, is evidence that the common people believed that the king needed their goodwill. Some verses written probably about 1450 expressed the sentiments of a commoner frustrated by his political impotence in the face of court corruption:

> Trowth and pore men ben appressed
> And myscheff is nothyng redressed.

Meanwhile, another poem of the same time, the so called *Advice to the Court*, undertook to advise the king and his councillors on behalf of the common people, warning them, significantly, 'Loose not the loue of alle þe commynalte'.[9] This assertion of the king's need for his common people turned up again in even bolder fashion in one of the manifestos produced by the rebel followers of Cade in 1450 in which, after a recital of all the wrongs done by the traitors of the realm, that is, Henry VI's evil councillors, the question is posed: if the common people were disposed against their sovereign lord, as God forbid, how might his favoured councillors help him?

Much of the explanation for the changed political atmosphere of the fifteenth century lies in the fact that the populace lived in a world so different economically and socially from that of their forebears in the fourteenth century. Economic changes set under way during the decades after the Black Death, which continued into the fifteenth century, created new social groupings with their own social aspirations. Severe depopulation did not, of course, significantly alter the proportion of governing class to governed, but the withering of servile bonds, the liberation of the labouring agricultural classes from their most irksome renders and services, the greater availability of land and the creation of a prospering peasant yeoman group, transformed the life of the villages and the towns. A more fluid society developed which lent itself less well to rigid distinctions, one in which 'the same person could equally well be classified as landlord, customary tenant, lessor, lessee, peasant farmer or merchant'.[10] Parish communities were now led by a yeoman group who as landlords and employers felt that they had a stake in society and who in the role of constables, churchwardens and jurymen took an interest in life both within and outside the parish.[11] It was not to be assumed either that that all the members of this upper peasant stratum had been born and raised in the parish in which they farmed, or that they were fit for no other livelihood. John Cathero of Salisbury described himself as pewterer, alias mercer, alias chapman, alias organ-player, alias yeoman.[12] A characteristic of these late medieval communities, especially towns, was the 'pairing of individual economic assertiveness with group political activity'.[13] This could be the case in national as well as petty, local politics.[14]

A very significant feature of this acquisitive, assertive group, which must be thought of as including prosperous artisans and better-off husbandmen as well as yeomen, was its increasing literacy. It furthered the demand for elementary and grammar schools around the country, knowing what opportunities education offered. By the mid-sixteenth century these men would be idealized nostalgically by their successful offspring. Bishop Latimer, a child of Edward IV's reign, recalled affectionately, 'My father was a yeoman'.[15] England in the fifteenth century has been described as a 'relatively literate and much governed society'.[16] This could not be said of any earlier period, and it made a difference to political life. At the most obvious level it meant that the disaffected had the means to organize themselves more skilfully. They could write manifestos, employ letter carriers[17] or even send secret messages written in invisible ink.[18] It meant that the south-east of England could rise up in 1450 in an 'articulate and literate demonstration against bad government'.[19] However, literacy was not an essential prerequisite of revolt and the revolts themselves were temporary and sporadic. A much more permanent and all-pervasive influence exercised by greater literacy upon the politics of the nation was that it helped to produce a population who knew in rough outline what was going on nationally. This may help explain why, as a rule, mob violence was not of a random or indiscriminate nature. Presentments brought before the King's Bench for seditious speech reveal a population who talked politics in their homes and alehouses, be it in Alice Bentley's house at Ipswich, in The Tabard at Chichester, The Bell in Fleet Street or The Hart in Salisbury.[20] A yeoman who sat in a friend's house in Westminster in the late summer of 1457 was informed enough not only to know that the king had been hurt at the battle of St Albans but also to deplore the fact that the injury had not been fatal.[21] Some were interested enough to write down the information they gathered, as did Robert Reynes, a manorial agent and church-reeve active at the end of the fifteenth century, who included in his commonplace book the principal battles in the Wars of the Roses.[22]

Another indicator of the apparently rather high level of popular awareness of topical political affairs comes from the political verse which circulated among much of the general public. A good deal of this verse was densely allusive. It pre-supposed in its readers and listeners a certain amount of basic information. Its function was not as reportage or narrative. Major political figures were not always explicitly named but could appear symbolically in the guise of their heraldic badges or metaphorically as animals. One needed to know that the duke of Suffolk's badge was a clog and chain such as were attached to tame apes in order to understand allusion to 'Iack napys', or that Suffolk was reputed to have murdered the duke of Gloucester at the 1447 parliament at Bury St Edmunds in order to catch the significance of 'þis fox at bury slowe oure grete gandere'. Likewise, the meaning of the lines

> Witnes of Humfrey, Henry and Johan,
> Whiche late were one lyve, and now be they goon

would be opaque unless one already knew that the death of Henry VI's father and uncles, the dukes of Gloucester and Bedford, was being mourned. Admittedly these were very public facts. In a realm in which the political community was so small one did not have to be privy to court circles to recognize the badge of one of the most famous men in the country in his day, or to have heard the rumour about the duke of Gloucester's sudden death, or to know the names of the brothers of the hero-king, Henry V. Such facts evidently formed a basic common currency among the population. Some of them were taught by doggerel rhymes, such as a chronology offering an easily memorized guide to all the monarchs since the conquest which taught that the salient facts about the reign of Henry VI included,

> The duke of bedford wyth gode in tent
> Was hys uncle and of Fraunce Regent
> The duke of gloucetre hys uncle also
> Of Ingelond was protector thoo.[23]

The people gained their information about national affairs from a variety of other sources. There were the royal proclamations read aloud in English in the seaports and market towns of the land, telling of victories, truces and general pardons; also the sermons and processions at royal request to bolster royal messages.[24] But for the literate individual considerably more detailed information about persons or political issues could be gathered from reading the handbills and schedules of articles posted on doors, windows and town crosses. These were becoming an almost automatic part of rallying public opinion in local and national squabbles. Their contents would also reach the illiterate person in the street since readers read not silently but aloud. In 1431 a widespread poster campaign formed part of 'Lollardy's final attempt to achieve its ends by an appeal to public opinion'.[25]

Gossip and rumour also played a major part in the spreading of information and the formation, or indeed inflaming, of popular opinion, for seditious rumours were part of political life. There could be important repercussions to what was 'the common sayng withe euere markett man that cumes frome London'.[26] It tells of the seriousness with which rumour was treated that one form which the government's active discouragement of the common people's political awareness took was its employment of spies. This was justifiable anxiety in view of what Professor Ross has called the 'credulity and volatility of

the common people'.[27] Spies were paid to travel the roads and to eavesdrop in
villages and alehouses in order to keep those in authority informed of what the
common people were saying and doing. Villagers and townspeople were probably
well aware that not all itinerants, be they servants, musicians, merchants or priests,
were likely to be precisely what they appeared to be. In 1450 resentment at such
underhand surveillance burst into violence when John Wodehouse, a valet and
messenger of the king, was murdered in Lincolnshire on the suspicion of being a
royal spy.[28] With the onset of civil war spying intensified. In 1466 Edward IV
introduced the new financial practice of permitting sheriffs an allowance of
between £40 and £300 for their costs in detecting treason.[29] Spies were seen as
essential agents of government. In 1497, faced with an uprising from the West
Country, Henry VII from the safety of Surrey sent out half a dozen spies to keep
him informed of developments; then, once the rebellion was over, forty-six spies
were employed to serve the king's commissioners who worked their way through
the west of England, punishing it with fines.[30]

The government's desire to curb and supervise those it governed had also to
meet the challenge of the changing social stratification of society. This it did by
means of legislation, which in itself betrayed the alarming fact that the
boundary lines of political society had become blurred. No longer could it be
automatically assumed that the running of the country was in the hands of the
aristocracy and gentry if the matter had to be stated explicitly by statute.
Legislation of the parliament of 1429 stipulated that only those persons with
forty shillings or more income a year from freehold land could vote in the shire
elections for their member of parliament. In similar vein, the parliament of
1445–6 excluded those of the rank of yeoman and below from standing as
knights of the shire or as burgesses. County representatives were to be:

> notable knights of the same counties for which they shall be chosen, or
> otherwise notable esquires, gentlemen born, of the same counties as shall be
> able to be knights, and no man to be such knight which standeth in the
> degree of a yeoman or under.[31]

Acting as a JP was also something which had to remain in the preserve of the
ruling élite, an office to be filled by justices, magnates and, in increasing

numbers, the gentlemen of the county, the knights and esquires of the county 'establishment'.[32]

On the social side, labour legislation from the fourteenth century had attempted to hold down the wages that workers might command and in the mid 1440s parliament renewed its efforts at fixing wage rates. It was intended to stop the activities of such persons as the Middlesex labourer who during the 1430s attempted to charge his employer $8^{1}/_{2}d$ a day at a time when a skilled workman would command $6d$ or less.[33] Furthermore, sumptuary statutes of 1463 and 1483 tried to prevent the lower classes from dressing in a manner above their station. The common people were to look as common as they were. Similarly the countryside, as home to the greatest of all aristocratic passions, hunting, could not therefore be accessible to all and sundry. A hunting statute of 1390 banned hunting to lay persons with lands or tenements worth less than forty shillings a year, and new swathes of non-royal land were fenced off for the protection of deer. In 1447, Adam Moleyns, bishop of Chichester, was granted a royal licence to impark 12,000 acres of land, wood, meadow, heath and furze in Sussex, that is, three years before his death at the hands of an angry mob.[34] Governments viewed the preserving of game not merely as the protection of an aristocratic recreation but also as a matter of social control. Poachers were not just deer stealers but potential agitants meeting up in the woods to plot sedition. The preamble to the 1485 act recited how 'persons in great number had often times hunted by night as by day in divers forests, parks and warrens by colour whereof rebellions, insurrections, riots, robberies and murders had ensued'.[35]

Another time-honoured measure taken by the authorities to stem the growing political and social confidence of the populace, in addition to spying on them and legislating against them, was to terrorize them. In 1451, after a judicial commission had gone through Kent punishing rebels, over a score of heads stood on London bridge. The commission was known as 'the harvest of heads'.[36] Philippa Maddern is probably right in her view that historians have exaggerated the general level of violence in fifteenth-century society:[37] the distribution of human quarters certainly shocked the chroniclers who heard tell of them and the men and women who saw them. The town of New Romney bribed a man carrying a quartered rebel to pass on to some other destination, while at Norwich some persons unknown stole the city's alloted quarter of the rebel leader Jack Cade off the city gate by night.[38]

So feared was the avenging arm of government that even the threat of it could panic a population into angry, defensive revolt. When rebels in Kent in 1450 drew up a list of complaints and causes of their assembly together on Blackheath the first they mentioned was that it was rumoured 'that Kent shuld be dystroyed with a ryall power and made a wylde fforest' in punishment for the murder of the king's favourite, the duke of Suffolk, off the Kent coast.[39] Who made such an idea openly noised about the county is another question, but the point here is that people could find such an idea credible. Likewise the inhabitants of Sherborne, Dorset, engaged in a rancorous dispute with the bishop of Salisbury, came forward and paid a fine for a royal pardon when they were given to believe that otherwise the king would reap retribution from the whole shire.[40] In 1470 a similar scare about government attack was alleged to have roused rebels in Lincolnshire, not that the king would turn the country into a wild forest, but that there should be another harvest of heads. The rebel captain, Sir Robert Welles, had proclamations made in all the churches of the shire that the commons should resist the king as he was coming to destroy them. Royal judges, it was claimed, would sit and have a great number of the common people hanged and drawn. Such a threat was too plausible to be easily ignored.[41] Governments were there to protect their own interests, not those of the people they governed. In 1489 William Caxton sought to ingratiate himself with his patron Henry VII by complimenting him upon the fact that 'I haue not herd ne redde that ony prynce hath subdued his subgettis with lasse hurte'.[42] That was before Henry's suppression of the rising of 1497, the news of which left a forceful impression on the young Thomas More. He would later refer to it through one of his fictional characters as a 'ghastly massacre'.[43]

Despite living under a series of brutally repressive monarchs, the country had a resilient population. One of Bishop Fox's sayings to those he was training up in government service under Henry VII was to observe the circumstances and misery the English would abide and endure.[44] If on occasion temporarily crushed, they were never permanently deterred from talking and behaving as if they had a stake in the country's political life. Four factors are worth considering as contributions to this surprising belief of the general public in its own significance. First, although they may not have borne any of the burden of the country's administration they did play a clear part in its defence. They could be called up to fight for it. Since the later part of the thirteenth century the Statute of Winchester had obliged every free man to equip himself in accordance with his wealth and status in readiness to keep the peace within his respective county and to be prepared to defend the realm. The statute was reissued in 1437 and 1442. All men between the ages of 16 and 60 below the rank of knight or esquire had not only to be armed according to their status but to be trained in those arms.[45] Those next to the bottom of a descending scale were obliged to supply themselves with cutlasses, spears, knives and other lesser weapons, and all other men below that status were to have bows and arrows or bows and bolts. By a system of county levy, a selection of these men of the counties – yeomen, agricultural labourers and artisans – could be called upon to supply troops to the king when there were campaigns in Wales or Scotland and when there was a threat of invasion, although by the fifteenth century service abroad had long since ceased to be an obligatory service and was contractual.[46] The threat of a French invasion or raid on the south coast of England would have the county levies raised in Hampshire, Sussex and Kent as well as letters sent off to the nobility and gentry to resist invasion. An aspect of this local, county preparedness against attack was the network of beacons set up on prominent sites along the coast and inland which had to be constantly manned as a national security alarm system during times of alert. The beacons, like the system of county levy, were organized at hundred and township level. Hundred courts imposed fines upon those tithingmen who defaulted on their vigils.[47] During periods of active warfare in Scotland, Wales and France the country as a whole suffered the nuisance and disruption to life which it brought. It was not only the population of the North who were affected by border warfare and of the South who suffered attacks to the Channel ports, but all round the coast ships could be requisitioned and all over the country bitter resentment was aroused by the purveyance of foodstuffs and stores. Responsibility for the internal peace of the county and involvement in the national security of the country thus impinged very directly upon the lives of the common people. Their noble, military caste might lead them, but the whole realm was part of the war machine.

Intimately connected to this subject of the country's defence, taxation was another lever which hoisted the general population on to the political stage. The usual form of direct taxation of a fifteenth and tenth, based on an assessment of movable property rather than land or income, was requested of all the realm, not just of the well-to-do, usually having been granted to pay for the expenses of war. Among the common people these fiscal levies could be evaded only by the very poorest or by those living in special jurisdictions or under special dispensations, such as the inhabitants of the earldom of Chester or the Cornish tinners.[48] Since there was no regular imposition of this direct taxation it always carried a sense of a special grant, perhaps the more grievous for that. Moreover, the population could feel aggrieved that royal impositions of taxation were given the consent of a parliamentary commons which spoke not merely for the enfranchised forty-shilling freeholders and above but also on behalf of all the unenfranchised taxpayers of the boroughs and shires. Often it meant that the common people, as one chronicler put it, 'grucchid sore ayens thaym that hadde the gouernaunce of the land'.[49] It aligned the governors against the governed. Employed as royal collectors, the local county gentry were very conspicuously seen to be aligned with those who had the governance of the land. In 1446 some forty and more Hampshire villagers had their tax collector, a gentleman of the shire, taken to court for overcharging them for the half fifteenth and tenth he had gathered the previous year.[50] Taxation was such a perennial grievance that it was naturally exploited by those seeking political support. So in 1460 the would-be reforming Yorkist earls played to the political gallery, itemizing in their manifesto of complaints 'howe ofte the seyde commones have ben gretely and merueylously charged with taxes and tallages to theyre grete enporysshyng'.[51] However, paying taxes was a form of direct participation – albeit a reluctant, contentious form of participation – in politics. The common people were given a sense of being active participants, petty shareholders, in the running of the realm. It made them assertive. In 1416 in Cheshire armed crowds at townships in the hundred of Macclesfield prevented collectors of a mise from doing their duties on the grounds, so an indictment later said, that the subsidy should not be levied from them because it had not been granted by the assent of all the community of the county. They wanted to know whether it was the king's will that they should be taxed.[52] It was an extraordinary objection to raise, which provides a very clear example of the kind of desire for accountability which tax demands could generate. It is noteworthy too that the king was seen as the people's champion who it was believed did not want money from those who had not granted it. Elsewhere in Cheshire later that same month inhabitants demanded permission from the county authorities that they should not be taxed until they knew the king's will about the subsidy, and if it was the king's will that they should have the subsidy levied from them then they wanted to be asked whether they would contribute voluntarily.[53] More than any other issue, unduly heavy or misspent taxation goaded the king's subjects – and not just the humble – to revolt. Taxation was a grievance which figured in the revolts of 1403, 1450, 1489 and 1497.[54]

A third factor in political life which encouraged self-confidence among the populace, in addition to their roles as county levies and taxpayers, was the psychological benefit of oral tradition: the inherited memory of the events of 1381. The magnitude of that rising's destruction and of its aspirations could not but change attitudes among the governing and the governed classes who lived during the century of its aftermath. After 1381 nobody could characterize the common people as politically harmless. If common knowledge knew one fact ahout Richard II it was that

> In hys tyme the comenate of Kent
> Uppe a Rossen and to London Went.[55]

The Great Revolt set a precedent which caused the upper classes of English society to live in dread of another such upheaval, never mind that the impositions and burdens of serfdom were no longer a grievance for most workers on the land. It would seem that the commons of the fifteenth century looked back to 1381 as an important point of reference which encouraged and fortified potential insurgents. For the inhabitants of the south of England the events of 1381 would appear to have established a blueprint for the conduct of a regional uprising. The procedure was to rouse the counties of the south-east to ride upon London, pitch camp at Blackheath and then enter London where the king was to be petitioned and some of his evil counsellors slaughtered. In January 1450 men in eastern Kent planned such an insurrection, very soon detected and extinguished, which intended to do just that, to raise the counties of Kent, Surrey, Sussex, Essex and Hertfordshire to march upon London. A few months later, in June 1450, Cade's followers did successfully put into action a rising on the same plan as 1381. They rode up to Blackheath from Kent, Surrey and Sussex whilst others from Essex approached London from the east; they drew up a petition to present to the king; entered London and slaughtered some of the king's council. In 1471 Londoners, mindful of what they called sundry precedents, put up a stout defence against an attack by townsmen, yeomen and gentlemen of Kent led up to Blackheath and then to the city walls by the Bastard Fauconberg. The insurgents of 1497 apparently attempted a similar course of action when the Cornishmen marched across southern England to camp on Blackheath in the approved fashion, hoping to present their grievances to the government and to attack Cardinal Morton and Sir Reginald Bray. They were bitterly disillusioned when the county of Kent did not rally to their aid in the time-honoured manner.

For the fifteenth century the name of 'Jack Straw', one of the leaders of the rebels in 1381, came to epitomize the Great Revolt itself. It was a name to be conjured with by those with grievances. In 1407 troublemakers in Warwickshire protesting against the church authorities posted up schedules written in English which claimed to be written by 'Jack Straw and his companions'[56] and in 1452 protestors in Kent wanted to follow practices which they believed to have been done in 'the time of Jack Straw'.[57] Since uprisings were remembered by their leaders rather than by date or name, so in turn the memory of Cade, nicknamed John Amendall, was kept alive by insurgents of the later fifteenth century. In 1485 a group of rebels who rose up in the north dubbed three of their captains 'Jack Straw', 'Master Mendall' and 'Robin of Riddesdale', thereby saluting the memory of the risings of 1381, 1450 and 1470.[58] The success or otherwise of any of these uprisings would not seem to have been of much significance to those who looked back to them. They were celebrated high points in a tradition of dissent which could be traced back to 1381.

The fourth, last and perhaps most important factor to mention which may have increased the common people's sense of their own importance in national political life was the utter discrediting of Henry VI's regime during the 1450s and the coming of partisan politics fought out between Lancastrians and Yorkists. It led, during the second half of the century, to a corrosion of the bonds of loyalty which bound the people to their monarch, bonds which were so important a feature of the popular view of kingship. The Wars of the Roses were fought not only by lords, their tenants and retainers, but also by the shire levies, and brought a revivial of demand for these men of the towns and counties whom the chronicler Warkworth noted were called out from their own counties to fight at their own cost. In 1461 Henry VI's queen learnt at the second battle of St Albans that the men to trust were her own retainers, not the commons. A London citizen who fought as a foot soldier at the battle noted that Queen Margaret won that battle through the valour of the professional men-at-arms in her army since her county levies of northerners fled the field.[59] Civil war meant that more than one royal master or mistress demanded that the commons turn out to fight, as in 1470 when the invading Lancastrians issued their own commissions of array, and in the spring of 1471 when Edward IV sent commissions of array to fifteen counties in the West Country, West Midlands and Welsh Marches while Queen Margaret for her part mustered Cornwall and Devon.[60] Such conduct could only discredit the monarchy. It was not only the levies who were alienated. With armies moving about the realm, the non-combatant commons suffered damage and loss of property.

The damage done to bonds of loyalty meant that the Wars of the Roses involved a fight for popular support as well as for military victory. Thus political collapse at the centre elevated the importance of the views of the unenfranchised majority. By the middle of the century popular opinion became so important that it began to be wooed. During the 1440s, as Henry VI's reign slid towards disaster, the duke of Suffolk came increasingly to be depicted as a villain for his undue influence in the close circle around the king. It is likely that the ballads lampooning the duke and his associates at court which circulated the south-east in the early months of 1450 helped to create the climate for the popular revolt which subsequently took place against what had come to be regarded as Suffolk's administration. Of course, their author's names and identities are not known, but it was almost without doubt Suffolk's own political enemies who were behind the ballads of this defamation campaign, pouring out versified invective against him month by month as he moved from position of king's favourite, to prisoner in the Tower, to a corpse on Dover beach. Their manipulation of public opinion was relentless and effective. Moreover, contemporaries recognized it precisely for what it was. The view was that 'the name of the lord of Suffolk was distroyed be billes made of him and sette upp'.[61] The very success of the method inspired William Tailboys the following year to attempt the same against Lord Cromwell, having bills and letters set up on town gates throughout the country so that 'the comons of this land shulde engruege agayn þe said Lord Cromwell and ryse upon hym and so finally to distroye hym'.[62]

Ross clearly demonstrated the important role played by the seeking of public support during the period of the Wars of the Roses. He described the Yorkist dynasty as coming to power 'in the wake of a veritable flood of propaganda'.[63] There were genealogical rolls and anthologies of prophecies for the gentry to read,[64] but also political poems, manifestos and broadsheets for the common people. Edward also courted the popular 'vote', as it were, by his conduct (until his patience ran out). At the battle of Northampton the Yorkist soldiers were under orders to slay the lords, knights and squires but to spare the king and the commons. In similar vein Edward issued a proclamation in March 1461 announcing that any adherent of Henry VI who submitted within ten days would be pardoned; any adherent, that was, who possessed an income of less than 100 marks a year. Those with more did not enjoy such a pardon.[65] He wanted the validation of the people's support too, their public acclamation of him in a shout of a 'Ye Ye' before the formal acclamation of the coronation ceremony itself. And, indeed, just as much of the success of the earl of Warwick in 1460 had been due to his popular support, so much of Edward's humiliation in 1469 was due to his underestimation of the extent to which he had lost popular sympathy.[66] Richard III felt obliged to issue royal proclamations to fend off slurs to his name, while during the 1480s his future successor Henry Tudor made great play on his Welshness, such as it was, flying the banner of Cadwalader, the legendary last king of the Britons, in his attempt to drum up popular as well as gentry and magnate backing. These were all propaganda exercises of a less regal and confident sort than, for example, Henry V's ride into London in 1415 with its triumphant Biblical imagery.[67]

The picture sketched out in this essay is of a common people no longer quite as much in the political background as they had been. They had no politics in the sense of sustained agenda to pursue; their insurrections were reactive and conservative and needed aristocratic or gentry leadership – thus the rising of 1450 was 'a wasted opportunity' because it was not used by the leaders of political society.[68] However, their influence in political life should be measured less in the incidence of popular revolt than in the attention given to popular opinion by those who governed and in the volume of political propaganda produced. Those historians concerned with the influence of the parliamentary commons in the fifteenth century have had to acknowledge the importance at times of non-parliamentary opinion, the so-called 'people's authority', seen, for example, in Yorkist engineering of popular acclamations.[69] Emboldened by economic circumstances that made many of them more independent and more literate, and faced with increasingly brittle royal authority, the commons of the realm began in the second half of the century to see themselves less as the passive recipients of government and more as a politically aware taxpayers with a stake in society. Credulous and volatile they may have been, but their beliefs and actions told upon the politics of fifteenth-century England.

Notes

1.   H.L. Gray, 'Incomes from Land in England in 1436', *E.H.R.* XLIX (1934), p. 630; the returns do not include figures for the palatinates of Durham and Chester.

2.   R. Faith, 'The "Great Rumour" of 1377 and Peasant Ideology', in *The English Rising of 1381*, R.H. Hilton and T.H. Aston (eds.) (Cambridge, 1984), pp. 48–58.

3.   N. Orme, *Education and Society in Medieval and Renaissance England* (1989), pp. 101, 107.

4.   E.B. Fryde and N. Fryde, 'Peasant Rebellion and Peasant Discontents', in *The Agrarian History of England, III: 1348–1500*, E. Miller (ed.) (Cambridge, 1991), p. 799.

5.   *An English Chronicle of the Reigns of Richard II, Henry IV, Henry V, and Henry VI*, J.S. Davies (ed.) (Camden Society, old series LXIV, 1856), p. 107.

6.   McFarlane, *England*, pp. 254–5. Charles Ross developed this point in 'Rumour, Propaganda and Popular opinion during the Wars of the Roses', in *Patronage, the Crown and the Provinces in Later Medieval England*, R.A. Griffiths (ed.) (Gloucester, 1981), pp. 15–32.

7.   *The Historical Collections of a Citizen of London in the Fifteenth Century*, J. Gairdner (ed.) (Camden Society, new series XVII, 1876), p. 221.

8.   My following examples are taken from A.R. Myers, 'Parliamentary Petitions in the Fifteenth Century', in *Crown, Household and Parliament in Fifteenth-Century England*, C.H. Clough (ed.) (1985), pp. 5–6, 18–19.

9.   V.J. Scattergood, *Politics and Poetry in the Fifteenth Century* (1971), pp. 161, 163.

10. M. Mate, 'The East Sussex Land Market and Agrarian Class Structure in the Late Middle Ages', *P.P.* CXXXIX (1993), p. 64.

11. R.B. Goheen, 'Peasant Politics? Village Community and the Crown in Fifteenth-Century England', *American Historical Review*, XCVI (1991), pp. 46–62, an important article which addresses the subject in greater depth than is possible here.

12. P.R.O. C.67/40 m. 27.

13. M.K. McIntosh, *Autonomy and Community: The Royal Manor of Havering. 1200–1500* (Cambridge, 1986), p. 184.

14. L.R. Poos, *A Rural Society after the Black Death: Essex 1350–1525* (Cambridge, 1991), p. 292; M. Mate, 'The Economic and Social Roots of Medieval Popular Rebellion: Sussex in 1450–1451', *Ec.H.R.* XLV (1992), pp. 661–76.

15. J. Cornwall, *Revolt of the Peasantry, 1549* (1977), pp. 21–2.

16. J. Gillingham, *The Wars of the Roses: Peace and Conflict in Fifteenth-Century England* (1981), p. xii.

17. E.g. P.R.O. Court of King's Bench, Ancient Indictments, K.B.9/133, m.3.

18. E.g. P.R.O. K.B.9/955/2, m.2.

19. C. Richmond, 'After McFarlane', *History*, 68 (1983), p. 48.

20. P.R.O. Court of King's Bench, Plea Rolls, K.B.27/760, rot 3; P.R.O. K.B.9/237, m.24; K.B.9/996, m.55; K.B.9/133, m.5.

21. P.R.O. K.B.9/287, m 53.

22. E. Duffy, *The Stripping of the Altars: Traditional Religion in England c. 1400–c. 1580* (New Haven, 1992), p. 71.

23. Somerset R.O. DD/SF 836.

24. C. Richmond, 'Hand and Mouth: Information Gathering and Use in England in the Late Middle Ages', *Journal of Historical Sociology*, I (1988), pp. 233–52.

25. K.B. McFarlane, *John Wycliffe and the Beginnings of English Nonconformity* (1952), p. 182.

26. *Letters of Richard Fox 1486–1527*, P.S. and H.M. Allen (eds.) (Oxford, 1929), p. 44.

27. Ross, 'Rumour, Propaganda', p. 16.

28. I. Arthurson, 'Espionage and Intelligence from the Wars of the Roses to the Reformation', *Nottingham Medieval Studies*, XXXV (1991), pp. 144, 141.

29. Ibid. p. 138.

30. Ibid. pp. 136, 143.

31. J.S. Roskell, *Parliament and Politics in Late Medieval England* (1981) chapter V, p. 57.

32. A.L. Brown, *The Governance of Late Medieval England 1272–1461* (1989), pp. 126–7.

33. P.R.O. K.B.9/229/1, m.55.

34. *C.Ch.R.* VI, pp. 94–5.

35. *S.R.* II, p. 505.

36. *Great Chronicle of London*, A.H. Thomas and I.D. Thornley (eds.) (1938), p. 185; *Gregory's Chronicle*, p. 197.

37. A theme she develops in *Violence and Social Order: East Anglia 1422–1442* (Oxford, 1992).

38. *Historical Manuscripts Commission*, V (1876), p. 543; P.R.O. K.B.27/758, rex side rot.9.

39. B.L. Cotton Roll IV 50.

40. *Gregory's Chronicle*, pp. 194–5.

41. M.A. Hicks, *False, Fleeting, Perjur'd Clarence: George. Duke of Clarence 1449–78* (Gloucester, 1980), p. 68.

42. *The Prologues and Epilogues of William Caxton*, W.J.B. Crotch (ed.) (E.E.T.S. old series, CLXXVI, 1929), p. 104.

43. T. More, *Utopia*, Paul Turner (trans.) (Harmondsworth, 1965), p. 43.

44. *Letters of Richard Fox*, pp. 56–7.

45. Brown, *Governance*, pp. 93–4; M. Powicke, *Military Obligation in Medieval England* (Oxford, 1962). pp. 213–23.

46. H.J. Hewitt, *The Organization of War under Edward III, 1338–62* (Manchester, 1966).

47. For example, B.L. Additional Roll 32,472.

48. Brown, *Governance*, pp. 70–4; M.J. Bennett, 'A County Community: Social Cohesion amongst the Cheshire Gentry, 1400–1425', *Northern History*, VIII (1973), p. 39.

49. *English Chronicle*, p. 65.

50. P.R.O. K.B.9/254, mm.46, 47.

51. *English Chronicle*, p. 87.

52. P.R.O. Chester 25/11, m.9d; A.E. Curry, 'The Demesne of the County Palatine of Chester in the Early Fifteenth Century' (unpub. M.A. thesis, Manchester Univ. 1977), pp. 275–6. I am grateful to Anne Curry for bringing this Cheshire indictment roll to my attention and for her generosity in giving me access to the relevant section of her thesis.

53. P.R.O. Chester 25/11, m.10.

54. For the risings of 1489 and 1497 and a general discussion of fiscal revolt, see M.L. Bush, 'Tax Reform and Rebellion in Early Tudor England', *History*, LXXVI (1991), pp. 379–400. That the rising of 1497 was also political and dynastic is emphasised by I. Arthurson, *The Perkin Warbeck Conspiracy, 1491–1499* (Stroud, 1994), pp. 162–3.

55. Somerset R.O. DD/SF 836 m.4.

56. P.R.O. K.B.9/196/2, m.10. I am grateful to Maureen Jurkowski for this reference.

57. P.R.O. K.B.9/955/2, m.2.

58. I. Arthurson, '1497 and the Western Rising' (unpub. Ph.D. thesis, Keele Univ. 1981), p. 21.

59. C.D. Ross, *The Wars of the Roses* (1976), p. 116. The participation of the commons in the Wars of the Roses is discussed by A. Goodman, *The Wars of the Roses: Military Activity and English Society, 1452–97* (London, 1981), pp. 197, 203–8.

60. Hicks, *False, Fleeting, Perjur'd Clarence*, p. 85; Gillingham, *Wars of the Roses*, p. 202.

61. R. Virgoe, 'William Tailboys and Lord Cromwell: Crime and Politics in Lancastrian England', *B.J.R.L.* LV (1973), p. 477.

62. Ibid. p. 477.

63. Ross, 'Rumour, Propaganda', p. 23.

64. A. Allan, 'Yorkist Propaganda: Pedigree, Prophecy and the "British History" in the Reign of Edward IV' in *Patronage, Pedigree and Power in Later Medieval England*, C.D. Ross (ed.) (Gloucester, 1979), pp. 171–92

65. Gillingham, *Wars of the Roses*, p. 131.

66. C.D. Ross, *Edward IV* (1974), pp. 128–33.

67. C. Allmand, *Henry V* (1992), pp. 410–13.

68. Richmond, 'After McFarlane', p. 47.

69. For a discussion of views of late medieval parliament, see J.W. McKenna, 'The Myth of Parliamentary Sovereignty in Late Medieval England', *E.H.R.* CCCLXXII (1979), pp. 481–506.

8

Political and Constitutional History: Before and After McFarlane[1]

Christine Carpenter

New Hall, University of Cambridge

In the period between the 1860s and 1890s, when the history schools at Oxford and Cambridge were breaking away from the other subjects, like law and political philosophy, to which they had originally been yoked, and beginning to achieve intellectual respectability, they introduced a paper called constitutional history. This was to be taught and examined separately from political history. At Oxford they had no difficulty in defining constitutional history: it was to comprise the machinery of government, parliamentary institutions and national law. With political history they were less sure and it ended up being defined by default as everything else: 'the reign of monarchs, the development of the Church and the growth of foreign policy'.[2] At Cambridge, at the last but one major Tripos reform in 1966, political and constitutional history were for the first time explicitly incorporated in the same paper and, despite some further intervening changes to the Tripos, together they have remained. But it is now the status of constitutional history which is in doubt. The trouble is that, if, in the later nineteenth century, historians knew what constitutional history was, but were hazy about political history, the situation is now reversed: we are very clear about the nature of political history – many late medievalists spend most of their professional lives teaching it or doing research on it or both – but exceedingly vague about what we mean by constitutional history. Indeed, I have a strong suspicion that many late medievalists would like to deny its existence all together. Many might feel that this is entirely in keeping with McFarlane's attitude to medieval constitutional history. After all, he introduced his Ford lectures with a memorable dismissal of its founding father: 'If we are still too preoccupied with that far from helpful abstraction, constitutional history, it is thanks to the powerful mind of – let me utter his name for the last time in these lectures – William Stubbs'.[3] And yet, in a seminal paper of 1938, he wrote that 'constitutional history is concerned with men. That is to say it is not something distinct from political history; it *is* political history and the attempt to isolate it is vain.'[4] It seems then that, although, like the Cambridge History Tripos since 1966, he aimed at its integration with political history, he did not deny that it existed.

The purpose of this paper is to examine McFarlane's legacy in relation to constitutional history, as he found it and as he left it, and what has happened since. I hoped originally that I could make my definition of constitutional history emerge from my argument but in practice it was apparent that without a working definition I was sowing confusion, so I shall give it here. Self-evidently I do *not* propose to use the nineteenth-century definition, offered as late as 1936 by Lapsley: 'What for convenience sake I call "constitutional" must be taken to refer to attempts to solve the problem without, or following on, recourse to violence, whether by controlling the king through new and essentially revolutionary bodies or through his ministers and council by making them responsible to parliament'.[5] What I do mean is political and governmental structures, and the beliefs of those who participate in them about how those structures should operate. These are the more slowly changing parameters within which the daily and sometimes frenetic to and fro of politics occurs. Without a sense of the constitution, the history of politics or institutions can be no more than a series of isolated fragments, which, however interesting in themselves, add up to nothing more than a jumble of facts. Equally, a constitutional history which excludes or denatures politics is merely schematic concept-spinning. Thus, 'constitutional' means neither parliamentary nor institutional though, self-evidently, both may be part of the constitution, for, as McFarlane put it in a rather tetchy annotation to Chrimes's *English Constitutional Ideas in the Fifteenth Century*, 'All states have constitutions tho they may be difficult to define'.[6] By the same token all states or their equivalent must have some constitutional thought. In fact, although the nineteenth-century definition of constitutional history was profoundly misconceived, it passes *my* definition, since its protagonists firmly believed that medieval politics were primarily about institutions and representation.

The nineteenth century was, of course, the great age of constitutional history. It was constitutional history that gave history at the universities its academic respectability, after the subject had struggled in vain to show that it could compete on equal terms with the 'exact' and proper university subjects, classics and mathematics.[7] Thus, the justification of constitutional history as a fit subject for students, on the grounds that it forced them to master technical detail and foreign terminology, meant that, from the start, and as the Oxford definition implies, it was conceived in institutional terms.[8] However, the university did not invent the subject – only took it over – for, as is well known, constitutional history, written by amateurs like Palgrave and Macaulay, had been integral to English political thought, through the medium of 'the Whig interpretation', since the early years of the century.[9] Equally well known is the fact that the first great university practitioner of constitutional history, as well as the first great medieval constitutional historian, was Stubbs, Regius Professor at Oxford from 1866 to 1884, whose *Constitutional History* appeared in the 1870s. He was moreover the first professional historian to hold this post at either Oxford or Cambridge[10] and he was a participant in the movement to turn history in England into a professional discipline, one which owed a considerable debt to the great nineteenth-century German school of history.[11]

But, admire our founding fathers as we must, the monopolization of history by the constitutionalists in this period was to raise immense problems, for history in England in general, and for that of the late Middle Ages in particular. First of all, the Whig interpretation was, of course, profoundly present-centred. As Burrow and Blaas have shown, it veered with every political wind that blew in the great nineteenth-century debates over parliamentary reform.[12] This led to an obsession with a limited series of issues – those that were thought germane to the present state of England – which has probably been matched subsequently only by the more doctrinaire Marxists. As Southern put it, 'They left out that which is most interesting in the past in order to concentrate on that which was practically and academically most serviceable'.[13] As with the university examination papers, what they concentrated on was primarily the history of institutions. What got missed out was therefore real politics: it was all large-scale evolution, with very little room for real people or day to day upheavals. Secondly, it could easily lead to a contempt for the past when it failed to measure up to the present. It seems to me that *the* characteristic failing of all Whig history is the complete inability to meet the past on its own terms and value it for its own sake.[14] As Butterfield notes, it is from this 'that our textbook historians have inherited the top hat and the pontifical manner, and the grace with which they hand out a consolation prize to the man who, though a reactionary, was irreproachable in his private life'.[15] We shall see that this is highly germane to the importance of the McFarlane legacy.

This present-centred moral tone had particularly deleterious effects for the late middle ages, especially the fifteenth century. Let me give you Stubbs's verdict on this period: 'a worn-out helpless age, that calls for pity without sympathy, and yet balances weariness with something like regrets'.[16] Once the 'Lancastrian constitutional experiment' was over, indeed seen to be offering too much liberty to a country not yet ready for it, the century had nothing to offer Stubbs: 'From the accession of Henry IV to the accession of Henry VII, the baronage, the people, and the royal house, were divided each within itself, and that internal division was working a sort of political suicide which the Tudor reigns arrested, and by arresting it they made possible the restoration of the national balance'.[17] If the history of England was the fusion of England's ancient Germanic representative institutions with a revivifying feudal kingship, to produce the perfect balanced governmental system, safeguard against both tyranny and anarchy,[18] the combination of unstable kingship, noble conflict, pitched battles and, according to Stubbs, decline into despotism, had little to commend sustained attention. As Tanner put it in 1901, 'To read the first volume of Stubbs was necessary to salvation, to read the second was greatly to be desired, the third was reserved for the ambitious student who sought to accumulate merit by unnatural austerities'.[19] After all, Stubbs's *Select Charters*, the essential teaching vehicle for generations of medievalists, does not go beyond 1307.[20]

The trouble was that, if 'proper' history was the history of England's representative institutions, there was very little to celebrate after 1450 and, if the responsible use of power by the governing classes to advance the cause of these institutions was integral to the story, there did not seem very much to hold the attention before. So, the fifteenth century was glossed over as an 'Age of Transition'. We are assured that 'the dawn is approaching . . . the evil is destroying itself, and the remaining good . . . is already striving toward the sunlight that is to come'.[21] But that hardly commends the century itself. Green's contemporaneous invention of the 'new monarchy' did little to dent the orthodoxy, since it endorsed the unfavourable view of the Yorkists and early Tudors.[22] Even though Tudor despotism was acquiring some respectability at this time with Froude, the 'Tory Whig', as an essential step on the road to national sovereignty,[23] this did nothing for the fifteenth century either. It remained in a limbo. With the blitheness still common to early modern historians, Froude embraced the view that 'if you don't know about it, nothing happened', and cheerfully consigned late medieval England (apart from the Church, whose need for reform was central to his thesis) to the status of precapitalist idyll, a 'merrie England'.[24]

But there was a still more serious weakness in the work of these Whig constitutionalists. Schematic history with a clear story to tell remains convincing only so long as research remains at a superficial level, and what was to damage the great nineteenth-century syntheses beyond repair was, ironically, the next stage in the professionalization of history in England, of which they themselves had been the pioneers. This is a story that has two centres. The one is Manchester. The other is the Public Record Office, established in 1838, an early product of the concern to record the past.[25] Here the arrival of Maxwell Lyte as Deputy Keeper in 1886 was to initiate the first age of record history in England. It was Maxwell Lyte who by a series of radical innovations really began to make the voluminous records of the English government available. To him all of us who work on the public records owe an incalculable debt.[26] Because of Maxwell Lyte, it suddenly became possible to work from a far wider range of governmental materials than the limited sources, principally parliamentary and chronicle, that had been at Stubbs's disposal.[27] A new generation of historians was ready to take advantage of this. These were, in many cases, the men trained by the Stubbs generation at Oxford and Cambridge. They included Bury, Firth, Pollard, Prothero – who, together with Firth, turned the Royal Historical Society into a proper professional organization – Round and, one of Stubbs's first pupils, Tout.[28]

The aims of these men can be summed up as wanting to make research much more central to academic history in England.[29] Their models were now less the Germans, although in terms of professionalism these were still well ahead of England, than the new school of French administrative historians. By the 1870s the French were beginning to rival the Germans in professional training.[30] Pollard managed to found an institute of advanced historical training, on the French and German model, with the establishment of the Institute of Historical Research in 1921,[31] while Manchester, and eventually even Oxford and Cambridge, accepted the foreign notion of higher degrees in history and became training grounds for future members of the profession.[32] But it was at Manchester, under Tout's direction, that the hope of training undergraduates in historical disciplines was most fully realized and at Manchester that the principle that teaching and research were inseparable was earliest implemented.[33] The old system at Oxford and Cambridge was in fact the retrograde two-tier one to which, under government pressure, we are in danger of reverting; the professors brought lustre on the university by writing, while the college tutors did no research but endless teaching. This produced a farcical situation in which Stubbs lectured to empty lecture halls because all but a tiny number of Oxford men were unable to match the intellectual levels he demanded, while college tutors lectured 'Noddy' Stubbs to enthusiastic audiences and, in one case, even published and sold their lecture notes.[34]

The research of the new generation was as professional as their approach to historical education. Able to take advantage of the availability of so much more record material, they began to study the records of the English government in far greater detail, and in a far more systematic manner. Not only did they thus uncover the complexities of English administration. At the same time, influenced by the sceptical eye that was being cast on ancient English institutions at the end of the nineteenth century by people like the Webbs, and the associated drive for administrative efficiency, they cast serious doubts on the impeccable Whig pedigree of England's law and legislature.[35] Following on Maitland's epoch-making publication in 1893 of his work on the parliament of 1305, it became apparent that it was king, council and nobility that dominated parliament at that stage, not, as Stubbs had supposed, the commons.[36] The late medieval parliament and the historiographical tradition it had stood for, including even *Magna Carta*, were systematically debunked. The new heroes were the unsung administrators, whose records were being used *in extenso* for the first time. The great theme of English history was no longer liberty and the representation of the people but the creation of the nation state, and the state was built in public by great kings like Henry VIII, rescued from Tudor despotism by Pollard, and behind the scenes by the faceless apolitical 'middle-class' bureaucrats.[37] The greatest of all these expositions, so excellently accomplished that the work itself may never have to be done again, was, of course, Tout's massive and misleadingly titled *Chapters in the Administrative History of Medieval England*, published between 1920 and 1933, the first systematic investigation of the royal household and the king's seals in the Middle Ages.[38]

So, the nineteenth-century synthesis fell apart, under the combined weight of a *Zeitgeist* that was starting to lose faith in the special calling of England, and research that was showing that large parts of it were simply untrue. For late medieval history, this development at least had the merit that much of what was now acknowledged to be fruitful in England's past actually belonged to the latter part of the Middle Ages, while, if even *Magna Carta* was the product of self-seeking barons, the arrival of a whole lot more in the fifteenth century was routine rather than shocking. However, the professional revolution of the late nineteenth and early twentieth centuries in the end created more problems than it solved – for late medieval history in particular but ultimately for history in England as a whole.

Historians of the late Middle Ages, especially those concerned with the fifteenth century, continued, despite what I have said, to marginalize the period. Tout believed his story to be over in 1399, with what he saw as the failure of the last attempt by a medieval king to create absolute rule through the household. In general terms Stubbs's misleading version of the following century was accepted.[39] The next important episode, with a prelude for Henry VII, was the reign of Henry VIII, now seen as a pivotal period in the growth of the English state and incorporated into what survived of the Whig interpretation. According to Pollard and then Neale, it was under the Tudors that the real growth of parliament occurred. That naturally gave further arguments to downgrade the importance of the later Middle Ages.[40] Perhaps more damagingly, the content of the period continued to be marginalized. Whether it was the commons in parliament or the administrators who were being given centre stage, the nobility, the real central figures, were still being reduced to stereotypes or ignored.

Moreover, although the nineteenth-century synthesis could not withstand this onslaught, much of it remained, an incongruous survival, increasingly bereft of any philosophical basis and kept in place by the fact that nobody seemed to have any alternative to offer. Even the new state-building theme was really only grafted on to Stubbs. Thus, for example, not only did Tout accept Stubbs's version of the fifteenth century (as did Pollard)[41], but he also effectively absorbed the entire Stubbs paradigm for the thirteenth and fourteenth centuries – a struggle over the reins of power between would-be authoritarian monarchy and encroaching baronage – while transferring the scene of the action from parliament to household and administration.[42] And, as all these remarks imply, overwhelmingly the anachronistic vision that could value the past only for what seemed germane to the present had not shifted at all. One striking example will have to suffice: Tout's characterization of Edward II's reign as a great period of reform, in which 'the permanent civil service' was able to get on with the really important task of 'work[ing] out their own ideas on the basis of their practical experience', because king and magnates were too busy fighting each other to get in their way. Even more bizarrely, the younger Despenser is given some credit as the only 'real reformer' among these otherwise hopeless cases.[43] Only one contributor to the reaction against Stubbs was able to move beyond this limited vision. He was Maitland, and to him we shall return later.[44]

However, what had been overlooked in the rejection of the nineteenth-century vision was Stubbs's real and lasting contribution to English history, the merging of political and constitutional history. For him this took what we might now see as an anachronistic form, the union of the nation's Anglo-Saxon local representative institutions with the superimposed feudal monarchy, but as an analytical tool it was irreplaceable: the king who was simultaneously the public ruler of a nation and the private feudal overlord of its greatest men.[45] The section from the Conquest to Henry II, where this process is most fully charted, remains the best and most readable part of the book.[46] As we shall see, it is a fusion that historians have found it hard to recreate.

Thus, the absence of any credible alternative to Stubbs was only part of a wider problem – that is, the more general mislaying of conceptual tools for analysing the past. In a sense the dismantling of abstract generalizations had been an article of faith with the new school. They took their lead from the positivism of the scientists, believing that there was an absolute historical truth to which the combined scientific labours of professional historians, each in his own little corner, would bring them. In the words of Powicke, one of the later products of the Manchester school, 'Interpretation has to wait on scholarship'.[47] Or, as Tout put it, 'we are half-way towards solving a problem when we have traced it from stage to stage through the ages'.[48] Even at Cambridge, which never really became a fully paid-up positivist institution, there was the early archpriest of positivism, Lord Acton, who espoused, 'a vision of a new scientific history which would attain to the ultimate truth'.[49] In his inaugural lecture on his return to Oxford as Regius Professor in 1928, Powicke outlined the acme of positivism. Celebrating the pleasure that amateur historians could derive from tasks that were 'rather dull or seeming to lead nowhere, working towards a common goal', he called for massed armies of 'country gentry and clergy . . . ecclesiastical dignitaries . . . schoolmasters and mistresses . . . lawyers . . . public servants . . . persons of leisure engaged in historical work', all presumably moving in serried ranks towards the positivist nirvana.[50] One has to agree with Barraclough that this 'turns out to be the great illusion of a whole generation'.[51]

But this was a very powerful and influential generation. In English history – certainly in medieval history – the years from the period leading up to the First World War until as late as the 1950s can be summarized as the Manchester School era, or more accurately the Manchester-Oxford era. Let me name a few names: Powicke, Jacob, Galbraith, Roskell, Myers, Treharne, Cheney, and that is to omit the multitude who were linked to Manchester solely by their training at Oxford at the hands of former Manchester men.[52] In 1957 Trevor-Roper pointed out that he was the first Oxford Regius Professor for thirty years not to have a pedigree of medieval history, Balliol and Manchester.[53] Manchester provided generations of professional historians for other universities, even, in Cheney, a medieval professor for Cambridge, which has had a consistently less orthodox attitude to the subject than Oxford.[54] In this time, it goes without saying, some excellent work was done and many new records brought into use. In preparing this paper, I have looked again at Jacob's *Studies in the Period of*

Baronial Reform and Rebellion and Powicke's *Loss of Normandy*,[55] and have felt a proper humility in the face of work that is still so worthwhile and so readable. Nevertheless, as many people were starting to realize before very long, something had gone wrong.

Not everyone will want to be as forthright as Keith Thomas in 1966: 'Future histories of English historical writing are likely to reveal the first half of the twentieth century as a time when most historians temporarily lost their bearings',[56] but from 1930 onwards objections to 'scientific' history were beginning to come fully into focus.[57] Partly these were just that it was being achieved at the cost of history's literary traditions,[58] but more cogent were the genuine historical objections; that over-specialization was depriving historians of the broader view, that history could not be reduced to scientific principles, that there was no absolute historical truth to which historians might aspire, that records themselves carried hidden biases.[59] Trevor-Roper, in his inaugural lecture of 1957, summed it up using a brilliant extended angling image:

> . . . skilful riparian subdivision, devised by the genius of Manchester, to which we owe so much and where so many of our professionals throughout the country have bought their fishing tackle, has ensured that every man, within his narrowing reach, has the opportunity – without any tiresome controversy with his neighbour or exasperating entanglement of lines – to extract from the swollen stream of historical evidence some small conclusion which, though perhaps not very tasty to the lay palate, may yet be pickled in a thesis or potted in the transactions of a provincial learned society.[60]

In a similar vein, Thomas suggested that the acme of an English historian's aspirations was an article in the *English Historical Review*, 'scholarly and precise, but cautious in its conclusions, so as to delay its inevitable fate – supersession by another article, even more scholarly'.[61] And perhaps the most damning comment of all came from one of the central figures of the Manchester-Oxford school, Galbraith: '150 out of the 165 research students at Oxford would be better doing a proper job of work'.[62]

The partial dismantling of the Whig paradigm, while its agenda remained so fundamental to the way history in England was done, had deprived the history of England of a central point around which it could be organized.[63] The work of the great figures of the period exemplifies this unease. The British Academy obituaries of both Jacob and Powicke suggest that they were happier with the essay form and that even their larger-scale works tended to be more a series of essays.[64] Powicke's one really extended work, *King Henry III and the Lord Edward*, although a wonderful read, is, as Southern describes it in this obituary, 'history as perhaps Proust might have written it – episodic, fitful, haunting', or, as R.H.C. Davis put it more unkindly, 'I could not for the life of me say what was the thesis of the work', though he *had* greatly enjoyed reading it.[65] The content of *Henry III* – as much or more about foreign affairs and the papacy than about the political and constitutional struggles that were supposed to be at the heart of the book – indicates the way out that was already being taken.[66] Historians, especially medieval historians, were abandoning political, constitutional and administrative history and moving into the history of ideas, of religion and of culture, and that is where most of the really satisfying work on medieval history was done in England between the 1920s and the 1960s, by Jacob, Powicke, Knowles and Southern, to name only four of the most distinguished.[67]

The trouble was that there remained an uneasy sense that the abandonment of the high political and constitutional ground was, to put it crudely, a cop-out. Not least, it deprived history of the central position in politics and political ideas it had enjoyed in the previous century.[68] There was a not entirely unjustified feeling after the last war that in some way the insanities the world had just seen and academic history's retreat from attempts to make sense of the world, leaving the field to charlatans and ideologues, were not unconnected. There was also an instinctive feeling before and after the war that history *ought* to be concerning itself with great matters.[69] There was a general agreement that history was about men in society,[70] an idea which of itself invited generalizations, and to omit the means and the people by which those societies were governed was to retreat from any attempt at a proper synthesis. The question then was where the conceptual framework for the history of government and politics was to come from. In fact, as I shall argue later, as early as the late 1920s a possible solution to the problem of historical synthesis in the broadest terms was evolving in France. However, its impact in England, as I shall show, was delayed and limited and largely excluded political history.

But contemporaneously what has been likened to a Darwinian revolution in the study of English politics was being achieved by Lewis Namier for the eighteenth century[71] and, to some extent moving in his wake, in the 1930s McFarlane began to do the same for the fourteenth and fifteenth centuries.

Already in 1938 McFarlane was well aware that something had to be done: 'we have failed to do what it is the duty of every generation of historians to do, namely to rewrite the broad outlines of our subject in the light of those specialized studies which are our prime concern. To all intents and purposes the attempt to interpret the period as a whole . . . begins and has ended with Stubbs'.[72] And, of 'narrow and specialist' studies, he commented, 'they have discredited [Stubbs's interpretation] without putting anything coherent in its place. This failure to substitute anything for it *as a whole* [McFarlane's italics] has produced utter confusion.'[73] He was speaking in much the same tones as other historians, in varied fields, who were coming to doubt the efficacy of 'scientific history'. It could be argued, however, that the need to break free would be felt most strongly by someone who had chosen to devote himself to the period within the Middle Ages that had been most deprived of meaning by both Stubbs and his successors.

Perhaps it was inevitable that the mould would be broken by an alien, a Polish Jew, Lewis Namier, curiously yet another with a Balliol and Manchester pedigree.[74] There the resemblance ends, although if ever there was a fervent believer in the virtues of professional research it was Namier, the constructor of countless biographies of insignificant men and founder of the biographical History of Parliament. But in his case this really was the prelude to a larger vision.[75] He was able to dismantle completely the Whig version of the eighteenth century and to show the nuts and bolts of politics at both electoral and parliamentary level. This was a world inhabited by real people and held together not by the anachronism of parties pursuing abstract principles but by patronage networks and 'interest'.[76] But there was much more than the mere destruction of a received idea. The key lay essentially in some of those revolutionary foreign thinkers of the turn of the nineteenth century whom the generally insular English intellectual establishment – and in historical studies it had become particularly insular – had mostly failed to take seriously.[77]

For Namier these were first of all three of the great nineteenth-century founders of modern sociology, Weber, Durkheim and Pareto. He had indeed attended the latter's lectures during a brief sojourn at the university of Lausanne before he came to England.[78] As was pointed out in a retrospective article in 1950, what Namier had was something English historians had almost consistently lacked, the ability to treat the past on its own terms, at least the eighteenth-century English past in which he was not emotionally involved. 'Corruption', for example, was not something to be condemned with the Whig loftiness that Butterfield mocked, but rather to be analysed as a necessary part of a system.[79] All this he learned from the new sociology, with its emphasis on social function and its rejection of an evolutionary approach to human society.[80] As he himself put it, 'The first and greatest task of a historian is to understand the terms in which men of a different age thought and spoke, and the angle from which they viewed life and society'.[81] The very title of his first book, *The Structure of English Politics at the Accession of George III*, was a sociological challenge to the traditions of English history, which had recognized neither structures nor, really, politics.[82]

The other great influence on him was Freud. Central to Namier's concern to comprehend a past society was the need to understand the individual people whose lives he had recreated, and, for Namier, psychoanalysis, to which he was himself addicted, was a fundamental part of this process.[83] It was also fundamental to another, and, as we shall see, more problematical part of his work, the rejection of political ideas as a primary motivating force.[84] But let me leave Namier for the moment with a quotation which seems to me to show that he had in large measure found a method of turning detailed research into large-scale generalisation and which at the same time brings me to the central figure of this paper. According to Namier, the problem was to deal with 'aggregates otherwise than in vague generalisations; to treat them as entities in which each person retains his individuality'.[85]

Namier's *Structure of Politics* was published in 1929. As we have seen, by 1938 another Oxford historian was wrestling with the same problem, and his answer was very similar. At first it owed its largest intellectual debt to another alien, Karl Marx, although by the 1930s McFarlane was not of course alone amongst English intellectuals in his attraction to Marx's ideas, even if this was, and remained, unusual amongst historians of medieval English politics. At this point he was concerned with underlying economic factors; with the rise of a new class which destabilized Lancastrian England; with bastard feudalism as the growth of a new cash nexus.[86] But what has more lasting importance is that, as the Marxist influence shows and as he put it as early as 1929, history must deal with 'man as a member of society'.[87] This may have been a historical commonplace in England, but to McFarlane it had real meaning and purport.

By 1940 he was beginning to move into that study of aristocratic society that we associate particularly with his name.[88] His lectures on parliament in that year[89] are at times more a study of the social groups represented in parliament than of the institution itself, an approach signalled very clearly in his sixth lecture when he denied that it was 'either possible or desirable to study the history of institutions apart from the activities, opinions and passions of the men who made and used them!'[90] This is of course an early shot across the bows of the Tout school.[91] In a paper delivered in the same year he wrote in similar vein, 'If we wish to understand the nature of the English state, what is necessary is a study of the evolution of its governing class'.[92] During the 1940s his interest gathered pace. Interestingly, it was then that he reread one of the few medieval works of that time with an aristocratic focus, Stenton's *First Century of English Feudalism*, which he had first read and annotated in 1932.[93] This came of course from a different tradition, dating back to Round, but in 1944, when McFarlane made far more extensive notes on it, he was clearly looking for parallels with noble society three hundred years later.

For its time this is all most unusual: the wholesale rejection of the old constitutional history, rather than the tinkering with it that the previous generation had done, the focus on the governing class and the investigation of this class through its own records and on its own terms, without judgement, and the attempt to build a new synthesis based on integrating political history with the social history of the ruling élite. Where did it all come from? Well, partly from the fact that he was a great rejecter of established orthodoxies.[94] But I do not think there can be very much doubt that the initial germ came from Namier, another habitual iconoclast,[95] and that much of McFarlane's greatness as a historian stems from the fact that he grasped the significance of what Namier was doing, and how it might be applied to the late Middle Ages, some two decades before 'Namierism' became the height of historical fashion.

Indeed, McFarlane bought both Namier's works on politics under George III when they were published in 1929 and 1930.[96] What I have already said about the two men and the quotations I have read make this debt clear. Both tried to understand the ruling classes of the past on their own terms, as an anthropologist or sociologist would. McFarlane sought an answer to 'the question how the nobility of later medieval England saw itself as a group and how this group was to be defined by the historian',[97] an aim almost identical with that expressed by Namier in the quotation cited earlier. He shared the same prosopographical interests and the same obsession about pursuing his individual members of the governing classes through the archives.[98] And, if McFarlane's discussions of bastard feudal patronage networks were not in themselves sufficient evidence that he had read Namier's analyses of similar eighteenth-century groupings, in one of those lectures on parliament from 1940, he explicitly stated that 'these groupings were . . . "connections" in the 18th century sense, not parties in the modern sense'.[99]

While Namier explored this society in order to put reality into the history of parliamentary politics, McFarlane had moved from an inherited parliamentary focus to the study of political society. Both had found a way out of the tyranny of institution-centred history. McFarlane may have owed something to Ronald Syme's exposition of the politics of patrons and clients in ancient Rome, published in 1939, but this was much more narrative-led and much less of a social study than the work of either McFarlane or Namier.[100] We should realize that Namier and McFarlane remained almost unique amongst English historians in their interest in the governing classes and their records until well into the 1950s, because unless we do so we can grasp neither their profound originality nor the extent of the revolution that they might have brought about.

Placed in this context, the Ford Lectures of 1953 show most clearly what might have been. It is a large step towards what the author himself called for during the course of those lectures: ' what we need is a more detailed study than we have at present of English society in the age of bastard feudalism'.[101] Here we have the beginnings of a portrait in the round of a governing class, on the basis of which it would be possible eventually to rewrite the history of late medieval England. Here is a history that can do full justice to the high ground of rulers and ruling élites and therefore of politics, and that does not dissolve into a series of isolated pieces of research, but is itself based on just such research, of the most meticulous kind. The synthesis in the political history of medieval England, lost since Stubbs came under attack, could have been achieved. The conceptual tool is no longer the history of institutions but a grasp of the interaction of people, society and institutions.

And it is indeed constitutional history. I repeat this pivotal quotation, 'If we wish to understand the history of the *English state* [my italics], what is necessary is a study of the evolution of its governing class'.[102] As is apparent in the Ford lectures, this study was to include those 'opinions and passions' which he had already proclaimed to be inseparable from the study of institutions, and these he understood to be part of the constitution.[103] To McFarlane, political, social and constitutional history were not separable subjects, for constitutional history was not the history of institutions.[104] The history of the evolution of the governing class of England was what he was trying to achieve.[105] So was Namier, who was engaged on 'a study of the British "political nation" during the American Revolution . . . by concentrating on that marvellous microcosmos, the British House of Commons'.[106] If Namier and then McFarlane could be said to have created the first schools of real political history in England, here was potentially that fusion of political history with a larger conceptual grasp of the structures of governance and politics, which we must call constitutional history, and which could have led to a revolution in English history that would have been accomplished by the historians of high politics.

However, that is not how it has worked out, in either the later Middle Ages or the eighteenth century, or in English political history as a whole. Until very recently, with the possible exception of the special case of the seventeenth century, it has generally remained resolutely unconceptual.[107] Even in the seventeenth century, despite the plenitude of intellectual fireworks, not to say atomic bombs, the constitutional framework of politics remains largely unexplored. McFarlane's legacy has been a barrage of detailed studies of nobles and gentry, an immeasurable enrichment of what was once a destitute period, but one which has taken us no closer to a synthesis than we were at McFarlane's death. Paradoxically, now into the third generation of the 'children of McFarlane', even if our focus has altered radically, we are still in the same situation which so excited our progenitor in the 1930s and 1940s: encumbered by a mass of detailed research from which it seems impossible to generalize. How did this situation come about?

Partly it has been through a misunderstanding of the legacy of both historians. Both left their work incomplete – McFarlane sadly so – so neither was able to demonstrate its full implications. Then, in the post-war period, the horror at what ideas had done to mankind led to a general dismissal of the role of ideas in politics among most historians of England. It was then that Namier's study of 'interest' became the basis for a fashionable preoccupation with patronage politics, and that to deny the reality of ideas, other than as a cloak for self-interest, 'epiphenominalism', became a historical commonplace.[108] Given the work of its founder, it is hardly surprising that the new political history of late medieval England should subscribe wholeheartedly to these assumptions.

But in many ways it is a bastardization of both McFarlane and Namier, bastard McFarlanism, in fact. We have seen that these two did not subscribe to the overweening individualism implicit in the work of their successors – far from it – and that they were both immensely interested in people's ideas and attitudes. What they were hostile to was the notion that crudely formulated political ideas, often modern conceptions foisted on the past, could be seen as freestanding motivators in politics.[109] Namier produced a wonderful series of rich multi-dimensional character vignettes: Lord Bute, for example, who 'had his eyes fixed all the time on the grand, moving scene of his future resignation'.[110] It is difficult to believe that either historian would have subscribed to the prevalent 'common-sense' approach that denies all subtlety of motivation, when Namier was such a keen apostle of Freud, and McFarlane chided 'the habit of assuming a simplicity of behaviour and of motive in medieval politicians that is wholly unwarranted by our knowledge. It is . . . the prevailing vice of English medievalists. This want of psychological penetration is especially noticeable in Stubbs.'[111] 'Common sense' is acutely deflated in Horace Rumpole's dealings with its bluff, northern, self-styled apostle, Mr Justice 'Ollie' Oliphant:

'Mr Rumpole,' Ollie Oliphant answered, 'you know we have a saying up in the North where I come from: "There's nowt so queer as folks"?' 'Do you really my lord? Down here, in the Deep South, I suppose we're more inclined to look for some sort of logical explanation.'[112]

Logical explanations, combined with deep insight, in dealing with the vagaries of the human impulse, however irrational, rather than instant formulations, seem to me to be the stock in trade of these two historians.

Once the 'Namierite' model of politics had become standard in late medieval political history, there could be no conceptual basis for a synthesis. First, no generalizations about political motive would be possible beyond the fairly banal statement that everyone was out for what he could get. Secondly, the extreme individualism of the approach has inhibited worthwhile generalisation about nobles and gentry as social groups, and, combined with the emphasis on self-interest, has made it difficult to investigate the ideas of the political classes – precisely those things that McFarlane was trying to do. This means that neither the political structures created by collective action nor contemporary beliefs about how those structures ought to function can be explored. Finally, late medieval history is still so scared by the spectre of the Whigs that the institutions by which the realm was governed have all but disappeared, leaving politics devoid not just of conceptual structures but of the institutional framework within which they operated: politics are held to be about lordship, operating in a governmental vacuum. In sum, we now have the politics in full measure, but we have lost the constitution, and with it an intellectual point of focus.[113]

McFarlane himself cannot be entirely exonerated from what has happened to his legacy.[114] We must remember that he was both very excited by the analysis of 'interest' and in profound reaction against the aridity that had taken human beings out of late medieval history. Quite rightly, he wanted to put them back in again. As he wrote famously about the reign of Edward III, hitherto dominated by the study of parliament, 'the real politics of the reign were not confined to the short if frequent parliaments; they were inherent rather in Edward's daily personal relations with his magnates. The king's service was profitable; his favour the only sure road to honour and success; men went to court and to the royal camp, not to express unacceptable views, but for what they could get.'[115] As this quotation suggests, he never quite lost his early Marxist sense of the later Middle Ages as a period of striving ambitious individuals, of politics as a 'business', or as a 'joint-stock enterprise'.[116] It has led to a bizarre intellectual development in which Karl Marx, filtered through McFarlane, and Margaret

Thatcher have met in a depiction of late medieval society as one where individualism and the profit motive reigned supreme.[117]

Moreover, McFarlane applied this management metaphor to kingship as well, which seems to me to be the one serious weakness in his history.[118] From this follows a reluctance to analyse the nature of late medieval government. By contrast, Namier, who was actually involved in politics and diplomacy at the highest levels, never forgot the governmental dimension.[119] In a famous phrase, McFarlane spoke of the nobility's need 'to rescue the kingdom from the consequences of Henry VI's inanity'.[120] What he did not do was ask precisely what those consequences were and how they manifested themselves. There is not a great deal of acknowledgement in his work as we have it that kingship was something different, that the king was not just 'the good lord of all good lords',[121] but that there was a public dimension to ruling which had profound implications for both what the king gave and what could be got out of the king. It is this, Stubbs's most important bequest to us, that I find most lacking in both McFarlane and much of the post-McFarlane work: the analysis of how public transmission of power worked and how it interacted with private power structures, and the acknowledgement of a public element in the political morality of the ruling classes. It has obvious implications for the problems with the legacy that I have just discussed.

That the heirs of Namier and McFarlane have chosen this particular road has been especially unfortunate, because, since the 1960s, and by a completely different route, in other areas of history there has been the sort of revolution that these two looked likely to make in the 1930s and 1940s in the history of politics. Contemporaneously with Namier's and McFarlane's revitalizing of a jaded subject, two French historians, Bloch and Febvre, were doing the same thing in France. I refer of course to the *Annales* school, named after the periodical founded in 1929, the year of Namier's first major work.[122] Indeed, so similar was the approach that at one point I toyed with the idea that McFarlane had known this French work at an early stage, before I realized that the same, or very similar influences, had come through Namier, another foreigner. Again, there was the impact of the social sciences, the study of society on its own terms, the valuing of the past for its own sake, even if the ultimate implications went far beyond political history.[123] I mentioned earlier that English historians had agreed that history was about man in society, but in practice they had lacked the conceptual tools to make good this laudable definition and social history had remained Trevelyan's 'history with the politics left out'.[124] Because the *Annales* school was deeply steeped in the social sciences,[125] it was now possible to write a real history of society.[126] As Cantor noted, while English historians agonized over how to restore the lost synthesis, Bloch was producing just such a synthesis, in *La Société Féodale*, published in 1940.[127]

Yet the early reviews of Bloch and Febvre in England show how little their work was understood. These are mostly deeply respectful, especially towards Bloch, but oblivious of their revolutionary implications. Let me give two examples. In 1926 the *Times Literary Supplement* reviewed *Les Rois Thaumaturges*, one of the most mould-breaking historical works ever published. It was applauded for its scholarship and 'careful documentation' and provoked a minor antiquarian correspondence on the subject of cramp rings. The review of *La Société Féodale* in the *English Historical Review* of 1940–1 is again complimentary. But the writer is unaware that Bloch's approach to feudalism as a social phenomenon makes his detailed criticisms of Bloch's discussion of feudalism in England by reference to an *institutional* interpretation out of place.[128] After the war, historians of English politics, multiplying in the wake of the Namierite revolution, were not generally inclined to take an interest in what was becoming the great area of development in historical studies in this country.[129] If the legacy of their gurus, Namier and McFarlane, could not interest them in aggregates or in politics placed within the social context of the ruling élite, then it was unlikely that some foreigners – most of them not yet translated – would succeed in doing so.[130] And yet Bloch had after all written a major work in which government, politics and the ruling classes were central. Another path to the integration of political and constitutional history, which would in fact have brought practitioners back to Namier's and McFarlane's placing of politics in a social and structural context, had been rejected.

It was as the history of the lower classes, the politically powerless, that the *Annales* really took root in England. Apart from the extraordinarily receptive Trevor-Roper, the tiny number of English contributors to the *Annales* before the 1960s were nearly all Marxist historians.[131] Then the young Turks, led by Keith Thomas, arrived in the mid 1960s and 1970s.[132] I have already quoted from his profoundly influential article in the *Times Literary Supplement* in 1966. Echoing the *Annales*, and with complete truth, he wrote that 'the social history of the future will therefore not be a residual subject but a central one, around which all other branches of history are likely to be organized.'[133] However, one particular branch would take a back seat: this would lead, he said, with some satisfaction, to 'the dethronement of politics'.[134] Sadly, that is what has happened. With one or two notable exceptions, mostly recent and mostly confined to the seventeenth, eighteenth and nineteenth centuries,[135] across the whole of English history at the moment, nearly all the most exciting work is taking place outside political history. Social history offers the conceptual structure that has enabled this work, despite the vast proliferation of subjects for historical research in the wake of the *Annales*, to retain an intellectual coherence. And yet, I cannot be unique in believing that, however intellectually ambitious, history that neglects the people who at the highest level actually made things happen, and the means by which they made them happen, can only be a rather maimed kind of history.

So, finally how can we put back into our subject that conceptual edge that it seems to have lost, by adding a constitutional dimension to our burgeoning knowledge of political events? The answer must be to return to our McFarlanite roots: not patronage and individual strivers, but aggregates and beliefs and McFarlane's interest in 'the complex organism' of 'the English body politic'.[136] But now we can take this further. We must include the public dimension neglected by McFarlane. We must look at public institutions, and at how private power and private interests focused around them; at those structures of power and government that are integral to constitutional history. And, as Powell has argued, we must study 'political culture', the terms and currency of political action and beliefs.[137] To do this, we must, on the one hand, return to an even earlier legacy, and cease to be so dismissive of the splendid work on the institutions of government done by our distinguished forebears. But unlike them we must treat these as living institutions, not, to quote Powell, as 'fish on a slab',[138] and see how they were shaped to the needs of the governors and the governed (who were often, of course, the same people).

On the other hand, we can make use of newer approaches. We should no longer allow the historians of the lower orders their exclusive use of the *Annales* clothes that belonged once to a historian of the ruling classes of early medieval Europe. After all, what was McFarlane doing much of the time but studying the *mentalités* of the late medieval nobility? We should furthermore be looking at the language of politics, at words used in context, in documents of high policy and debate, in letters, in literary and theoretical works. Here we have the dazzling work of Skinner and his school to follow, and indeed the pioneering interest of Namier, Bloch and Febvre.[139] As Skinner has said, it does not really matter whether the ideas used in politics are cloaks for self-interest or not; what does matter is that it was these words and ideas that were used and not others.[140] Watts in his work on the reign of Henry VI has already shown how much can be done by these means.[141]

Finally, embracing almost all these approaches, we have a subject which is perhaps the single most exciting area in English history at the moment and whose founder was a medievalist. I refer to the study of law in society and, of course, to the greatest of all medievalists, Maitland. It was Maitland, uniquely among English historians before Namier and McFarlane, who broke through the Whig inability to value the past on its own terms.[142] Much of the reason for this was, I think, that Maitland's primary expertise lay in the law, an area that, from the reign of Henry II, if not earlier, was fundamental to English society and to the beliefs and practices of its ruling classes. Moreover, in the Year Books, in legal texts, in statutes and the records of the courts, he had access to the vocabulary of this central province of medieval experience.[143] From Maitland there ran an academic chain, through Plucknett to Chrimes, that might have given late medieval politics an alternative way out of the impasse of the 1930s, for, in his *English Constitutional Ideas in the Fifteenth Century*, published in 1936, Chrimes explores the late medieval constitution in very un-Stubbsian terms and his definition of a constitution is in some ways close to McFarlane's.[144] In practice, as McFarlane noted,[145] his work was too much a lawyer's view of the constitution and, being published not long before the war, by the time it might have made an impact in peacetime England McFarlane was well launched on an alternative course.

But it is time we returned to Chrimes's work. McFarlane was I think too dismissive of it and of the promise of the Year Books – perhaps his prejudice against Fortescue got the better of him here[146] – and his neglect of legal evidence, despite his admiration for Maitland, is an aspect of his failure to render due attention to the public domain in late medieval England.[147] The law can serve us in several ways. Legal history in its present form, using manorial, honorial, ecclesiastical and common law records, owes much to the *Annales* school and has become a key tool for exploring social stability and the *mores* of a society.[148] Indeed I would go so far as to say that it informs most of the best social history being done by historians of England at the moment. It is a particularly promising field for late medievalists, for law was the single most significant aspect of government for late medieval landowners.

Thus, how it functioned and was enforced is integral to the public mechanisms of rule. The use that was made of it by landowners is central to our understanding of their ideas about governance, both private and public. Moreover, some of them were lawyers, many had at least a smattering of the law. Consequently, as long as we remember that it is the consumers of the law, not the lawyers, that we want to learn about, the vocabulary of the law may tell us a lot about political ideas amongst the landed classes. Since most medieval political thought was fundamentally bound up with legal thought, and even the most mundane theoretical discussions of law could not escape some reference to the standard categories of divine, natural and positive law, we might use this as an avenue to explore the extent to which 'high' political and constitutional theory had filtered down to the world of nobility and gentry.[149] Here then we have a field which offers access to the study of political and governmental structures and political culture. And its records are vast and still to a large extent unexplored: difficult, often heavy and always dirty, but full of hidden treasures.

When Deutscher gave the Trevelyan lectures in Cambridge in the year of the fiftieth anniversary of the Russian revolution, one Cambridge historian said that his last lecture, a call to arms to bring about the real Marxist revolution, had sounded like a revivalist meeting, and I may have given the same effect today. But I do think that late medieval political history, the subject that above all we owe to McFarlane, is in need of a revival. It is in danger of dying in its centre of origin, Oxford, and has died in one of its earliest offshoots, Bristol. Many of the first generation of McFarlane pupils have retired and, in my own generation, despite the fact that it was with us that the subject really took off numerically, very few have achieved permanent posts within the university system. We need to regenerate a subject that can too easily come to seem an intellectual backwater. To do so, we must place our studies of politics firmly within the parameters of constitutional history; not the history McFarlane inherited from the Whigs and rejected but, following McFarlane, something far more difficult and challenging, a constitutional history conceived in terms of the world that our late medieval protagonists knew and grappled with.

Notes

1. Like E. Powell, 'After "After McFarlane": The Poverty of Patronage and the Case for Constitutional History' in *Trade, Devotion and Governance: Papers in Later Medieval History*, D.J. Clayton, R.G. Davies and P. McNiven (eds.) (Stroud, 1994), pp. 1–16 (originally a given as a paper at Manchester in 1989), this chapter takes its title from C. Richmond's influential review article, 'After McFarlane', *History*, LXVIII (1983), pp. 46–60. Reading Powell's paper after I had written this piece, I realized how much some of our ideas overlapped. I decided to leave my paper as it stood, since the similarities represented convergence rather than plagiarism. I am most grateful to Dr Powell for letting me have a manuscript copy of his paper. I must also express my thanks to Dr Gerald Harriss for arranging access for me to the McFarlane Library and papers at Magdalen College, Oxford and to my colleagues at New Hall, Dr Zara Steiner for reading and commenting on this paper and, above all, Mr Patrick Higgins, for historiographical guidance, especially towards the riches of inaugurals, British Academy obituaries and *T.L.S.* reviews.

2. P.R.H. Slee, *Learning and a Liberal Education: The Study of Modern History in the Universities of Oxford, Cambridge and Manchester, 1800–1914* (Manchester, 1986), chs.1–6 and pp. 90–1.

3. McFarlane, *Nobility*, p.1.

4. Ibid., p. 280.

5. G. Lapsley, 'Some Recent Advance in English Constitutional History (before 1485)', *C.H.J.* V (1936), p. 138.

6. S.B. Chrimes, *English Constitutional Ideas in the Fifteenth Century* (Cambridge, 1936) (copy in McFarlane Library, Magdalen College, Oxford). On the denaturing of politics by traditional constitutional history, see G. Kitson Clark, 'A Hundred Years of the Teaching of History at Cambridge, 1873–1973', *H.J.* XVI (1973), p. 547: 'Gaillard Lapsley . . . presumably knew what human nature was like, but he was determined that this irrelevant factor should not blur his account of the ideas and principles involved in constitutional history'.

7. Slee, *Learning*, parts 1 and 2, passim; R.W. Southern, 'The Contemporary Study of History' (inaugural, given 1961), in *The Varieties of History: from Voltaire to the Present*, F. Stern (ed.) (2nd edn, 1970), p. 412.

8. Slee, *Learning*, p. 91.

9. J.W. Burrow, *Learning and a Liberal Descent* (Cambridge, 1981), chs. 2–4; P.B.M. Blaas, *Continuity*

and Anachronism: Parliamentary and Constitutional Development in Whig Historiography and in the Anti-Whig Reaction between 1890 and 1930 (The Hague, Boston, London, 1978), pp. 78–9.

10. Burrow, *Learning*, pp. 97–8.

11. 'I am proud indeed to be an instrument, in the humblest way, in repaying the debt which English history owes to German scholarship': M.D. Knowles, 'Some Trends in Scholarship, 1868–1968, in the Field of Medieval History', *T.R.H.S.* 5th series, XIX (1969), p. 142. Also Burrow, *Learning*, pp. 119–25; Southern, in *Varieties of History*, pp. 413–14. Stubbs relied heavily on the Rolls Series for which he was a prolific editor. It was founded in 1857 as the English answer to the great German *Monumenta Germaniae Historica*, which had been begun in the 1820s: D. Knowles, 'The Rolls Series', in *Great Historical Enterprises* (1963), pp. 99–134, 'The *Monumenta Germaniae Historica*', ibid., pp. 63–97; Blaas, *Continuity*, pp. 154–7; N.F. Cantor, 'Medieval Historiography as Modern Political and Social Thought', *J.C.H.* III (1968), pp. 56–7.

12. Burrow, *Learning*, especially pp. 22–35, 99–102, 266–7; Blaas, *Continuity*, especially pp.101–3, 174–9, 183, 197–211.

13. Southern, in *Varieties of History*, p. 418.

14. A point made in V.H. Galbraith, *Historical Study and the State* (Oxford, 1948), p. 4.

15. H. Butterfield, *The Whig Interpretation of History* (1931), p. 4.

16. W. Stubbs, *Constitutional History of England*, III (5th edn, Oxford, 1903), p. 638.

17. Ibid., III, p. 520.

18. Blaas, *Continuity*, p. 158, quoting Stubbs's comment that 'it was in England alone that the problem of national self-government was practically solved'; Burrow, *Learning*, pp. 126–44.

19. J.R. Tanner, 'The Teaching of Constitutional History', in *Essays on the Teaching of History*, F.W. Maitland (ed.) (Cambridge, 1901), p. 54.

20. A point noted in ibid., p. 55.

21. Stubbs, *Constitutional History*, III, pp. 634, 635.

22. Blaas, *Continuity*, pp.190–2.

23. Burrow, *Learning*, pp. 239–50.

24. Burrow, *Learning*, pp. 265–7.

25. R.B. Wernham, 'The Public Record Office, 1838–1938', *History*, new series, XXIII (1939), p. 222.

26. Wernham, *History*, new ser. XXIII, pp. 228–35; Knowles, *Historical Enterprises*, pp. 128–9; *idem*, *T.R.H.S.* 5th ser. XIX, p. 144; Blaas, *Continuity*, p. 51.

27. A point made by J.G. Edwards in defence of Stubbs, *William Stubbs* (Historical Association Pamphlet, 1952), pp. 11–12 and similarly by H. Cam, 'Stubbs Seventy Years After', *C.H.J.* IX (1948), p. 131.

28. Blaas, *Continuity*, pp. 1–2, 37–8, 51–61, 63–5, 70, 346; Slee, *Learning*, pp.129–35; V.H. Galbraith, Obituary of A.F. Pollard, *P.B.A.* XXXV (1949), p. 259; F.M. Powicke, Obituary of T.F. Tout, *P.B.A.* XV (1929), p. 492; E.S. de Beer, 'Sir Charles Firth', *History*, new ser. XXI (1936–7), p.1; Galbraith, *Historical Study*, p. 4. Bury was a notable outsider, both by origins and by subject: N.H. Baynes, Obituary of J.B. Bury, *P.B.A.* XIII (1927), pp. 368–78.

29. Blaas, *Continuity*, pp. 64–5, 268, 275–6; Slee, *Learning*, pp. 129–30; C.H. Firth, *A Plea for the Historical Teaching of History* (Oxford, 1904); Galbraith, *P.B.A.* XXXV, p. 261.

30. Knowles, *T.R.H.S.* 5th ser. XIX, pp. 140–1; Blaas, *Continuity*, pp. xv–xvi, 51, 67–70, 350–5. The École des Chartes, which had become an institute of advanced training for historians, had been established in 1829: Knowles, loc. cit., p.141.

31. Blaas, *Continuity*, pp. 276–7, Galbraith, *P.B.A.* XXXV, pp. 261–4.

32. Slee, *Learning*, pp. 133–4; Blaas, *Continuity*, pp. 61–2; R.W. Southern, Obituary of F.M. Powicke, *P.B.A.* L (1964), p. 289; W.A. Pantin, Obituary of E.F. Jacob, *P.B.A.* LVIII (1972), p. 454; Powicke, *P.B.A.* XV, pp. 501–6; C.N.L. Brooke, *A History of the University of Cambridge, IV: 1870–1990* (Cambridge, 1993), p. 280.

33. Slee, *Learning*, pp. 129–49, 153–60; Galbraith, *P.B.A.* XXXV, p. 261.

34. Slee, *Learning*, pp. 95–100, 107–110.

35. Blaas, *Continuity*, pp. 216–38, 244–9, 263–5.

36. Blaas, *Continuity*, pp. 167, 266; J.G. Edwards, *Historians and the Medieval English Parliament* (Glasgow, 1960), pp. 8–9, 10–24; Lapsley, *C.H.J.* V, p. 121; *Records of the Parliament Holden at Westminster 28th Feb. (1305)*, F.W. Maitland (ed.) (R.S., 1893).

37. Blaas, *Continuity*, pp. 287–96, 345–7, 357–61; Burrow, *Learning*, pp. 142–4, 226–8, 295–7; Lapsley, *C.H.J.* V, pp. 122–35; Edwards, *Historians*, pp. 13–40; T.F. Tout, *Chapters in the Administrative History of Medieval England* (6 vols, Manchester, 1920–33), I, p. 2 ('even under modern conditions, administration is more important than legislation'). For a quintessential 'debunk' of the period, see C. Petit-Dutaillis and G. Lefebvre, *Studies and Notes Supplementary to Stubbs' Constitutional History*, trans. W.E. Rhodes (3 vols, Manchester, 1908–29).

38. Full reference in preceding note 37.

39. Tout, *Chapters*, I, p. 21 and V, ch. 16.

40. Edwards, *Historians*, pp. 24–40; Blaas, *Continuity*, pp. 292–320, 335–7; A.F. Pollard, *Henry VIII* (1902); K. Pickthorn, *Early Tudor Government: Henry VII* (Cambridge, 1934).

41. Blaas, *Continuity*, pp. 287–9.

42. Cantor, *J.C.H.* III, p. 68; Tout, *Chapters, passim*; Petit-Dutaillis and Lefebvre, *Studies and Notes, passim*. See also Lapsley, *C.H.J.* V, who comments that 'Stubbs' "system" has been completely rejected' (p.119) but offers a still essentially Stubbsian account of the Middle Ages (pp. 130, 135–46).

43. Tout, *Chapters*, II, p. 189.

44. Below, p. 196.

45. Burrow, *Learning*, p. 140; Blaas, *Continuity*, pp.155–62.

46. Burrow, *Learning*, pp.139–42.

47. G. Barraclough, *History in a Changing World* (Oxford, 1955), p.14; Slee, *Learning*, pp. 132–3; Blaas, *Continuity*, p. 279; Firth, *Historical Teaching*, p. 6.

48. Barraclough, *History*, p. 28.

49. V.H. Galbraith, *An Introduction to the Study of History* (1964), p. 13; Cantor, *J.C.H.* III, p. 68; Knowles, *T.R.H.S.* 5th ser. XIX, p. 144; G. Parker, Obituary of G.N. Clark, *P.B.A.* LXVI (1980), pp. 407–25; Kitson Clark, *H.J.* XVI, pp. 541–51; Brooke, *History of Cambridge*, pp. 227–39.

50. Southern, *P.B.A.* L, p. 287; F.M. Powicke, *Modern Historians and the Study of History* (Watford, 1955), p. 184.

51. Barraclough, *History*, p. 28. Note that as early as 1931 Powicke himself was expressing some unease about what was happening: Powicke, *Modern Historians*, p. 191.

52. Galbraith, *Historical Study*, p. 4.; Pantin, *P.B.A.* LVIII, pp. 453–4, 457–8, 461; *idem*, 'Frederick Maurice Powicke', *E.H.R.* LXXX (1965), pp. 2–3; Southern, *P.B.A.* L, pp. 276, 286, 291; *idem*, Obituary of V.H. Galbraith, *P.B.A.* LXIV (1978), p. 398; C.N.L. Brooke, Obituary of C.R. Cheney, *P.B.A.* LXXIII (1987), pp. 430–2.

53. H.R. Trevor-Roper, *History: Professional and Lay* (Oxford, 1957), p. 3. This lecture is both extremely funny and as acute an analysis of the state of English history at that time as one is likely to find.

54. Brooke, *P.B.A.* LXXIII, p. 433. For Manchester, see references above, n. 52. For some references to Cambridge history, see above, n. 49.

55. E.F. Jacob, *Studies in the Period of Baronial Reform and Rebellion, 1258–67* (Manchester, 1925); F.M. Powicke, *The Loss of Normandy* (Manchester, 1913).

56. K. Thomas, 'The Tools and the Job', *T.L.S.* 7 April 1966, p. 275.

57. Knowles, *T.R.H.S.* 5th ser. XIX, p. 147; Blaas, *Continuity*, pp. 362–9.

58. Powicke, *Modern Historians*, p. 189; Blaas, *Continuity*, p. 367.

59. Galbraith, *Introduction*, pp. 13, 73–6; *idem*, *Historical Study*, pp. 7–8, 11–12; Edwards, *William Stubbs*, p. 20; 'History Becomes Co-operative', *T.L.S.* Special Issue, 29 August 1952, p. xix; G. Barraclough, 'The Larger View of History', *T.L.S.* Special Issue, 6 January 1956, p. ii; Trevor-Roper, *History: Professional and Lay*, pp. 14–17; Blaas, Continuity, pp. 362–9.

60. Trevor-Roper, *History: Professional and Lay*, pp. 12–13, and also p. 22. This was very specifically an attack on professionalism in the terms in which the Manchester era had defined it: 'Research is not the same as professionalism': ibid., p. 19.

61. Thomas, *T.L.S.* 7 April 1966, p. 275.

62. Barraclough, *T.L.S.* 6 January 1956, p. ii.

63. See, more generally, N. Annan, *The Curious Strength of Positivism in English Political Thought* (L.T. Hobhouse Memorial Trust Lecture, 28, 1962).

64. Pantin, *P.B.A.* LVIII, especially p. 463; Southern, *P.B.A.* L, especially p. 281.

65. Southern, *P.B.A.* L, p. 294; R.H.C. Davis, 'The Content of History', *History*, LXVI (1981), p. 363.

66. F.M. Powicke, *King Henry III and the Lord Edward*, (2 vols, Oxford, 1947).

67. Cantor, *J.C.H.* III, pp. 68–9 (but he dates the start of this reaction too late); Southern, *P.B.A.* LVIII, pp. 282–6, 290–2; *idem*, in *Varieties of History*, pp. 417–21; Pantin, *P.B.A.* LVIII, pp. 463–8; C.N.L. Brooke, Obituary of David Knowles, *P.B.A.* LXI (1975), pp. 439–77; *T.L.S.* 29 Aug. 1952, p. xix; Knowles, *T.R.H.S.* 5th ser., XIX, pp. 151–2.

68. See Southern's comment on Powicke: 'He loved the ramifications of history more than its wide avenues': *P.B.A.* LVIII, p. 295; Blaas, *Continuity*, p. 369; Barraclough, *History*, pp. 1–2; Burrow, *Learning*, *passim*; Slee, *Learning*, p. 4.

69. Barraclough, *History*, pp. 1–30; *idem*, *T.L.S.* 6 January 1956, p. ii; Galbraith, *Introduction*, p. 20; 'History in England', *T.L.S.* Special Issue, 25 August 1950, pp. iv–v; Blaas, *Continuity*, pp. 364, 368–9.

70. Galbraith, *Introduction*, p. 3; A.L. Rowse, *The Use of History* (1946), pp. 59, 62–3, 74–80. The latter work is dedicated to McFarlane, 'scholar, mentor, friend'. It is not entirely clear that he would have approved its contents.

71. 'The Namier View of History', *T.L.S.* Special Issue, 28 August 1953, p. xxiii.

72. McFarlane, *Nobility*, p. 279.

73. Ibid., pp. 279–80.

74. J.P. Cooper, 'Lewis Namier: A Biography', in *Land, Men and Beliefs*, G.E. Aylmer and J.S. Morrill (eds.) (1983), pp. 256–7. Cooper's piece is a review of J. Namier, *Lewis Namier: A Biography* (Oxford, 1971), which should be consulted for a full account of his life.

75. J.P. Cooper, 'Recollections of Namier', in *Land, Men and Beliefs*, pp. 252–3; L. Colley, *Lewis Namier* (1989), pp. 22, 28, 73–9, 82, 102.

76. L.B. Namier, 'Human Nature in Politics', in *Varieties of History*, pp. 385–6; *T.L.S.* 25 August 1950, p. iv; 'The Structure of Politics: 1929' and 'Namier View', *T.L.S.* Special Issue, 28 August 1953, pp. xx–xxii; Colley, *Namier*, pp. 46–61.

77. Cantor, *J.C.H.* III, p. 68 (if rather overstated); Annan, *Curious Strength, passim*. A notable exception to the insularity were of course the economic historians but their view, limited in other ways, was inimical to the study of high politics: M. Postan, 'Economic Social History', *T.L.S.* Special Issue, 6 January 1956, p. vi; Thomas, *T.L.S.* 7 April 1966, pp. 275–6; Blaas, *Continuity*, pp. 43–50; below, n.128.

78. Colley, *Namier*, pp. 24–7, 74.

79. Colley, *Namier*, p. 58; *T.L.S.* 28 August 1953, pp. xxii–iii. See also a similar comment, probably by the same writer, 25 August 1950, p. iv.

80. A.P. Cohen, *The Symbolic Construction of Community* (Chichester and London, 1985), p. 116; Annan, *Curious Strength*, pp. 8–13.

81. Colley, *Namier*, p. 58.

82. L.B. Namier, *The Structure of Politics at the Accession of George III* (lst edn, 1929); L.S. Sutherland, Obituary of Sir Lewis Namier, *P.B.A.* XLVIII (1962), pp. 381–2. Note also the later anti-positivist statement, 'The function of the historian is akin to that of the painter and not of the photographic camera': Namier, 'History and Political Culture', in *Varieties of History*, p. 379.

83. Colley, *Namier*, pp. 26–31.

84. Namier, in *Varieties of History*, pp. 384–8; *T.L.S.* 28 August 1953, pp. xx–xxi, xxiii; Cooper, in *Land, Men and Beliefs*, p. 259; Colley, *Namier*, pp. 26–7, 65.

85. Sutherland, *P.B.A.* XLVIII, p. 382.

86. McFarlane, *Nobility*, pp. ix–x, xii–xiii; K.J. Leyser, Obituary of K.B. McFarlane, *P.B.A.* LXII (1976), p. 490.

87. McFarlane, *Nobility*, p. x.

88. Possibly even earlier: Leyser, *P.B.A.* LXII, p. 490.

89. Magdalen College, Oxford, McFarlane papers, VI/3b.

90. Ibid., Lecture VI.

91. J.P. Cooper, 'K.B. McFarlane 1903–1966', in *Land, Men and Beliefs*, p. 245.

92. McFarlane, *Nobility*, p. xx, quoting McFarlane Papers II/7: 'From Feudalism to Whig Oligarchy or the real Middle Ages'.

93. F.M. Stenton, *The First Century of English Feudalism* (lst edn, Oxford, 1932) (copy in McFarlane Library).

94. Cooper, in *Land, Men and Beliefs*, p. 244; Leyser, *P.B.A.* LXII, p. 493.

95. Cooper, *Land, Men and Beliefs*, p. 252; Colley, *Namier*, p. 46.

96. McFarlane, *Nobility*, p. xii; Leyser, *P.B.A.* LXII, p. 497.

97. Leyser, *P.B.A.* LXII, p. 497 (the quotation is by Leyser rather than McFarlane).

98. McFarlane, *Nobility*, pp. xxviii–ix, 297; Leyser, *P.B.A.* LXII, p. 495; above, n. 75.

99. Magdalen College, Oxford, McFarlane papers, VI/3b, Lecture IX; also Lecture V. See also McFarlane, *Nobility*, pp. 293, 297 and the title of the paper from 1940, cited above, n. 92. The influence was noted implicitly in *T.L.S.* 25 August 1950, p. iv.

100. R. Syme, *The Roman Revolution* (Oxford, 1939); Cooper, in *Land, Men and Beliefs*, p. 245; McFarlane, *Nobility*, p. xviii. The debt to Syme over that to Namier is emphasized in a commemorative talk given at Magdalen College by Karl Leyser (which also explains why it was not possible to examine McFarlane's annotated copy of The Roman Empire at Magdalen: Leyser was given it). Perusal of the work of all three, Namier, Syme and McFarlane, confirms the views expressed here, as, in some measure, does the fact that Namier was the other great influence on one of McFarlane's most distinguished pupils, J.P. Cooper: Cooper, 'Introduction', in *Land, Men and Beliefs*, pp. ix–xiii. I am most grateful to Dr Harriss for sending me a copy of this talk and allowing me to mention it here.

101. McFarlane, *Nobility*, p. 296; see also p. 3.

102. Above, n. 92.

103. McFarlane approved of Chrimes's definition of a constitution as 'that body of governmental rights and duties which exist in a state at any given time in virtue of their recognition by law, custom, convention, practice or opinion', including 'opinions, ideas and assumptions as to the nature and distribution of constitutional rights'. But he complained that the book does not try to attempt a definition of what was meant by 'good and abundant governance' : Chrimes, *English Constitutional Ideas*, pp. xix–xx; K.B. McFarlane, review in *E.H.R.* LIII (1938), pp. 707–8.

104. McFarlane, *Nobility*, p. xii; *idem, E.H.R.* LIII, p. 708; Cooper, in *Land, Men and Beliefs*, p. 248. Similarly with Namier: Colley, *Namier*, p. 89.

105. Note the approving annotation to his copy of J.H. Hexter, *Reappraisals in History* (1961), p. 19, where a similar approach is advocated (copy in McFarlane Library).

106. Namier, *Structure of Politics*, p. vi; Colley, *Namier*, pp. 70, 82–3.

107. For a discussion of the Namier legacy up to 1953, see *T.L.S.*, 28 August 1953, pp. xxii–iii. One exceptional (in every sense) work of medieval English history is J.C. Holt, *Magna Carta* (1st edn, Cambridge, 1965) whose author, interestingly, was an early espouser of Namierism amongst medievalists: *idem, The Northerners* (Oxford, 1961, reissued 1993).

108. Colley, *Namier*, pp. 93–6; *Meaning and Context: Quentin Skinner and his Critics*, J. Tully (ed.) (Cambridge, 1988), *passim* and p. 109 (for 'epiphenomenalism').

109. Cooper, in *Land, Men and Beliefs*, p. 259; McFarlane, *Nobility*, p. 120; *idem, England*, pp. 111–13, 247; Colley, *Namier*, pp. 26–31.

110. L.B. Namier, *England in the Age of the American Revolution* (1st edn, 1930), p. 151. See a similarly effective character summary in McFarlane, *England*, p. 176.

111. McFarlane, *Nobility*, pp. 280–1; Cooper, in *Land, Men and Beliefs*, p. 249.

112. J. Mortimer, *Rumpole on Trial* (Harmondsworth, 1992), p. 68. See also Keith Thomas' damning comment on 'common-sense': *T.L.S.* 7 April 1966, p. 275.

113. For amplification and references, see Carpenter, *Locality*, pp. 4–7.

114. Modernists would probably say the same about Namier: see Colley, *Namier*, pp. 31–3, 95–7.

115. McFarlane, *Nobility*, p. 120.

116. See, for example, McFarlane, *Nobility*, pp. 119, 121, 231, 290; *idem, England*, pp. ix, xxvi–vii, 25, 231; *idem, Lancastrian Kings and Lollard Knights* (Oxford, 1972) p. 60. Despite the rider: 'I am not suggesting that there were no politics save jobbery' (*Nobility*, p. 119), he does come perilously close to suggesting that this was in fact the case.

117. Carpenter, *Locality*, pp. 6–7.

118. See the references above in note 116.

119. Namier, *Lewis Namier*, chs. 7–18. This point was made to me by Dr Zara Steiner. But note Colley's comments on Namier's 'lack of interest in sources that would illuminate administration and policy rather than the individuals behind them': *Namier*, pp. 33, 79–80.

120. McFarlane, *England*, p. 240

121. McFarlane, *Nobility*, p. 119.

122. P. Burke, *The French Historical Revolution: The 'Annales' School 1929–89* (1990), p. l.

123. Ibid., *passim*.

124. Ibid., *passim*. Note the perceptive comment, that Trevelyan's definition 'implies that politics is not a social activity', an assumption wholly alien to the work of Namier and McFarlane: *T.L.S.* Special Issue, 25 August 1950, p. iv. See also *T.L.S.* 28 August 1953, p. xxii on Namier and social history. Powicke, *King Henry III* has the laudable aim of being such a social history (see pp. v–vi) but lacks the conceptual framework to succeed.

125. Burke, *French Historical Revolution*, pp. 16–25.

126. As Bloch put it, 'le terrain si mal défriché de l'histoire sociale': Burke, *French Historical Revolution*, p. 22.

127. Cantor, *J.C.H.* III, pp. 64–5; M. Bloch, *La Société Féodale* (2 vols, Paris, 1939–40).

128. Burke, *French Historical Revolution*, pp. 17, 24–5, 96–7. Review of 'Les Rois Thaumaturges, *T.L.S.* 11 March 1926, p. 177 and letter, ibid., 18 March 1926, p. 219; D.C. Douglas, review of *La Société Féodale, History*, new ser., XXV (1940–1), pp. 255–6. Other reviews of Bloch include *E.H.R.* XL (1925), pp. 267–70, XLVII (1932), pp. 655–7, LV (1940), pp. 449–51, LXV (1950), pp. 384–7; *History*, new ser., XXXV (1950), pp. 197–201; *T.L.S.* 24 December, 1954, pp. 829–30, 23 June 1961, p. 386, 21 November 1963. Both the last two, probably by the same writer, are very appreciative but treat him primarily as an economic historian; see also Hobsbawm's comments on Burke's contribution in *Review*, I (1977–8), p. 158. Reviews of Febvre include *T.L.S.* 26 October, 1922, 14 May 1925, 13 November 1930. See too P. Burke, 'Reflections on the Historical Revolution in France: The Annales School and British Social History', *Review*, I (1977–8), pp. 147–8. Braudel was, however, reviewed, soon after publication in French, by someone who understood his purposes (*T.L.S.* 1 September, 1950, pp. 541–2) and a conference of younger British and French historians soon after the war left no excuse for ignorance: P. Wolff, 'French Historical Writings on the Middle Ages in the Years 1940–47', *History*, XXXIII (1948), pp. 203–10. Note that, agonising between 1947 and 1955 over the disintegration of history under 'scientific' positivism, Barraclough, a medievalist, did not see fit to mention the 'Annales' school: *History, passim*.

129. Burke, *French Historical Revolution*, ch. 5; below, n. 132; for 'Namierite' political history in the postwar period, see above, n.107.

130. *T.L.S.* 25 August 1950, p. iv.

131. Burke, *Review* I , p. 148. Note also E.P. Thompson's very limited definition of social history: Thompson, 'Social History', in *Varieties of History*, pp. 423–30. Trevor-Roper, *History: Professional and Lay*, pp. 19–22; he names Namier and Bloch amongst the three examples he cites of 'the greatest professional historians of our century' (p. 22).

132. The list of works is too long to attempt here, but see summary in Burke, *Review* I, pp.148–9. Perhaps the most seminal of all these was K. Thomas, *Religion and the Decline of Magic: Studies in Popular beliefs in Sixteenth and Seventeenth Century England* (1971); also *idem*, 'History and Anthropology', *P.P.* XXIV (1963), pp. 3–24. Burke fails to mention the enormously influential P. Laslett, *The World We Have Lost* (1965).

133. Thomas, *T.L.S.* 7 April 1966, p. 277.

134. Ibid. p. 277; also the article as a whole (pp. 275–7) and note the reference here to the influence on continental history of Durkheim, one of the formative influences on Namier (above, p. 187) .

135. For example, the work of J.S. Morrill, M.A. Goldie, Jonathan Scott (all seventeenth century), Linda Colley, John Brewer (eighteenth century), J.P. Parry, Boyd Hilton (nineteenth century), and work on élites in relation to diplomatic history e.g. by D.C. Watt (drawn to my attention by Dr Z. Steiner).

136. McFarlane, *Nobility*, p. 25.

137. Powell, 'After "After McFarlane"'.

138. Remark to author.

139. *Meaning and Context*, Tully (ed.), *passim*; Namier, in *Varieties of History*, p. 373; Burke, *French Historical Revolution*, pp. 13, 25, 29.

140. *Meaning and Context*, Tully (ed.), pp. 109–18; Q.R.D. Skinner, 'The Principles and Practice of Opposition: The Case of Bolingbroke versus Walpole', in *Historical Perspectives: Studies in English Thought and Society in Honour of J.H. Plumb*, N. McKendrick (ed.) (1974), pp. 93–128.

141. J. Watts, 'Domestic Politics and the Constitution in the Reign of Henry VI, c.1435–61' (unpub. Ph.D. thesis, Cambridge Univ. 1991) and forthcoming book.

142. Cantor, *J.C.H.* III, p. 68; Cam, *C.H.J.* IX, p. 145; Powicke, *King Henry III*, pp. v–vi. Note also Maitland's extraordinarily prescient conception of history in 'Introduction', *Essays on the Teaching of History*, pp. xi–xxx.

143. See the comment in Cantor, *J.C.H.* III, p. 68.

144. Chrimes, *English Constitutional Ideas*, pp. xv, xvi, xix; McFarlane, *E.H.R.*, LIII, p.707. Chrimes's observation that by his definition (above, note 103) 'even the most extreme despotism is a constitution' (p. xx) is marked 'obvious' by McFarlane in the margin of his copy. See too T.F.T. Plucknett, 'The Lancastrian Constitution', in *Tudor Studies Presented . . . to A.F. Pollard*, R.W. Seton-Watson (ed.) (1924), pp. 161–81.

145. McFarlane, *E.H.R.* LIII, p. 707.

146. Ibid., pp. 707–8; McFarlane, *England*, p. 23.

147. McFarlane, 'Mount Maitland', *New Statesman*, 4 June 1965, pp. 882–3.

148. See, for example, the references in Carpenter, *Locality*, p. 2, n. 7, in E.W. Ives, 'English Law and English Society', *History*, LXVI (1981), pp. 50–60, and in L. Bonfield, 'The Nature of Customary Law in the Manor Courts of Medieval England', *Comparative Studies in Society and History*, XXXI (1989), pp. 514–34. See also, for example, M. Ingram, *Church Courts, Sex and Marriage in England 1570–1640* (Cambridge, 1987).

149. For example, G. Ashby, 'Active Policy of a Prince', *George Ashby's Poems*, M. Bateson (ed.), E.E.T.S. LXXI (1899), pp. 34–5; *Four English Political Tracts of the Later Middle Ages*, J.-P.Genet (ed.) (Camden Society, 4th ser., XVIII, 1977); Sir John Fortescue, *The Governance of England*, C. Plummer (ed.) (Oxford, 1885).

INDEX